DARING be DIFFERENT

An Experiment in Busing — Verona, New Jersey, 1968-1969

DARING *to be* DIFFERENT

An Experiment in Busing — Verona, New Jersey, 1968-1969

by
Kurt Landsberger

Sunflower University Press®

1531 Yuma • P.O. Box 1009 • Manhattan, Kansas 66505-1009 USA

Amie Goins, Technical Editor

Layout by Lori L. Daniel

ISBN 0-89745-250-X

Sunflower University Press is a wholly-owned subsidiary
of the non-profit 501(c)3 Journal of the West, Inc.

*To the parents who want to
improve the lives of their children
through education . . .
and to those who understand.*

Contents

Acknowledgments

To NAME ALL those who helped in the creation of this work would take too long to list. My thanks go to those who agreed to talk to me, or who wrote to me, and whose stories appear. But special thanks go to Jack and Lois Grebe, who offered their home and an invitation to some of the host parents for a meeting that started me on a different tack, steering towards more than dry minutes and transcripts. It was Ethel Melvin who patiently sifted through the records of the Hawthorne School, and never with the slightest inflection seemed annoyed by my constant phone calls. Rosalyn Bernstein-Harnes kindly arranged for me to sit down and break bread with four former Hawthorne teachers who gave me insight into their Newark school. Ben Veal introduced me to the invisible black community of Verona. There were many, not named, who in one way or another suggested that I call someone who might have information, or who knew someone who in turn might have sent me to others in a seemingly endless chain. There were some I could not reach by phone, and my thanks go to those who then answered my letters.

I gratefully acknowledge the collection of clippings, scrap books, etc., loaned to me by Dick Heaslip, Edward Wizda, and

Hilda Jaffe. Also valuable was the scrap book of the Verona Board of Education.

Quoted throughout this book are interviews with various individuals who all played a major part in this story. Nearly all interviews were conducted in person, a limited number in writing, and a few over the telephone. Those interviewed in person received a rough copy of what I thought I had heard. Minor corrections were suggested by some.

For the brief history on Newark, I wish to thank Jean-Rae Turner and David Wiesen. Robert Blackwood, of the Newark Public Library, was essential in making contacts for me, and also helped with my research on the Hawthorne Avenue School.

And my special thanks to Verona, the town where Anny and I — and many of the others I have mentioned — raised our children. In many ways I have been involved with this community, whether fighting to keep the nearby 300 pristine acres of Hilltop green, nudging to retain historic buildings before the few remaining are torn down, making sure that our public buildings are accessible, or just doing my best to irritate, cajole, and push the ever-changing crop of local politicians. Verona is special to me, and even though it was tempting to relocate as my wife and I grew older, we stayed. Through circumstances not of our making, even though Anny and I grew up in the old country, we both have found a home in Verona, New Jersey.

Kurt Landsberger

Foreword

by Dr. Robert L. Crain

*I*N 1975, a scientist at Educational Testing Service, Dr. Stanley Zdep, published a technical article in a scientific journal describing the educational impact on inner-city African American children who volunteered to be bused to white suburban elementary schools — in this case from Newark, New Jersey, to the suburb of Verona. The move was done as if it were a scientific experiment. Because there were more parents waiting to send their children to the suburbs than were vacant seats in Verona, the students were selected randomly, and both they and the unselected Newark applicants were tested at the beginning and end of the year. The result was important to scientists of education. The students who transferred to Verona made sizable gains in reading scores, significantly higher scores than the scientific "control" group of students who were not randomly selected to make the transfer. Although the students who entered as second graders were a bit confounded by the "new math" being taught in suburbia, those who transferred at the beginning of first grade adapted quickly. These results have influenced other scientists, who have used this and other

evidence to recommend school transfers be made in first grade or kindergarten.

But what looks like a small, highly technical scientific experiment is actually the exposed tip of the iceberg — a dramatic story about a group of whites, led by a group of concerned citizens in the town of Verona, who decided that it should take on its share of righting the wrongs of discrimination and bring 37 of Newark's ghetto children into their schools, only to create a furor that undid the program within a year of its beginning.

This book is that story — one of only a very small number of books about a white community volunteering to help, only to find its efforts stifled when anti-integrationist whites organized to kill the program. This book portrays in great detail, but nonetheless on an understandable scale, the differences between those who wanted to make a small effort in the long process of creating a nation dedicated to the proposition that all men are created equal, and others who were able to end those dreams.

Dr. Robert L. Crain is a sociology and education professor in the Teachers College at Columbia University, New York. He has co-authored five books on school desegregation, including *Stepping Over the Color Line: African-American Students in White Suburban Schools* (New Haven, CT: Yale University Press, 1997).

Preface

by Frank Nunziata

*W*ITH THE PASSAGE of time, I have come to better appreciate the psyche of the townspeople of Verona. Like many small towns in America, Verona's idyllic setting did not exempt it or its citizens from facing the urgent social issues of the era. It is a different world now, as we look back on that turbulent period through more mature eyes and an ever-evolving sense of social justice. "Time heals all wounds," the adage goes — issues of great passion have become less so and the ebb and flow of life has smoothed the emotional peaks and valleys of the past 30 years.

A friend suggested that I consider running for a seat on the Verona Board of Education in 1972. I agreed, all the while thinking that it would be an excellent opportunity to give something back to my newly adopted hometown. My wife Marlene and I have strong education backgrounds, so it seemed like a logical step. First, I met with former Board members and interested citizens to offer my candidacy. Though some have suggested that the meetings were clandestine in nature, I was able to pass through the screening process with little noticeable suspicion. My willingness to become a part of the school process was appreciated by the

"Liberal" element of the town. My recollection of conversations with supporters at every end of the town failed to bring into focus any serious question of the busing issue, which, although generally resolved by that time, still burned in the very heart of the town.

As I eventually learned, the busing project still held a great share of supporters, who believed in a higher sense of social purpose and justice. The detractors still burned with the notion that the issue was an intrusion of their personal property and private domain. The fervor with which they expressed their opinions cut deeply into every aspect of town life. There was no middle ground, even by the 1972 election.

Verona, like many towns, was effectively polarized in its social beliefs. Many still feared retribution for the failed project, while others vowed to ensure that the issue would never again have enough support to be brought to a public forum. Each faction had agendas they were sworn to uphold.

Ethnic slurs and political epithets during the election of 1972 seemed always to have a reference to the busing issue and to the support of the "Liberal elements" responsible. Fortunately I was the recipient of a great effort by a moderate movement in town, and unseated a popular conservative Board member. My three years on the Board was not noted for individual accomplishments, but rather for a greater sense of cooperative effort between the citizens' governing body and the educational establishment. Though personal attacks continued, they eventually waned. The townspeople laid down their arms, as it were, and turned their focus back to what brought prominence to our town in the first place — our exemplary educational system.

Introduction

*N*O HISTORY OF Verona, New Jersey, would be complete without exploring the involvement of its nearly all-white population with a small segment of Newark's black population.

In years to come, as Verona's population changes due to the passing of generations, a record should remain of more than the very distant past. Several booklets, including one of my own, delve into the township's beginning and early years. There may have been slight differences, but most West Essex County communities started in a somewhat similar fashion: the first settlers arrived, built their homes, started commerce, built churches, schools, and libraries, and interconnected with other struggling neighbors. Only slight nuances made one town distinct from another. Rarely were there cataclysmic events that would suddenly differentiate one municipality from all the others.

But such a thing can happen. Verona in the 1960s was thrown into unexpected turmoil, through a coincidental convergence of a few idealists from different ethnic and religious backgrounds. On July 13, 1967, the city of Newark, only a few miles from Verona, erupted in racial violence. The riots devastated the community, leaving 21 dead and hundreds injured. A year after the 1967 Newark riot, the Verona Board of Education voluntarily, without government coercion, offered to share its educational facilities with children from a blighted area in Newark. The experiment lasted a year, and then had to be abandoned. Verona is usually mentioned in the numerous studies about busing and integration, but this particular case differs not only in the unusual offer by this board of education, but — even more astonishing — the voluntary involvement of many of Verona's citizens.

At the time, Verona's public schools did not have cafeterias, so the children walked home for lunch. During the 1968-1969 school year, the 37 black children who came daily from Newark were invited into the homes of Verona's volunteer host parents for lunch. There were many more interested hosts than children. Several of the students made friends with their host's children, and a few were even invited over on weekends. Some volunteers met the Newark parents, others conversed via telephone. For a short time these parents, who lovingly cared for and fed the students, seemingly found a bond.

For three years, after the original plan to educate the Newark children had been discontinued and the students had reluctantly returned to their original school, Hawthorne, in Newark, a group of Verona volunteers, parents, and teenagers conducted a camp at Verona Park, entertaining and keeping the Newark children busy when school was closed for the summer. In addition, a group of four Verona women worked voluntarily as teacher's aides in the Newark school, and for some time, groups of Verona High School students were chauffeured by volunteers to the Hawthorne School to tutor the children.

Yet amidst this spirit of community and sharing was an ongoing travail, not anticipated by the men and woman who had been elected to the Verona Board of Education. A sizeable group of residents that had originally opposed busing the children went to court to stop it. The Board of Education had not expected that through their actions they would open their forum not only to discussions of busing of black children, but, soon afterwards, to discourse on the Vietnam War and sex education. Public School Board meetings became a battleground where long hours were spent fighting over the importance of sports, teachers' rights, and, again and again, money.

The decade of the Sixties was a manic time. Quiet moments were rare, for it was an age of causes. It seems as though there were daily demonstrations for peace in Vietnam, civil rights, and against nuclear power, police brutality and busing. Questions were raised about schools, churches, government and corporations. Spirits soared and then plunged as unforgettable events unfolded. The decade teemed with charismatic leaders, triumphs and defeats. The trademark of the Sixties was extremism in everything from politics to fashion to art.

— Carol A. Emmens, *Album of the Sixties*

Chapter 1

The Era of the Sixties

IT WOULD NOT BE much of a guess that the causes of the turbulent years of the Sixties were responsible for strife within families, pitting children against parents, neighbors against neighbors, communities against communities. The influence of national happenings, in addition to a changing culture, reverberated even in the smallest town. It did not take much to raise the decibel of arguments, even in tranquil places like Verona, New Jersey. It only took a letter to the editor, a rally at the local high school, or a speech by a local candidate to interrupt the normal peace and quiet.

The 1950s was the era of high expectations, when many workers reached what is called the "middle class" and were able to move to the suburbs, when television was considered wholesome entertainment, and the young belonged to the so-called "silent generation," who did not seem to care what was happening.

The election in 1960 of President John F. Kennedy started the transformation of many segments of society to a more proactive participation. The young volunteered for the newly formed Peace Corps and for various civil rights causes. Then came the Cuban missile crisis, and our open involvement in Vietnam. On November 22, 1963, the climate of America started to change with the assassination of President Kennedy — only the first of many emotional disturbances of the Sixties.

The assassinations in fairly rapid succession of Malcolm X, Martin Luther King, Jr., and Robert Kennedy added to our inner turmoil. What was happening to our America? Where were we going?

It was the leadership of President Lyndon B. Johnson, who succeeded President Kennedy and served until 1969, that pointed the country in a new direction. For a time, the majority — though some with misgivings — followed him. At the urging of President Johnson, the 1964 Civil Rights package was passed by Congress as a memorial to the late President Kennedy, who had introduced the bill some six months before his death. This was followed by the Economic Opportunity Act, the War on Poverty, and the Great Society programs, and with all of it, the expansion of government services. The success of President Johnson having these programs passed seemed to confirm that the nation approved of the direction America was heading.

We watched the headlines and the TV coverage on the civil rights march on Selma, the black sit-ins at restaurants, the refusal of black citizens to sit in the rear of segregated buses, and, later, the riots in Watts and in other cities — Cleveland, Chicago, and Detroit.

What we could not see, but most could feel, was the demise of the almighty American dollar. A tax cut was ordained, also as a memorial to the late President. Business did well in those years, unemployment was practically non-existent, and credit cards were the novel way to purchase the unattainable.

But the escalation of the war in Vietnam created economic problems for the nation. For the moment, let us not consider what the war did to the psyche of the nation, but what it did to the financial status of the recently empowered new middle class. In simple terms, not until it was too late to curb the ensuing inflation did Congress raise sufficient money to pay for the war. As Tom Shachtman wrote in his *Decade of Shocks*:

> . . . Inflation rubbed salt in wounds. It accelerated the middle class's disenchantment with government programs which aided the poor and the minorities. It made workers more resistant to moderating their wage demands and made the possibility that the unemployed would be hired less likely. . . . Inflation made the generation of the parents intolerant of their children's efforts to change the work ethic. It set the blue collar against the poor, the old against the young, the middle-class managers against the working stiffs, whites against blacks, and American-born against new immigrants.

Rowland Evans and Robert Novak, in their *Lyndon Johnson: The Exercise of Power*, reported that the Vietnam War had become the President's all-consuming passion, "a war he had not started and could not end, a war that broke his consensus, alienated the liberal wing of his party and threatened to undermine his higher purposes . . . ."

Rapidly becoming a larger percentage of the total population, the sons and daughters of the World War II generation, led by college students, were the first to object to the Vietnam War. And the students were joined by more and more segments of the populace. Idealism still reigned during the Sixties; a fair percentage of the citizens were passionate in their beliefs, especially the young. Idealists were convinced that events could be changed by participation. And thousands did participate; they marched, they protested, they rioted. Those marching for civil rights for a time merged with those marching against the war in Vietnam.

Protests were rampant, especially during 1968. In *The Year the Dream Died*, Jules Witcover characterized these years as "a cauldron of dissatisfaction and dissent." That it was, and more a year of unusual politics, of assassination, of unexpected happenings that had historic impact.

After the 1967 riots in the ghettos, Governor Otto Kerner of Illinois, who headed the Commission on Civil Disorders, issued its report:

Our nation is moving towards two societies, one black, one white — separate and unequal.

Subsequently, 1968 was also a presidential election year. Senator Eugene J. McCarthy, with his anti-war stance, captured the spirit of the young, the college crowd. Through their hard work and efforts, he won the first primaries of the year. Robert Kennedy, who had not thought of opposing a sitting president and had watched from the sidelines with interest, now decided to enter the fray. Nelson Rockefeller of New York, the hope for a moderate voice in the Republican Party, withdrew from the race early. And populist Governor George C. Wallace of Alabama, then an avowed segregationist, decided to run for president as an Independent.

At the same time, President Lyndon Johnson, disappointed in his dismal approval rating, announced that he would not run again. This pushed Vice President Hubert H. Humphrey to the forefront. Humphrey's liberal, pro-civil rights stance was well known, but as a loyal and supportive Vice President, he had supported Johnson's Vietnam policies. As Jules Witcover put it, "Johnson's war remained Humphrey's main albatross."

The riots that had occurred in so many American cities during these years had been counter-productive. President Johnson, who had been able to enact civil rights legislation such as the Civil Rights Act of 1964 and the Voting Rights Act of 1965 — which prohibited discrimination in public accommodations, schools, employment, and voting — as a result of the riots, faced increasing opposition. The population in general had either agreed or remained silent under President Johnson's efforts to stop overt discrimination. But the riots and the unrest at the campuses allowed opposition candidates to be heard as they garnered support. To quote Witcover:

> The demonstrators in the years up to and including 1968 saw their activities as the legitimate exercise of their rights in the quest to move society, in the case of civil rights and the government, in the case of the war in Vietnam, to do what was right and just. Success in civil rights encouraged them that similar success could be achieved with similar methods to try to end the war. At the same time, foes of civil rights, or those who believed the movement had gone far enough,

and supporters of the Vietnam War saw the street protests as distasteful, disruptive, disloyal, even disgusting.

Then, just after Robert F. Kennedy had narrowly won the California primary in 1968, edging out McCarthy, he was assassinated. Two brothers were gone; the third, Senator Ted Kennedy of Massachusetts, refused to entertain a candidacy. And thus the Democratic leadership, if not the masses, united now behind Hubert Humphrey. Despite strong pressure, especially from the Liberal wing of the party, Humphrey, loyal to the bitter end, still did not differentiate himself from his President.

The unrest of the late Sixties was global — from England to Japan to South America. There were strikes in France, and Russian forces ended Alexander Dubcek's "Prague Spring" in Czechoslovakia when Moscow ordered an invasion on August 20. But it was the riots in Chicago during the 1968 Democratic convention, and the behavior of the Chicago police, that really polarized the nation.

Richard Nixon, having learned from his previous loss in 1960 to John F. Kennedy, ran a fairly quiet presidential campaign, and the Republican Party presented a more unified front. But Hubert Humphrey, who had won the Democratic nomination, faced a splintered party. The Liberal wing opposed him, and the President refused to let him speak his mind on Vietnam. There also was Governor Wallace, the candidate of the American Independent Party, who threatened to take away votes from both candidates — blue collar workers who usually voted Democratic, and right-wing Conservatives, who usually were in the Republican fold.

It was quite late — very late — in the campaign, when Humphrey finally abandoned President Johnson and declared himself willing to stop the bombing of Vietnam. And it was at that precise moment that his campaign began to roll. Money started to come in, and polls finally were moving in his direction. LBJ, too, decided to help. A few days before the election, he announced that he had, indeed, stopped the bombing and that negotiations for peace would start. Our ally, South Vietnam, however, declared it would not attend such a conference. The day before the election, even though Richard Nixon was ahead by a percentage point or two, most polls indicated that it was a virtual tie — too close to call — that

Humphrey's campaign had caught up and that Governor Wallace was losing support.

The majority in Verona, New Jersey, rarely had voted for a Democratic President. Nor had much of an effort had been made for Hubert Humphrey by the local Democratic Party. Many Liberals decided not to vote at all, and because the Democrats were usually in the minority anyway, Richard Nixon easily won the town.

Local elections were then still partisan, and once in a while the sometime independent spirit of Verona voters produced a surprise. As the hometown paper stated two days after the election, "Verona Democrats were successful in placing their third candidate in 60 years on the Borough Council. . . ." The local Democratic winner polled 3,625 votes. Richard Nixon, heading the Republican ticket, out-polled Hubert H. Humphrey by 968 votes: 3,995 to 3,027. A total of 7,535 votes were cast — 87 percent of the registered voters.

The total 1968 election vote in the United States was extremely close. Nixon edged out Humphrey by only 500,000 votes, but it was enough to win the Electoral College. And thus he became the next President, facing a Democratic House and Senate.

The war in Vietnam lingered on for some time, and eventually Spiro Agnew, the Vice President, and later President Nixon himself, would resign under a cloud of scandal.

As Tom Shachtman points out in *Decade of Shocks*, the new generation were children of the bomb, prosperity, and television. And with this new generation came changes: drugs, sex, and rock-and-roll — not that these changes were noticeable all at once. Little by little America was evolving, and with it came resistance from part of the population who wanted America to remain as it had been.

Those of us who lived through the Sixties often recall the era in single words or phrases: Berkeley, Haight-Ashbury, LSD, hippies, "don't trust anyone over thirty," *Hair,* Woodstock, Weathermen, silent majority, My Lai, body count, and — probably the ultimate memory of this period — Watergate.

We had moved to Verona in 1952. It was then a small suburban town, a bedroom community. Most breadwinners left the community in the morning to return in the evening. The population of Verona, like that of so many other towns throughout the country, was increasing rapidly a decade after World War II. Newly married couples ventured forth to buy their dream house, to beget and rear their children. These same children, some of whom would be college students or new workers during the turbulent Sixties, would be the instruments of change.

Those who moved into the suburban community followed their diverse interests — volunteers for the PTA, for the local rescue squad or fire department, Little League, service clubs, and a multitude of various other organizations. But there were no major events that roused the majority of the residents "to man the barricades."

Complacent, quiet, neighborly — that was Verona. But our town was no different from the rest of the country. On a much smaller scale, and at least until May 1968 in a much more civilized way, the anti-war and pro-civil rights forces were opposed by what is now known as the silent majority, those who felt they stood for law and order and for the *status quo*.

The Verona Board of Education changed all that.

Citizens of Verona had a higher level of educational attainment than the region as a whole, which is reflected in household income statistics. . . . in fact, Verona's 1979 household income was about 29 percent higher. . . . The figures of those who completed four years of college rose considerably from 1970 to 1980, from 23.4 to 31.3 percent.

Chapter 2

Verona History Update

THREE HISTORIES OF Verona have been written and published, but not widely distributed. Grace Kaas's booklet, *History of Verona, New Jersey 1702-1907*, was published in 1940 and is currently out of print. My own booklet, *Between the First and Second Mountains: Verona, New Jersey*, published in 1996, is available through the Verona Public Library. And a booklet by Bob Williams, entitled *The Other Side of the White Mountain; Another Verona — The Early History of Verona, New Jersey from 1700-1907*, is available at the Verona Public Library and mentions the Lenape Indians as the first inhabitants of the Verona area. Williams writes:

When the Dutch arrived, the Indian population of New Jersey numbered at least ten to twelve thousand, although this population was quickly reduced by contagious diseases such as smallpox which were introduced by the Europeans.

In 1758, the first Indian reservation in New Jersey, consisting of some 3,000 acres, was established in Burlington County. In 1802 this reservation was sold, and the few remaining Indians departed, leaving some geographical names as their only heritage. Again quoting Williams, *Wachtschunk*, or as it is spelled now, *Watchung*, means "on the hill" and is the name given to the First and Second Mountains. The name of the Peckman River, which meanders through Verona, is believed to be derived from the Indian word *pakihm* meaning "cranberry."

"The Watchungs: Jersey's Jurassic Backbone" was the feature story of the Sunday edition of Newark's *The Star-Ledger* on August 31, 1997. The Watchungs, according to the accounts, were formed about 200 million years ago by one of the largest volcanic eruptions in history. Several violent convulsions over a long period of time created the minor elevations and ridges, all part of the Watchungs — officially named Orange, Preakness, and Hook Mountains, but mostly known now as the First, Second, and Third Mountains.

Verona lies between the First and Second Mountains, which gives it a somewhat insular quality. But the area's boundaries are fairly modern. Beginning in 1666, huge tracts of land were acquired through purchases from the Indians, and in 1702, a deed was secured for the 13,500-acre tract known as Horse Neck, which included a good part of modern day West Essex. It was purchased for roughly two and one-half cents an acre.

The area was settled slowly, mostly by descendants of English, Dutch, French, and Scottish immigrants. Research by Bob Williams turned up a 1787 map in the New Jersey State Library in Trenton, depicting the Ashfield tract, which shows all of Verona and parts of the neighboring towns. The sparsely settled area of Verona proper had only about five roads and was still a part of the Caldwell Township, created in 1798. It is quite probable that George Washington rode through Verona on his way from Camptown (Montclair) to his headquarters in Morristown. Certainly the First Mountain was used as a lookout during the Revolutionary War, to oversee activities between the enemy-held New York area and the swamps and plains between the Hudson River and these high ridges.

Verona was originally called Vernon, but the application for a post office revealed another Vernon in New Jersey, so the town's name was officially changed. In 1892, the approximately 800 people of Cedar Grove and Verona, unhappy with the local government and how its money was being spent, seceded from Caldwell Township to form Verona Township. The two separated in 1907, creating the Borough of Verona, when the residents of Verona proper wanted potable water and those living in the Cedar Grove area deemed potable water a luxury. In order to take advantage of state tax laws, the name was finally changed on September 10, 1981, to the Township of the Borough of Verona. But regardless of the changes and the passage of time, money and drinking water still occasionally flare up as campaign issues during local elections.

The first railroad arrived in the area by 1890, and six years later, the trolley car connected our rather secluded village to the rest of Essex County. Modern transportation and the introduction of the automobile early in the 1900s brought an influx of new settlers to the West Essex area. An 1892 news release trying to sell Verona building lots extolled,

> The elevation of this beautiful section of country, its picturesque mountain ranges, rolling hills and romantic valleys, watered by cool streams and sparkling rivulets, its invigorating atmosphere and pure spring water, make it eminently healthful and entitle it to special consideration from workers of nearby Suburban Residence for the overcrowded in New York, Brooklyn and Newark.

This was not hyperbole.

The population mix in Verona has changed since the early days. In *History of Verona*, Grace Kaas devotes a chapter to the "First Families," in which names like Mr. Butters, Nathaniel Baldwin and his son Lucas, DeWitt C. Calvin, I. Shaffer, Zenas Crane, Charles A. Smith, Marshall Baldwin, and Peter Raabie are mentioned as the first settlers. George Personette, after whom a street is named, was of Huguenot extraction, and two of his ten children are identified with local history. Stephen Personette followed Dr. Bone — Verona's first physician who practiced for years as the sole doctor at the corner of Bloomfield Avenue and Grove Street.

Dr. Bone was a native of Hesse Cassel, Germany. He owned a large part of what is now the center of Verona and also was the first to dam the Peckman River, which resulted in Verona Lake. These days, the lake is surrounded by Verona Park, which was designed by the architectural firm of the famous landscape architect Frederick Law Olmsted.

Grace Kaas estimates that by 1830 the population of Verona was only about 50 families. According to Kaas, the school history goes back as far as 1770, when two log buildings served that purpose. One was located in West Caldwell, the other in what was then still called Vernon, but the exact location of either structure is not known. The schoolhouse erected in 1816 was moved twice, each time apparently during the night by unknown persons. The one-room building known as the Little Red School, which was built in 1831, was located in what is now the Civic Center. The next school was built 50 years later.

By 1953, the school population had reached 2,066. Beginning October 15, 1953, the *Verona-Cedar Grove Times* printed a series of articles prepared by the League of Women Voters entitled, "Know Your Town," which each week examined a different aspect of Verona. The December 10 issue discussed the evolution of the school system and related how, through the efforts of a few dedicated citizens, elementary schools were built in each of the four corners of the town. No small child needed to cross Bloomfield Avenue, the main street which divides Verona from north to south. As the article states:

> The classrooms on the whole are of adequate size, are well-ventilated and lighted and according to some parents, almost too well heated. The administration tries to keep classes from becoming too large for effective individual attention but at present the average number of pupils per teacher is higher than normal — 30 per teacher.

The Census of 1910 listed Verona's population as 1,675, and the community experienced a greater than average rate of growth. The first master plan for the Borough of Verona was published in December 1946, and submitted under the signature of Kenneth W. Burnett, chairman of the planning board. According to the board's estimates, Verona's rate of expansion would reach its limit in 1970 with a population of about 10,200. But, as the League of Women Voters pointed out in 1953, that figure had already been reached by 1950, 20 years earlier than estimated. The population increased again between 1950 and 1970, according to the background studies for a 1991 master plan by Queale and Lynch, Inc., called *Housing Element and Fair Share Plan*, but it "declined in each of the two following decades so that in 1990 the total population of the township [13,597] was about the same as it was in 1960."

Modern-day Verona contains a total land area of 275 square miles, or 1,760 acres. Looking at the map, Verona has fairly straight boundary lines, and with the exception of one area in the northeastern part, is nearly rectangular. By 1977, 51 percent of the land use was residential, 4.2 percent commercial and industrial, and only 5.1 percent was vacant. Land not in use decreased to only 2.7 percent 11 years later.

Verona's population density is higher than both the region and the state, partially due to the lack of land, as well as to the proliferation of subdivided lots and a few conversions of single to two-family houses. Over half of the total housing units in Verona were built before 1950. During the 1950s, there was a considerable amount of construction, which continued through the 1960s; but at that point, the township's land supply diminished and construction activity declined considerably after 1970. According to the Queale and Lynch study, nearly three-quarters of the housing units are owner occupied.

The scarcity of vacant land in Verona had a decided influence on the makeup of the population. The lack of new development meant there were fewer children to attend school. Or, as the *Housing Element and Fair Share Plan* study states,

> Verona's median age is much higher than both the region and the state, whose age group distributions are almost identical. The major disparities between Verona and the other two geographic areas are that Verona has a pre-school ratio about 27 percent lower than the region and state, and its older population is from one-third to 40 percent higher in proportion to the ratios

found in the region and the state. The median age is about six years older than the region and the state.

Overall, the township had a population loss of about 900 between 1970 and 1980, in spite of an increase in the number of households and a continued low vacancy rate. This pattern continued even after 1980, and by 1990 households increased in number by over 300 while the population declined by 569. This is largely a result of the "emptying out" of housing units as children mature and start their own households, plus the overall "graying" of Verona's population.

This aging trend, which dramatically decreased the number of school children and young parents, began in the years between 1960 and 1970. In 1960, less than 20 percent of the population was over age 55, while in 1980 this age group had increased to almost 30 percent. According to the U.S. Census figures quoted in the Queale and Lynch study, the age group of 5 to 14 peaked in 1970 with 2,729 children. In the township and the region in 1960, children under 14 accounted for about 28 percent of the total population. By 1980 the township's ratio dropped to 18 percent, and the region was at 21.9 percent. The year 1970 also showed the highest number of births in Verona, a figure which declined nearly every year thereafter, until the ratio changed again somewhat 17 years later.

All of the elementary schools in Verona were built many years ago. Brookdale Avenue Elementary School, which serves the southeast portion of town, was constructed in 1927, with some additions in 1962. It has a capacity of 219 students and has about three acres, which are used for recreation. Frederic N. Brown Elementary School, located on busy Grove Avenue, serves the northwest quadrant. It was built in 1931, with an addition in 1963. Its capacity is 408 students, with two acres of land. The northeast area of town is served by Laning Avenue Elementary School, on Lanning Road [*sic*], which was constructed in 1918 and expanded in 1955 and 1966. It has a capacity of 304 children, with three acres for play area. Students in the southwest part of town attend Forest Avenue Elementary School, which was built in 1927, with one addition in 1966. The school, which sits on nearly five acres, has a capacity of 284 students.

Citizens of Verona had a higher level of educational attainment than the region as a whole, which is reflected in household income statistics. One would expect Verona's higher proportion of elderly to lower income levels when compared with the region, but, in fact, Verona's 1979 household income was about 29 percent higher. Comparing the educational attainment of persons over 25 years, there is almost no difference between 1970 and 1980, with two significant exceptions. First, in 1970, more residents had a minimum of one to three years of high school as their total education. Ten years later, this percentage fell from 10.5 to 7.4. Second, the figures of those who completed four years of college rose considerably from 1970 to 1980, from 23.4 to 31.3 percent. This change in the percentage of people with higher education moving to Verona after 1970 may also reflect the national "urban flight" trend of the time.

Prior to the building of regional shopping malls, Newark was the hub of not only Essex County, but the entire region. Major department stores (which were easily accessible by trolley), tall office buildings, theaters, and hotels, maintained Newark for many years as the state's most vital city. It was in Newark where many of the residents of Verona, including my family, did their major shopping well into the 1950s and early 1960s. But a decided change was taking place in the population mix in Newark. This, plus the events that were about to unfold, along with the advent of regional malls, changed the habits of most suburbanites, who had looked toward Newark as their shopping and recreational center. Instead, Newark would soon become the city to avoid.

There are suburbs with many more blacks, but Verona's black population has not increased, and black citizens remain on the same two or three streets where they have lived for the past 50 years.

Chapter 3

Verona's Silent Minority — The Blacks

VERONA RESIDENT Alfred P. Harris was born in 1888 and moved to the township in 1893. Harris wrote his story about life in early Verona, entitled "The Priest Farm," when he was 63 years old. In his manuscript, which is reprinted in *Between the First and Second Mountains*, Harris wrote that the Priest Farm included an old rambling, tall, tenement-style building located about where Laning Avenue School is today. It was occupied when Harris was a child by the farm's black help — Br'er Jones, his wife Betsy, and their numerous progeny and relatives.

There were many of them of all ages, working here on the
farm and in the house. They had pigs and chickens and dogs
and cats all around there. . . . The colored man, Br'er Jones, had
charge outside and in the fields. His wife, Aunt Betsy, served in
the kitchen and laundry. I remember that there were quite a
number of smaller Jones youngsters, and some not so small,
who had jobs to perform in and out the house, in the gardens
and field and orchard, and some of the girls in the house under
Betsy's eye. Br'er Jones also marketed most of the farm produce in Montclair stores and to private customers on order. The
Priest Farm became widely known for its quality products.
There was a team of horses which was used to work the farm
on week days and also served on Sundays, hitched to the surrey
and driven by Br'er Jones, when the family attended the Presbyterian Church in Montclair.

Apparently Mr. Priest took title to the land around 1873, but did not
move to work the farm actively until the early 1880s. But at least we know
that black people lived in Verona early on, and have been living there ever
since.

Not far from where the Priests lived, George Martin owned a farm previously worked by his father, whose house was at the corner of Beach and
Martin Roads. It is on Martin Road and nearby streets that most, but not
all, of the black families reside. Verona, like many other communities,
used deed restrictions that kept out minorities, especially in areas considered to be of prime value. For that reason, most of the blacks congregated
in the area around Martin Road, though there were exceptions, like Dr.
Alex Ashe, a chiropractor, who lived at 202 Linden Avenue during the
1970s, the only black in the area.

Gloria Tillery actually lived in Verona on two different occasions. Her
mother, who had been born in Jamaica, came to this country during World
War I, suffering for seven long days on a banana boat. After a legal sepa-
ration, she worked as a domestic, trying her best to raise her two children.
Money was scarce, and for about one year, in 1934, the family moved in
with her mother's sister, who lived in a two-family house on Pompton
Avenue in Verona.

At age ten, Gloria was a student at Laning Avenue School and thoroughly enjoyed the experience. She was not the only black child in school

at that time. After that year, the family moved and both kids graduated from Verona's Bloomfield High School.

With three breadwinners in the family, a deposit of $1,000 was put down for a house at 39 Martin Road, and on Gloria's birthday, February 3, 1944, the family, now homeowners, moved in. A friend, Harrison Tate, who was a postman in Montclair and dabbled in real estate, had helped them obtain the house at a cost of $5,000. Gloria remembers the house well — after all, she lived in it for 48 years. She also remembers the soft coal they had to use for heat, all they could get during wartime. When the family moved in, they were not the only black people living in the area. She remembers Lucy Cox and a family called Hurling, who had a house built for themselves. And Reverend John C. Love, minister of the Union Baptist Church in Montclair, owned two houses on Pompton Avenue.

Gloria commuted via trolley to Newark for her first job at the Office of Dependency Benefit, a government department. Later, for a total of 34 years, she worked for Metropolitan Life, traveling to New York via bus and train.

Commuting did not leave Gloria much time to socialize or to be active in the town in which she lived. Like many blacks living in Verona, she went to church in Montclair on Sundays. Most of her shopping was done in a few small stores — a butcher, a baker, and an ice cream/newspaper store, near where Martin Road ends at Pompton Avenue. There are still some stores in this location.

Tillery praised all her neighbors, black and white, and told me that she had never heard an unfriendly word. Well dressed, well spoken, surrounded by books and the Sunday *New York Times*, Gloria is now retired. She lives in a beautiful large apartment not far from Verona, and spends her free time helping out as a volunteer. She remembers Verona well. After all, "those were forty-eight wonderful years."

Dr. Benjamin Veal moved to Verona in 1965. An educator who once ran for the Board of Education in Verona and who still lives far from where most other blacks live, Dr. Veal told me that 87 blacks lived in Verona in 1968. Like so many other Verona residents, Ben Veal worked his way up. Born in Paterson, New Jersey, in poorer circumstances, Dr. Veal, like many others I interviewed, used the G.I. Bill of Rights to further his education. Despite his having earned a Master's degree from Seton Hall and a doctorate in history from Rutgers, and although he is bright, articulate, and outspoken, Benjamin Veal is largely unknown in town.

Dr. Veal kindly loaned me his unpublished manuscripts, in one of which he wrote:

> Our search for and dream of owning our home was not an easy one. After trying for four years to relocate closer to our jobs, my wife and I had been shown six homes in the surrounding suburban communities. Both black and white real estate agents continue to steer us toward housing they believed was most suitable for black people. We simply refused to involve ourselves in this process once we found they had already selected what they termed "safe areas" . . . homes preselected for primarily black home seekers. After making many inquiries of real estate agents about property they had available for sale, we finally found a white real estate agent who treated us as any other prospective homeowner should be treated. John did not suggest where he thought we should live. He provided us with all of his present listings and encouraged us to "select" the homes we desired to inspect. Our "new home" was located in Verona, a small "integrated" community west of Montclair, on a street lined with oak trees. Our home had been vacant for almost six months and we later found out that some prospective buyers considered it to be overpriced. After inspecting the house with her mother, my wife and I were overjoyed and purchased it. Before the closing on the house took place, John informed us that most of the neighbors had submitted a petition to the former owners . . . requesting that they not sell the home to Negroes. The owners refused to concede to their demands.

Dr. and Mrs. Veal were the only blacks on that street, and never felt truly accepted. Soon after they had moved in, when all their fall leaves had been raked into one large heap in front of their home, someone started a fire during the night. They were surprised upon waking the next morning to find the smoldering remnants in front of their house.

Benjamin Veal first taught in Newark. He sent out over 100 resumes and received only two responses, from Springfield and Wayne. He accepted a post as a teacher in Wayne, and later became principal, one of only three blacks in New Jersey to hold that position. Dr. Veal feels that with his education and experience, had he been white, he could have become a college president. But even as a principal, Dr. Veal became a role model; during those years, not even towns with large black populations had black principals.

Even after his retirement, Dr. Veal continued his exciting lifestyle. Sponsored by the South Africa Forum, he flew to South Africa in 1987 as part of the effort to assist that country's peaceful changeover from the policies of apartheid. He met and discussed the country's problems with some of the most prominent officials. During the same trip, Dr. Veal flew to Namibia and trekked as far as the Angolan border.

During the 1967 Newark riot, Tom Rock, Verona's Chief of Police, warned local blacks not to stray very far from their homes. He advised them that white people with rifles lined Bloomfield Avenue; Chief Rock did not indicate whether they were armed police or vigilantes, and Dr. Veal did not want to ask.

According to Dr. Veal, the Fair Decision group, which opposed busing Newark children to Verona, showed what the town was really like. He viewed this group's statements as blatantly race-based, no matter how they camouflaged their arguments. Dr. Veal attended a meeting of the region's real estate agents, and was asked why he did not openly support the busing plan. He answered that he was not for or against it, but he certainly was against real estate people pushing all their prospective black clients to Montclair. It would be much better if all the towns were integrated, he felt, and then it would not be necessary to bus children.

In his manuscript, Dr. Veal quoted an article written in 1985 in *New York* magazine:

> The number of blacks living in suburbs has increased almost 100 percent in twenty years. A large percentage of blacks own their own homes. The number of blacks enrolled in college in 1960 was 227,000. In 1982, that figure had risen to 1,127,000.

This is supported by the study made by William G. Bowen and Derek C. Bok and published as *The Shape of the River*. According to this book, college and university leaders sought to enrich the education of all of their students by including race as another element in assembling a diverse student body. Also, they acted on the conviction that minority students would have a special opportunity to become leaders in all walks of life, and looked for supportive evidence for admittance.

The *New York* article's figures showed progress, Dr. Veal says, albeit limited progress. There are suburbs with many more blacks, but Verona's black population has not increased, and black citizens remain on the same two or three streets where they have lived for the past 50 years.

Samuel S. Cameron, who now lives on the West Coast of the United States, has a long list of professional achievements. Raised in and having attended public school in Red Bank, New Jersey, Cameron obtained no fewer than three degrees at Montclair State Teachers College. He furthered his education by taking courses at universities wherever his employment took him. Starting out as a teacher, he soon became a principal. Even after his retirement, he served as a principal on special assignments. He writes:

> My introduction and stay in Verona started while I was attending Montclair State Teachers College in 1951. I had observed a house for sale in Verona in 1951. [*The owners*] explained to me that they were building a new home and would not be ready to move for 9-12 months. I shared with them that I only had $10 to put down as a deposit and would bring them $25 to $30 a week until I had saved enough money. I also explained that I would be eligible for $2,000 in about 6 months. The arrangement worked well for me since I had little, if any, money and I had experienced some difficulty finding someone who would allow me to purchase a home in Verona. About 12 months later, I was able to close on the home and move in. This was accomplished with some degree of difficulty, since I was about $700 short at the closing.
>
> I should explain that I was in my first year of college when I entered into the agreement on the house, and I had just about completed my second year in college when I moved into Verona. In 1951, there were only four black families on Martin

Road. There were 24 white families on the street. As more black families started to move into the neighborhood more white families moved out. Black families had difficulty purchasing houses in Verona with the exception of the Martin Road, Nassau Road and Pompton Road areas.

During the first three years living in the area I had little time for anything else but school work, improving the house and church. When I went to City Hall to pay a bill, people were somewhat less than friendly. However, I started to demand that I receive a prompt response to my requests. I remember members of the police department being less than helpful. Police would stop you and ask, "What are you doing in this neighborhood? Where do you work?" And in general not give the kind of respect that a citizen should expect. I spoke with Chief Rock and the Superintendent of Schools on the phone and in person concerning things that needed improvements. I took an unofficial survey of all the black families in Verona, and to the surprise of the elected officials, there were close to 100 blacks in Verona in the 1960s. Dr. Veal and his family had experienced some of the same difficulties, and since we seemed to be getting little if anything moving in a positive direction, we decided to run for the Verona School Board.

We recognized that we stood little, if any, chance of being elected. We invited ourselves to both political party meetings and shared our concerns, our dream for a better town. As we started to move around in the community, many positive people encouraged us to continue our quest for equality.

Dr. Veal and I hosted several meetings in homes in Verona in both the black and white community. Many persons seemed interested in learning about the culture of black people. As a result we organized several meetings with educators, business persons, elected officials, etc., at Verona High School. We brought in speakers like Dr. Samuel Proctor of Rutgers, Rev. Dual C. Rice of the Union Baptist Church in Montclair, Rev. Matthew Carter, CEO of the Y.M.C.A. , and Mr. James Ransey from the Cedar Grove Public Schools. These meetings resulted in the city of Verona recognizing that black people had much to offer to a town like Verona. While some progress was being made, there were those forces in Verona who attempted to stop progress. Our children experienced some difficulty at school by adults who wished to discourage us.

The election itself was interesting. I don't remember how many votes we received. But one thing became clear. Black people had talent, black people had no intention of leaving Verona, and the power structure would be forced to deal with us in a fair way. We feel that some bridges were built towards a better understanding. As a result of some positive experiences in Verona I moved to Seattle, Washington, where I worked with multi-ethnic groups.

While working for the Board of Education as a principal in Palm Beach County, Florida, I worked with the Jewish Federation in Boca Raton on a program called "Hands Across the Campus." As of June 1996 I retired. I will continue to work for organizations which pull people together, building bridges for better understanding.

Our two children who attended the Verona Public Schools are working. Our daughter Colleen is a R.N. and our son Winthrop is a clergyman/educator serving as a principal in the public schools.

The best-known black family in Verona has long been the Hatchetts. Not only did they move here as early as 1939, they knew everybody in town, and, as one of the brothers states, "put Verona on the map."

In 1939, a number of blacks were already living in Verona, mostly in the same area where they live now. But Tom Hatchett also remembers the Green family, who had a home on the west side of town, near where the Senior Citizens complex now stands; the Dairyman family, who lived close to the bottom of Linden Avenue; and the Turner and the Wiggins families at the corner of Pine and Bloomfield Avenues, in what some of us call the "Flatiron Building," which is shaped similar to — but much smaller than — the famous in New York building of the same name. All these locations are far from the Martin Road area.

Tom Hatchett told me proudly and very emphatically that his family never had any problems living as blacks in Verona. But, later in the conversation, he also told me that he knew exactly what he could and could not do.

His parents rented a house on Pompton Avenue from white people. His father worked in construction and his mother did housework. Tom was five years old when they came to Verona, and his older brother William, known as Bucky, was ten. Both went through the Verona school system, Tom first at Laning Avenue School, then at the Junior High School, known then as the Red School (now torn down), and finally Verona High School (now the middle school). He, like his brother, excelled in sports, and that certainly made the brothers much more accepted. There were only two blacks in his graduating class. One went into service, while Tom spent the next two years at Grambling College. He remembers the advice of Nelson "Skip" Smith, his athletic director, who thought it would be better for Tom to enroll in an all-black school. He felt that since Tom had grown up in all-white surroundings, he probably should learn more about his roots.

Instead, Tom quit and found a job as a plant manager in nearby Parsippany, New Jersey, a position he still holds today. After his marriage, he bought a house in Verona and brought up his kids in his hometown. After all, he knew nearly everyone, was even offered a job as a policeman in town (though at a salary that he did not think was adequate) and was able to overlook occasional slights. As a matter of fact, for a short time the family had moved away. But they came back, primarily for the children to obtain the first-rate education he himself had received. All three of his children, though no longer living in Verona, are doing well.

Not everyone had it as easy, Tom remembers. The Crockets were an interracial family, a black husband and a white wife. The wife came to see the house, did all the negotiations and signed the contract. When the family moved in, the neighbors were in an uproar. They complained bitterly to the previous owner, but it was too late. As time went on, Mr. Crocket and most neighbors became friendly. And Bryan Crocket, at the high school, played on the same basketball team as my younger son Allen.

But it was Tom Hatchett's brother, Bucky, who was the famous one. *The Free Lance-Star*, the Fredericksburg, Virginia, newspaper, reported that Bucky Hatchett was

> the only man in the history of Rutgers to be inducted into
> two sports Halls of Fame, but the former Scarlet Knight

doesn't wear those honors on his crimson sleeve. In fact, his own wife didn't even know he was a football and basketball star until after their children were born.

At Rutgers, the 6-foot, 3-inch center was the first-ever 1,000-point scorer, a record that stood for 15 years (he had actually scored a total of 1,245 points). In his first football season, Bucky was named All-American and caught seven touchdown passes. He also set state records in the high jump and in the 120-yard hurdle.

Sid Dorfman, *The* (Newark) *Star-Ledger* sports writer, believes that Hatchett may be the best home-grown athlete in New Jersey history. "Bucky was a track zephyr, a collegiate football star and a guy who didn't play pro basketball only because he didn't want to." At that time, Hatchett was one of five black students at Rutgers, but race was never an issue until the team traveled to Johns Hopkins University. When a Baltimore hotel wouldn't let Hatchett stay there with his teammates, the story hit the radio waves and Rutgers graduates across the region offered him a place for the night.

During his senior year, Bucky Hatchett became the first black elected president of his class. Drafted by the Baltimore Bullets, he had to yield to a higher draft board. As an officer he spent a year in northern Japan during the Korean War, also guiding his football, basketball, track, and swimming teams to championships in their respective service divisions. For the next 16 years, Bucky was a mainstay of the Verona school system as a teacher, basketball coach, and director at the Verona Recreation Department. For 13 years he was an active member of the Verona Lions Club, a charter member and director of the Verona Community Little League Program, and served on the Board of Directors of the American Red Cross for the West Essex, New Jersey, chapter. With him on hand, Verona won four straight Suburban Conference and State Group 1 outdoor track and field championships! Sports is the great equalizer; everybody seemed to love him, and he would be highly electable, even in Verona, if he were to run for office.

In 1966, Bucky Hatchett left Verona to work for RCA at the electronics company's McCoy Job Corps Center in Wisconsin, where he set up and operated a complete program of recreation for 1,200 Job Corps young men. In 1968, he accepted a position as manager of the Special Employment Project for the RCA Corporate staff, where his initiatives and new programs in training the hard-core unemployed were widely praised. To date, he has made over 200 formal presentations to over 3,000 RCA management personnel. He has also spoken on college campuses and to business groups outside the RCA family.

He served as a commissioner of the New Jersey Public Broadcasting Authority, was on the Advisory Council on Economics in Career Education for the New Jersey State Boards of Education and Higher Education, and is a charter member of "Edges," a group of corporate executives working in concert to further the progress of equal employment opportunity.

His twin daughters, also All-Americans, were state high school champions in track, then went on to become members of the University of Virginia team that won the NCAA championship in 1981. Both earned Master's degrees and now work in New York City, one on Wall Street, the other for Xerox.

Bucky explained that he had left Verona after working there for many years because Verona refused him job opportunities. Twice there had been opportunities in Verona and he had been passed over. When the man who held the job as athletic director had moved to another job, Bucky applied. After all, in his Army days, he had provided similar duties to a whole division of men — more than the entire population of Verona. He did not get the job, and through the grapevine heard that higher-ups in the school district refused to be the first in the state to hire a black for that position. And this was not an isolated incident. When the job of head of the Verona Recreation Department opened up a couple of years before, a position for which he was eminently qualified, Hatchett was passed up by the Board of Education. And so, when a friend of his called to advise him of the job opening at the Wisconsin Job Corps Center, he knew it was tailor-made to his expertise. After visiting the town of Sparta, Wisconsin, which had a population of about 5,000, Bucky and his wife decided to make the move.

During his time in Verona, Bucky had been invited to attend a couple of meetings at the Verona Lyons Club, and then was asked to join, which he did. But once, over drinks, he was told by some of his fellow members that permission, which had been sought from the state or national organization to have Bucky join, had been refused. Nothing was said, the local members just ignored what they were told, and he was inducted anyway. It is Bucky's impression that he was the first black inducted in the

Lyons, a fact that he never really checked. (The Verona-Cedar Grove Kiwanis Club had a black member, Dr. Nash, for some time. However, the club was nearly terminated when it ignored the regional demand not to induct a woman as a member.)

Bucky Hatchett still has fond memories of Verona, and when he visits his brother, gets together with others from that era. He liked living in Verona, but knew that as an athlete he was different. Even so, he knew exactly what was required — keep his nose clean and know when to keep quiet. But even playing that game did not get Bucky the hoped-for promotions.

On February 8, 1994, the *Verona-Cedar Grove Times* printed the following letter signed by David and Sarah Love:

> There is an unsettling feeling in our home today. Though we live only a block away, a South Prospect Avenue resident called the police stating that our son was a suspicious character in the neighborhood.
>
> Now we know that in these modern days, neighborhoods no longer exist. But it is not that fact which is unsettling. My son was carrying a shovel on the snowy Saturday morning going from house to house trying to raise money for his sister's birthday presents. Most people would be extremely proud of the work ethic exhibited by such a young man. All too often our modern children expect things without having to work for them. However, rather than being seen as hard working, he was seen as suspicious.
>
> What is more unsettling is my other child came home having been offered many more jobs than she could possibly handle. Why would one child be seen as hirable and the other suspicious? Well you see, my daughter is white and my son is black.
>
> Verona has a very unsettling attitude exhibited within its boundaries. Don't dare to be different. This bigoted neighbor is not an asset to the community but rather a cancer that weakens us. The police would not identify this neighbor, citing that it

would do no good to introduce our son to these people; if they hate blacks they will always hate blacks.

We can only hope this suspicious person reads this letter and can understand the hatred that is exhibited by people of their type. Our son will recover, but we are not sure that he will ever feel comfortable in his own neighborhood.

Mrs. Love assured me later over the telephone that this had been an isolated incident and that their son was happy at the high school in Verona.

The riots of 1967 are thought to be the defining moment of the decline of Newark. But the truth lies somewhere else — the results of two world wars, the recession, the rise and fall of manufacturing, federal and local government policies, the impetus of residents to move to the suburbs, and the change to an information-oriented society.

Chapter 4

The Short History of Newark and the Clinton Hill/Weequahic Section

*T*HE POSSIBILITY OF A late-night, sit-down franchise restaurant opening in Newark — the first since the riots not including fast-food chains — warranted a headline in the Essex section of Newark's *The Star-Ledger* on November 26, 1997. The current Mayor, Sharpe James, visited a small business that had begun making knishes in a little South Ward shop on Hawthorne Avenue in 1947, employing 60 people, and was now looking for land in Newark to enlarge. This warranted another headline! This shop's planned move was big news in New Jersey's largest city, the third oldest of larger cities in the United States, a city that once boasted famous manufacturing plants like Engelhard, Edison, Hyatt, Weston, Tiffany — a city associated with an unbelievable array of industrial firsts and inventions that have changed the face of America.

At one time, the population of Newark exceeded 400,000. It has since dropped to fewer than 260,000, but the city is still the largest in New Jersey. Newark's decline started long before the riot of 1967, but the early changes were subtle.

When we moved to Verona in 1952, there were no shopping malls in the suburbs. Newark was the place to go, with six major department stores and over 1,000 other stores, legitimate theater downtown, and, at one time, some 50 movie houses scattered throughout in the various sections of the city.

Everyone laments the decline of Newark as a shopping center. But this has happened to many other communities of all sizes where small stores could not compete with regional malls or giant retailers like Wal-Mart. Newark, however, fared worse than most cities; banks left, all new car dealerships left, as well as supermarkets and department stores, and, at one time, every movie house had closed other than a couple of X-rated theaters.

Lately, there has been a reversal. The downtown office buildings are occupied; the New Jersey Performing Arts Center has opened; a stadium is on the drawing boards; restaurants, especially those featuring Spanish or Portuguese food, are crowded; Rite-Aid and other larger markets have opened. There is renewed hope.

Newark is one of the oldest cities in the United States. John T. Cunningham and Charles F. Cummings (who is the official Newark Historian and Assistant Director for Special Collections for the Newark Library), authors of *Remembering Essex: A Pictorial History of Essex County*, write:

> Several small boats worked slowly up the Passaic River in mid-May of 1666, weighed down by thirty families, household goods, livestock, fruit trees, and weapons. These were fundamentalist Puritans from Connecticut, hopeful that they had at last found their Zion, where church and government would be

one forever. No written record of the arrival survives, but tradition sets the date as May 18. Assuming each family had an
average of at least six children, usual in those days, about 250
people landed that day to found Newark and eventually, Essex
County.

The immigrants who settled Newark were industrious, and the city soon
became an industrial leader, known for large and small factories selling
worldwide. As the stores and factories crowded the center, those who
could afford it moved to the outskirts of the city. Soon, electric trolleys
made it possible to live farther away, in sections known as Forest Hill,
Vailsburg, Roseville, Clinton Hill, and later Weequahic. All these were
absorbed as parts of Newark.

A French visitor called Newark in the late 1700s "the most beautiful
village on the continent." Landscape artists pictured Newark and its surroundings. However, about 150 years later, industrialization and lack of
planning made Newark among the unhealthiest of cities — one notable
exception being that Newark always had an adequate supply of good
water. Three large reservoirs had been built in Passaic County, and, by
1892, a 48-inch steel pipe carried millions of gallons to Newark. The
Pequanock River storage area, together with the Wannaque Reservoir,
supplies good water to this day.

Blacks have lived in Newark almost since its beginnings; there were a
few slaves in the Newark area around 1730. As early as 1791, the local
newspaper spoke out against slavery, and in 1804, New Jersey started to
abolish the practice. According to John D. Cunningham, 75 free black
men with their own businesses were among the taxpayers of 1814. Eight
years later, the first black church was organized, the forerunner of St.
John's Methodist and Clinton Memorial AME Zion churches. By 1835,
the black population had increased to 112 adult blacks, whose occupations
included teaching, blacksmithing, carpentry, and restaurant owners. About
a score of black families owned their own homes. And while sentiments
in Newark were for the South prior to the Civil War — mainly due to the
strong trade ties for much of Newark's output — all of Newark's blacks
were free by 1860, working in jobs or in their own businesses and attending their own churches. According to a 1900 Rand, McNally & Co. atlas,
the population of New Jersey in 1890 was 1,444,933 of which 48,352
were black. At that time, the population of Newark, called the metropolis,

was 250,000. According to Helen M. Stummer, author of *No Easy Walk: Newark 1980-1993*, there were about 6,000 African Americans living in Newark when her grandfather arrived there in 1903.

During World War I, the Newark factories needed workers, and they came willingly — many of them black tenant farmers from the South. During the Depression of the 1930s, Newark became a town of unemployed — close to a third of the workers could not find jobs. The children of the more recent immigrants, with various European backgrounds, and the children of the blacks who had moved in to work in the factories, began to overwhelm the school system. The black population continued to increase, and during economic downturns this group suffered the most.

Newark saw a return to prosperity during World War II, as manufacturing demand brought full employment and a new influx of workers, again many of them black. But the good times also brought renewed pressures on the school system. Newark, like many other large cities, had lost "ratables" — property that is taxable. The tax base had shrunk due to the large-scale emigration to the suburbs of its wealthier citizens. To this day, the city abounds with tax-free institutions — colleges, private schools, hospitals, churches. Property taxes are high, and the city's tax system has not been revised since the late 1950s.

Helen M. Stummer writes that as early as 1925, about 40 percent of the city's attorneys already lived in the suburbs. By 1932, fully 86 percent of the officers and board members of the Chamber of Commerce lived outside the city. Quoting a 1944 planning report, John T. Cunningham states that Newark had lost its employment dominance: in 1909, it had 20 percent of all the jobs in New Jersey; by 1939, the figure was only 11 percent. Similarly, wages had slipped from 25 percent of the state to only 10 percent. The city budget was slashed, and still property taxes increased. And, even more importantly, nearly one-third of all dwelling units were estimated to be below "the generally accepted minimum standards of health and decency."

In the late 1940s and early 1950s, thousands of returning veterans looked for their own homes, driving their newly acquired cars along newly built highways. Every weekend freshly created subdivisions were crowded with home seekers. The real exodus to the suburbs had started. In *The Prize*, Daniel Yergin writes about the changes in U.S. cities after the war, brought on by the availability of cars and gas.

Suburbanization quickly gathered amazing speed. The number
of single-family new housing starts rose from 114,000 in 1944
to 1.7 million in 1950. With the developer's magic, every kind
of terrain, broccoli and spinach and dairy farms, apple orchards,
avocado and orange groves, plum and fig groves, old estates,
racetracks and garbage dumps, hillside scrub and just plain
desert gave way to subdivisions. Between 1945 and 1954, 9
million people moved to the suburbs. Millions more followed
thereafter. Altogether, between 1950 and 1976, the number of
Americans living in central cities grew by 10 million, the number in the suburbs by 85 million.

But this trend, so new to the rest of the country, was already established
in New Jersey. *Picturesque America or the Land We Live In*, printed in
1874, states,

In no part of the country has speculation in real estate been
carried on more vigorously or more successfully than in Northern New Jersey, and many a hard-working farmer has found
himself unexpectedly rich through the marvelous rise in the
value of the land which his father considered as only adapted to
the raising of cabbages or potatoes.

The movement to leave Newark accelerated after the 1967 riot. Even
before the unrest, this outward migration from Newark — and from many
other inner cities — was actually assisted by the worry about the influx of
the black population, and the fear of loss in real estate value due to the
practice of red-lining, or color-coding, by the Federal Housing Administration. As Helen M. Stummer vividly describes, the FHA believed that
density, ethnic and racial mixing, income mixing, and old buildings, were
undesirable and would, even in small quantities, depress property values:

The presence of Jews would demote even the best neighborhood to blue or yellow, but black neighborhoods were colored
red no matter what their condition.

This added to the detriment of cities like Newark, in which the population mix was predominantly immigrant, including Jews, and where, later,

large groups of blacks moved in. In addition, most of the buildings were old. Soon, nearly all of Newark was red-lined. Real estate values dropped, as did the income the city needed to sustain services, including education.

Along with the population, many factories left, too, finding greener pastures in the suburbs where the infrastructure was available. Federal tax regulations benefited new construction, not renovation, and the former Newarkers readily found employment without the hassles of long commutes and limited parking. Only recently have these errors been realized, and city planners everywhere are urging the redevelopment and rezoning of many of the older, now empty factory buildings. Indeed, the New Jersey Department of State set up Brownfield Remediation, which seeks to bring about the re-use of polluted factory sites by joint actions or new owners, and Big Box Development which oversees the rezoning and remodeling of former factories.

Venal politicians, first white and later black, did not help Newark or Essex County, either. Even though the black population had increased dramatically during the years, in 1967, the city was still governed mostly by whites. Blacks were excluded from many city jobs, including those in the police and fire departments, nor did they run the school system.

Writer-historian Jean-Rae Turner, a life-long resident of the Weequahic section, offered a wealth of historical information on the Hawthorne School area and its residents, who were to partner with Verona in the busing experiment. Many of those who lived in Newark's so-called South Ward — where the school is located — were forced to move prior to the riot when Route 78 was built. The South Ward, which also includes Clinton Hill, is now one of the city's poorest neighborhoods. But it was not always that way.

The section of Newark from Hawthorne Avenue to the Hillside line in the South Ward was admitted to the city in 1902. Originally, this area was known as Lyons Farm, because at one time early in the 18th century, 14 families by the name of Lyon lived there. Divident Hill, at the foot of Lyons Avenue — once the site of Dr. I. M. Ward's farm — was the traditional border between Elizabethtown and the Town of Newark. This border was agreed upon on May 20, 1668, when the representatives of the two settlements met on top of the hill. Divident Hill is supposed to have served as the traditional boundary between the Hackensack Indians to the north and the Raritan Indians to the south. Both were part of the Lenape tribes who occupied New Jersey. (Current plans for the area include the Lenape Trail, which, while not yet connected in all sections, will eventually offer a walking tour through all of Essex County.) Elizabethtown pioneers were granted land, which included all of Union and Essex and parts of Passaic, Morris, and Middlesex counties, by Captain Richard Nicolls, who captured New Amsterdam, New York, from the Dutch in 1664. Two years later, the Town of Newark made an agreement with Elizabethtown, taking about half of the grant. The early settlers, mostly Protestant and second-generation Americans from England, Scotland, Holland, or France, moved from Massachusetts via Connecticut and Long Island to the two New Jersey settlements. Irish Catholics formed Clinton Township in 1834. This new community, which did not last very long, cut a three-mile-wide and eight-mile-long wedge through Lyons Farm. It was dissolved on March 11, 1902, and the remainder of the Lyons Farm was merged into Newark.

Horse racing was one of the favored sports of the people of Lyons Farm. A track had been built about 1856, northeast of the present Weequahic Park. The section was named Waverly Park by Mary Mapes Dodge, an author who loved Sir Walter Scott's *Waverly* novels (Dodge wrote *Hans Brinker*, or *The Silver Skates*, and was editor of *St. Nicholas Magazine*). The horse races would be interrupted by the Civil War, but thrived again afterward.

The races also brought Gypsies into the area. They settled both across from the Lyons Farm Schoolhouse (which was built in 1784 and is now part of the Newark Museum) on the "Upper Road" — what is now Elizabeth Avenue — and Pot Pie Lane (Chancellor Avenue) in the area now called Weequahic Park, and on an island off Frelinghuysen Avenue. The men traded horses and the women told fortunes. They were among the first snowbirds, arriving with their wagons in April and leaving for the South in October.

The annual state fair was held in Waverly Park by the New Jersey State Agricultural Society from 1866 to 1898, when it was moved to Trenton. The Essex County Park Commission, the first such commission in the United States, purchased the fairgrounds and the adjacent swampy land, and began developing a 75-acre lake and the 311.24-acre park. It was completed with the dedication of a huge monument on Divident Hill in 1916. The park was named Weequahic, meaning the "head of the cove."

Horse racing continued until World War II, when an Army Air Corps hospital was placed in front of the stadium and staffed with physicians from Beth Israel Hospital. The barracks later were converted into homes for returning servicemen. Racing was resumed in July 1955, and moved to Robert L. Johnson Park in Highland Park about ten years later.

Until about 1910, the Lyons Farm-Weequahic area was farmland, primarily known for its apple trees. Twenty years later, little was left of the open land. One parcel was the house and garden of Dr. William Ward, Jr., at 112 Chancellor Avenue. Later a temple was built there, then a Baptist Church, and several dwellings were erected on the site.

The Weequahic and Clinton Hill area, where Hawthorne School is located, was initially populated by the children of new immigrants, who were later replaced by Jewish families — to the point that some sections became about 90 percent Jewish. Clinton Hill boasted of one-family homes, while in Weequahic, in addition to one-family houses, large and elegant apartments were built. Until the 1960s, Newark's school system was excellent.

Mr. and Mrs. David Wiesen, who purchased their home in the Weequahic section in 1966, told of the westward move made by more and more residents. While they remained in Newark, most of their friends left. First, those with real money purchased large estates in western Morris County. Mr. Wiesen surmised that Newark was never "fashionable." Sandwiched between Philadelphia and New York City, Newark always appeared "inferior" to those interested in the arts and the theater. Unless one was in or close to Manhattan, the location was considered less desirable, just like Brooklyn or the Bronx — not "with it."

Irv Newman, a former Verona resident, feels that growing up in the Clinton Hill section of Newark was a good experience. "There was a pervading sense of community and shared encounters," he said. It was like being related to everyone, or like being a part of one big family. And even though the big city of New York, and the busy section of Newark were close by, Clinton Hill felt like a small neighborhood town.

Of growing up during that time, Newman writes,

> Peshine Avenue School, my grammar school and Weequahic High School were predominantly Jewish; and even in those days the schools closed for the Jewish High Holidays. There were only three or four black kids in my grammar school and maybe five or six at my high school. Safety was never a question. We played in the streets, hung out in the school

playgrounds, or sat on the stoops of homes. Probably the worst crime committed was stealing a package of gum from the local candy or grocery store.

Very few people owned cars. We either walked to our schools or spent a nickel for a bus or trolley car. It seems that every child knew the parents of their classmates. Sundays were visiting days for friends, neighbors or family. Simple refreshments were served; there was no money for pretentious offerings. For a real treat we saved our pennies to accumulate a dime for a movie admission — and then we all chipped in a couple of pennies to buy and share some candy. In the evening families gathered around the radio for entertainment.

And even those who had very little money still had the opportunity to work their way through college. For a nickel they commuted to some of the local schools: University of Newark, Montclair State Teachers College or Rutgers Pharmacy. Newark also had a Hebrew Free Loan where in an emergency one could borrow.

I still am in touch with some of the kids of those days. And when we get together we still talk of the good old days.

The first black families moved into the area after World War II. In 1967, Clinton Hill already had a racially mixed group of residents, while Weequahic was still more white than black — and also more Jewish than most other areas. Even at that time, there was a connection between Newark and Verona — the owner of the Weequahic Diner, Morris Bauman, opened the Clairmont Diner in Verona. For some time the restaurant made Verona famous; people came from all over to eat there, including many from Newark.

The 1967 riot did not start in that area, but the South Ward was not spared, and part of Clinton Avenue suffered damage. All reports seemed to indicate that the riot was self-feeding. Though at one time contained, it again became ugly when the National Guard and the New Jersey State Police took over from the local authorities. Most of those killed were black, and although the papers at that time reported heavy sniper activity, later investigations denied this.

The Star-Ledger, New Jersey's largest paper, concluded its series on Newark the last day of 1997 with a full-page editorial. It stated that during the past 30 years, Newark had lost a large part of its population. Jobs were scarce at a time when employment had increased in the rest of the state. Newark authorities complained about the state takeover of the school system, but had no ideas for a remedy. Newark's leadership had not spent the time and money to plan for a better future, the article said. Though there were indications of change for the better, the paper complained, as long as only one-quarter of the residents bothered to vote in local elections, as long as there was no leadership with vision and a definite plan, those isolated improvements would not bring Newark back to its former glory.

The riots of 1967 are thought to be the defining moment of the decline of Newark. But the truth lies somewhere else — the results of two world wars, the recession, the rise and fall of manufacturing, federal and local government policies, the impetus of residents to move to the suburbs, and the change to an information-oriented society. All these factors have contributed to the changes of most major population centers, and especially to the inner cities. Newark may rise again, but it will have changed drastically.

"The pattern of racial violence that had scarred city after city across the nation." . . . had finally reached Newark.

Chapter 5

Response to a Ghetto Exploding

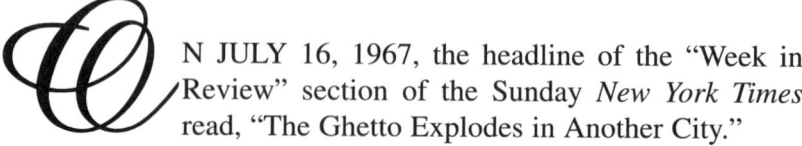N JULY 16, 1967, the headline of the "Week in Review" section of the Sunday *New York Times* read, "The Ghetto Explodes in Another City."

The Times noted "the pattern of racial violence that had scarred city after city across the nation." Streets filled with debris, shops burned and looted, and "the dead and the injured — and always new legacies of hatred and bitterness —" had finally reached Newark.

On August 8, 1967, three weeks after the riot, Governor Richard J. Hughes asked his commission to "examine the causes, the incidents and the remedies for the civil disorders which have afflicted New Jersey." Six months later, in February 1968, the Governor's Select Commission on Civil Disorder issued its "Report for Action." The report started with a short history of Newark and noted the change of the population mix. In 1911, it said, the predominant nationalities were Italians and Jews, with each claiming about 50,000 residents. Germans, Irish, and Slavs also had sizable groups. "Negroes" — the term used by the commission and one that was common at the time — numbered only 11,000. After World War I, blacks moved north to apply for available jobs in industry. That trend continued during and after World War II. "In the postwar era, young Newarkers began moving to the suburbs," the report continued, "commuting to their jobs in Newark. Negroes from the rural South flooded into the city." By 1967, Newark's black population had reached 52 percent. Newark and Washington, D.C., were the only large cities to have reached that stage.

The riot started on July 13. *The New York Times* reported: "Bands of Negroes Smash Windows and Stone the Police in Ghetto Area." It was not a major news story as yet, occupying a short column on page 1, and continued to page 26:

> Racial tension in Newark has been heightened in recent months by two issues: the selection of a new secretary for the school board and plans for the construction of a College of Medicine in the predominantly Negro Central Ward.

These issues may have lit the match, but judging from the report by the commission, these were but two of many problems. The next day, July 14, the riot commanded the lead story of *The New York Times*. "NEWARK'S MAYOR CALLS IN GUARD AS RIOTS SPREAD" was the banner headline, above the subheadings "Downtown is Hit" and "Scores are Injured — Police Instructed to Return Fire."

> The National Guard was called into this riot-torn city early today as Negro mobs spilled from their Central Ward Ghetto into the heart of the downtown business district.

It was at that time that Newark's Mayor, Hugh J. Addonizio, telephoned Governor Richard J. Hughes and asked for help, admitting that the police could not control the outbreak. Shotgun-wielding police guarded firemen who were fighting a raging fire in the center of the business district. The blaze drew hundreds of black onlookers, who then broke from the crowd to race through the business district, smashing windows and looting. Scores were injured, more were arrested.

It was a three-column headline on July 15:

11 DIE, 600 HURT IN NEWARK RIOTS; TROOPS USED TO CURB NEGROES; GOVERNOR SEES "INSURRECTION"

Underneath the headline, a large photo pictured police and national guardsmen searching prone blacks for weapons and stolen merchandise. One feature story told of soldiers exchanging "sporadic" gunfire with snipers at the Stella Wright housing project; another was about the curfew imposed on the city, stating that one sniper had killed a policeman at the same housing project. In a third story, a reporter watched a group of young black women looting a supermarket under the heading, "Leisurely Looters Defend Acts As Way To Deal With 'Whitey'."

Newark had now become a major story, and it continued to be for the next several days. On July 16, the front page of *The New York Times* read:

NEWARK RIOT DEATHS AT 21 AS NEGRO SNIPING WIDENS; HUGHES MAY SEEK U.S. AID.

Four persons had been killed that night, a total of 21 as the rioting was into its fifth day. The Governor was considering an appeal for federal intervention as "bursts from machine-guns" were heard in downtown Newark. "The police used so much ammunition," the article noted, "that 20 cases of rifle cartridges were borrowed from nearby Union City."

There were long reports, augmented by shorter stories on the prohibition of visitors to the City Hospital, the complaint of "home-grown" ills cited by blacks as the reason for the "insurrection," and the closing of major stores downtown due to lack of customers. The last article cited a parking attendant who complained that there were only ten cars instead of the usual 150 in the lot, and a bus driver who drove a nearly empty bus.

The following day, the riots were no longer the top story; a rail stoppage tying up commuter lines took a more prominent position. The coverage of the riot told of a house-to-house search for snipers and stated that nearly half of Newark's 23.7 square miles had become an occupied zone.

During the next few days, the local news included stories on the city's efforts to restore calm, and the panel that was set up by Governor Hughes to study the rioting. On the national scene, Congress voted for a bill which would have made it a federal crime to use interstate facilities or cross state lines to incite to riot. The vote on the same bill in the Senate was in doubt.

The 160-page report by the Governor's commission detailed the problems found within the political framework, the police, the courts, economics, housing, employment, etc., and set forth more than 12 pages of recommendations.

The report found that black neighborhoods were not taken care of by the local government. Slum landlords did not maintain homes, people lived in hovels, streets were dirty. Cars and buildings were abandoned in the neighborhoods. The report painted a bleak picture of corrupt city administration, high unemployment, and neglect.

But perhaps the report's strongest language concerned education. It was the commission's considered judgment that Newark's public school system was in an advanced state of decay.

> . . . The ills of the ghetto will not be permanently cured until the people of the ghetto have the same opportunity as other citizens to choose where they want to live, and the economic means to exercise this option. . . . And since education is perhaps the single most important key to escape from the ghetto, this Commission, as a matter of immediate urgency, is addressing itself to reform and improvement of ghetto schools in the immediate future. Each day that a child is poorly educated or miseducated postpones and in many cases precludes the possibility of escape.

The commission learned that Newark had reached its bonded indebtedness limit, that new school construction had to be delayed indefinitely, and that the system was some $250 million behind in capital funds needed to bring physical plants up to date. Overcrowding was a severe problem, with schools short more than 6,000 pupil stations the previous year and likely to be closer to 10,000 stations short the year of the report. Schools were averaging 112 percent of capacity, with some elementary schools operating at 101 to 151 percent of capacity. Part of this problem was caused by an ever-increasing student population, with one-third of the new arrivals coming from the Southern states and Puerto Rico. Because many of the children received their education in rural segregated schools of the South, or spoke Spanish, they were ill-equipped to cope with the demands and systems in the North. In addition, the commission found that each year 28 percent of Newark's school children left the district, many of them to seek better education in parochial or suburban schools. In 1961, 55 percent of Newark's pupils were black and 4 percent Spanish-speaking. Five years later the ratio was 69 percent black and 7 percent Spanish.

A table showed that Newark students' median reading and Stanford arithmetic test scores were below the national norm. Further, the gap between Newark children's student performance and national levels were widening as the students moved up in grades. The commission noted the high dropout problem, the dissatisfaction of Newark's population — black and white — with the state of education in the city, and the pressing need for additional fully certified teachers. Nearly one page was devoted to the

> lack of any meaningful relationship between the people in the ghetto and their schools. The situation contrasts sharply with that in many suburbs, where parents, and particularly mothers, are in touch with teachers and principals, and active in or on behalf of the schools.

The commission recommended that the state of New Jersey take over the administration of the Newark public schools, and asked for additional money to fund personnel, facilities, and special training for existing personnel. The panel urged the state to "take whatever measures the Governor, through the Commissioner of Education and with the advice of the Newark school authorities, deems necessary to resolve the crisis."

Other suggestions included the decentralization of the Newark public schools, a revised school aid formula to help impacted school districts, the development of additional sources of revenue, and an immediate review of teacher certification requirements.

Nowhere in this report did the commission recommend the busing of some of these children to more affluent suburban schools.

The National Advisory Commission on Civil Disorders — which was established in 1967 by President Johnson and chaired by Illinois Governor Otto Kerner — was charged with discovering the causes of the riots. The commission's findings were stated bluntly in its report, released on February 29, 1968:

> What white Americans have never fully understood — but what the Negro can never forget — is that white society is deeply implicated in the ghetto. White institutions created it, white institutions maintain it and white society condones it.

This may have been true about the majority, but there were concerned whites everywhere — even in some of the suburban areas.

"Thousands of Negroes and whites walked side by side through Newark's Central Ward yesterday in an historic demonstration of concern for the ghetto and commitment to the dream of Dr. Martin Luther King," reported the *Newark Evening News* in April 1968. The crowd — "more than half whites" — was estimated at approximately 25,000, in a column more than a mile and a half long.

> The walk, conceived six weeks ago as a demonstration by suburban whites of concern and goodwill for the city, was turned into a memorial to Dr. King after his assassination in Memphis last Thursday.

Originally, the two-mile walk had been conceived as a Palm Sunday gesture of concern by white suburbanites for black residents of Newark's Central Ward.

It was after the second Vatican Council that the Catholic Church decided on a closer relationship with other denominations. Joseph Thomas of Verona, active in church affairs, had suggested an increase in local contacts with other religions to Father McDermott of the Lady of the Lake Church in Verona. Thomas sent a formal letter to his pastor, while at the same time contacting other Verona religious leaders about opening an ongoing dialogue. It took a while, but finally all but the Jehovah's Witnesses were in agreement.

For the next three or four years, the group — either through voluntary means or at the request of a pastoral leader — met in homes, using texts of various religions to explore the concepts of each. Once a month, group members visited different services, and these were discussed at subsequent meetings. This finally lead to the formation of the Council for Inter-Religious Activity. The organization continued for about ten years, and was chaired the first three years by Joseph Thomas. It was this group that the *Verona-Cedar Grove Times* endorsed in its lead editorial on March 28, 1968, under the heading "A Walk in Newark." The editorial asked all residents to join the Verona Council for Inter-Religious Activity on Palm Sunday, April 7, in the walk through the black community of Newark.

Weeks earlier, in mid-February, some 250 Verona citizens had met to discuss inter-racial relationships, and on April 4, the *Verona-Cedar Grove Times* reported that the citizens decided to form a new group that would "devote itself toward improving attitudes and understanding in this area." A temporary steering committee was formed, which consisted of a group of residents to be advised by a panel of Verona clergymen and other prominent citizens. The newspaper went on, ". . . there is hope still among those trapped in the ghetto by discrimination, poverty and lack of opportunity. Despair has not yet claimed all possible victims. . . ." The local newspaper agreed that this gesture of the walk in Newark would do a great deal to let the black community know that they did not hope alone.

A "hastily formed *ad hoc* committee," Concerned Citizens of Verona, also supported the walk, according to the local paper. About 400 residents, mostly from Verona, filled eight buses, with an additional hundred or more citizens who used their own cars. According to the local paper of April 11,

> . . . residents showed indications of some apprehension in the early stages of their march . . . walking hesitantly at first, awaiting the impact their presence would have on the residents of the impoverished area. A confident spring soon replaced their hesitance as residents of the ghetto welcomed and waved to them from windows.

Clergymen as well as young students were among the Verona participants. One 12-year-old, Carolyn Thomas, was quoted as saying, "I think the people from the suburbs who came down were encouraged to do even more by the warm reception they received from the residents of Newark." Carl Erickson said, "It can't end here. We can't just return to Verona and forget all about Newark. If we don't do something more, then we never should have come down." John Grebe noted that "we have to follow up with direct action. If we abandon Newark now, after we've built up the hope of the people there, then despair will return. . . ."

The clergy of the Lutheran, Methodist, and Catholic churches, as well as four nuns of Our Lady of the Lake Convent, were among those who participated. I, too, was one of the walkers.

We did it not only to show that we cared, but also to see with our own eyes the torched streets, the slums, the depressed neighborhoods. Few of those who walked with the other 25,000 will forget. It is said that Verona had more participants per capita than any other suburb. This is quite possible; the community had formed citizens groups prior to the walk. This support from Verona may also have given the wrong impression of the true feelings of many of the residents of the town.

Memorial services for Dr. Martin Luther King were held in the churches of Verona. At the Whitehorne school, students gathered to hear a recording of Dr. King's famous "I Have a Dream" speech, while at the high school a lay minister of the Union Baptist Church of Montclair delivered a talk entitled "There Must Be a Better Way."

Dr. Carl L. Marburger, the recently appointed New Jersey Commissioner of Education whose photo appeared in *Saturday Review* magazine on April 20, 1968, said,

> We are trying to educate the rural Southern poor, and now their children, in a Northern urban environment. We are trying to educate children with little tradition of education. We are trying to teach them in aged, neglected buildings. We are often using obsolete textbooks and equipment. We are expected to send forth decent, industrious citizens imbued with the American ideal of equal opportunity and the notion of a classless society. And we are asked to do all of this in a world where junkies and prostitutes, street gangs and muggers, tenements and rats are commonplace. . . . [*Yet*] the cities are too often

told by their suburban neighbors, "Sorry, that's your problem, not ours."

One hundred Verona residents turned up at the meeting of the newly formed Concerned Citizens, according to the *Verona-Cedar Grove Times* of April 25. Six operating committees and a temporary steering committee were formed. The temporary chairman, James M. Hughes, who worked for Merck & Co. in Rahway, emphasized that "the group's aim is a Verona in which all residents are accepted on their own merit and not on the basis of race, creed, color, national origin or ancestry."

"Verona Citizens Unite Seeking Better Town" was the heading in a story in the *Newark Evening News* of April 27. "There's a tremendous amount of good will in the town which we hope to tap to achieve better understanding among races and creeds," said Hughes. According to the newspaper, the idea of organizing the group grew out of an ecumenical meeting of the Family Life Apostolate of Our Lady of the Lake Church in February. Some of their members already had been working voluntarily in Newark prior to the establishment of the group in Verona.

A seven-hour program sponsored by the Verona Education Association was also written up in the *Newark Evening News*. More than 350 teachers, school administrators, and clergymen listened to lectures and participated in group discussions at a "Human Relations Study Day" at Verona High School. In discussing "The Problems of Negro Youth," Dudley Cawley, assistant director of the eastern region of the National Urban League, stressed the low academic achievement norms of black elementary and secondary students, often in overcrowded and poorly equipped schools when compared to their white classmates. Benjamin Veal, who was principal of Preakness School in Wayne, and Samuel Cameron, assistant principal of Beech Street and Fairmount Elementary Schools in Hackensack — both Verona residents — lectured on difficulties encountered by blacks seeking teaching positions. Dr. George Sternlieb, professor at the Rutgers Graduate School of Business, concluded that a booming postwar economy, rather than the immigration of blacks, has caused the decline of large industrial cities such as Newark. A general panel suggested that elementary and secondary schools must return to the fundamental tasks of education, with an emphasis on the humanities. Several organizers of the program expressed disappointment at the absence of all municipal and county lawmakers.

On the surface, at least, there was public opinion to help the less fortunate neighbors in Newark. Soon, the residents of Verona would need to make a decision on how far this helping hand would reach.

Reflecting the national concern with the educational deficits suffered by children in many large cities of this country, and our own concern with the educational problems of our neighboring community, Newark, the Verona Board of Education [is] studying a proposal for sharing Verona's educational opportunities with a small number of Newark children.

Chapter 6

A Watershed Decision

ACH YEAR, the last issue of the *Verona-Cedar Grove Times* prints a recap of the happenings of that particular year for the two cities it covers. The Verona news for December 28, 1967, was headlined, "Swimming Pool Big News in '67." Describing the year drawing to a close as a "normal" one for Verona, the paper added,

> The multi-faceted manner in which the community scene unfolds amidst PTA affairs, church socials, Boy and Girl Scout programs, Little League and women's clubs was heightened by a new activity in the form of a

municipal swimming pool. Otherwise life in the borough was not much different in 1967 than it was the year before.

The article also recapped other city issues that year. Verona's tax rate was the fourth lowest in West Essex. Even so, the school budget had been defeated twice. There had been some complaints that the water supply was somewhat discolored, and other minor "rumblings" had been heard. But the paper pointed out there was "Pride in Stability." Walter D. McKinley had been elected Mayor, and Borough Councilmen Samuel E. H. France and Philip Vadeboncoeur were to take office as the successful Republican candidates in the November election. Other than the completion of the first high-rise — the Clairidge House on First Mountain — no major realty development had disturbed the peace, "the days of the builder's bulldozer upsetting the quiet of residential areas long having past."

Dr. Carl Marburger, the state's new Commissioner of Education, made the headlines in the *Verona-Cedar Grove Times* during 1967 with a speech to school administrators in Atlantic City. The paper summed up the speech:

> Essentially, Dr. Marburger made it known that he is irrevocably committed to integrating the city and suburban districts as the answer to Negro ghetto students receiving equal educational opportunities. He indicated that it was possible legislative enactment might offer financial incentives to cooperating urban and suburban districts. . . .

John E. Mattis, Verona's Superintendent, imagined this to be "a structural proposal only," while Ken Bechtold, the Cedar Grove Superintendent who had not attended the meeting but read about the speech, was not in a position to state his views at the time. Superintendent Mattis questioned funding and whether this would be a voluntary action, and stated that he had not reached any kind of conclusion on the subject unless much more information were forthcoming. Hilda Jaffe, president of the Board of Education of Verona, said she was not aware of the proposal and hoped to receive a report in the future. She also wondered about the availability of the necessary funds. Dr. Kenneth Bartlett, the president of the Cedar Grove Board, said he was not authorized to speak for the Board. He thought that the proposal could eventually lead to an educational "megalopolis" and if pursued would lead to considerable public debate.

In February 1968, Verona voters returned Hilda Jaffe to a third term on the Board of Education and re-elected Edward P. Wizda to a second term. Five candidates filed for the two offices; losers were Hrant Yousoufian, former president of the Citizens and Taxpayers League, and Samuel Cameron and Dr. Benjamin Veal, both Verona citizens who were educators in out-of-town schools. Jaffe carried all districts but two and received 1,192 votes. Wizda ran a close second with 1,111 votes. Yousoufian came in third, receiving 889 votes. It was a quiet election with no major issues, and even the proposed budget passed easily with nearly two-to-one support for the measure. The voters approved the expense item of $2,197,082 and the capital outlay proposal of $52,151.

Jaffe was re-elected to the position of president of the Board. During a subsequent meeting, it was decided — by a four-to-one vote — to update, revise, and outline the functions of the Board and that of the administrative personnel. A prior motion by Board member Emil Tomecek to require the Superintendent of Schools to furnish the Board with routine reports, without the need for approval of such requests by a Board majority, had been defeated. This was probably the last quiet meeting of the Board for the next few years.

There has never been an official explanation of how the Sharing Plan evolved. According to a story in Newark's *Star-Ledger* printed about a year later, its impetus was the urging by many different organizations to do something — anything — for the residents of Newark after the riots. The paper quoted Jaffe as saying,

> On a rainy night early in March of 1968, Newark school superintendent Franklyn Titus was invited to sit in on a secret board meeting [*and asked if*] all this about the Newark schools [*was*] true. . . . "Yes," Titus told them, and that it was true about the decay and the shortage of space and the lack of money and all the other items the Commission's report had to say. And yes, the Newark School Board would welcome any attempt by any suburb to lighten Newark's load. The board, again secretly,

asked Verona superintendent John Mattis to work with Titus to develop such a program. They would work intensely together in the coming weeks to develop what was to become the "Sharing Educational Opportunities Program."

During their regular Board meeting on April 30, 1968, Jaffe made the following announcement:

> Reflecting the national concern with the educational deficits suffered by children in many large cities of this country, and our own concern with the educational problems of our neighboring community, Newark, the Verona Board of Education [*is*] studying a proposal for sharing Verona's educational opportunities with a small number of Newark children.
>
> It is proposed that up to forty children from Newark be transported daily to the four public elementary schools in Verona, beginning in the fall of 1968. The children — in Grades 1 through 5 — would be invited to take part in the Verona school program; their parents would be offered the free choice of accepting or rejecting the invitation according to their own best judgment. Up to four Newark children would be placed in a Verona classroom, only when they could be accommodated without bringing class size over twenty-five, the number established as the desirable class size by the Verona Board of Education.
>
> Two major purposes recommend this proposal. First, it would aim at providing an educational program and environment which has promise for correcting some of the serious educational deficiencies experienced by some Newark children. Secondly, while the proposal involves only a small number of youngsters directly, it would provide an opportunity for research and evaluation which might serve many other children locally and across the nation.
>
> The children to be invited to fill empty seats in the Verona schools would be selected at random from a school which would be identified as appropriate by the Newark Board of Education — on the condition that the Newark Board feels that this proposal has promise. All children, Negro, Puerto Rican,

and white, attending a regular classroom of the Newark school would be eligible for participation.

The educational program for the incoming youngsters would be the same as that offered to resident Verona children. No special curriculum would be designed. A supplemental teacher would be available to help the Newark children make a smooth transition into the suburban classroom.

Because primary school youngsters in Verona ordinarily go home for lunch, volunteer mothers would be needed to provide a "home-away-from-home" for the Newark children during the noon hour.

No locally-raised tax monies would be used to support this program. All costs, including tuition, transportation, employment of a supplemental teacher, consultant services and research, would be paid from federal, state, and Newark funds.

If there is evidence that such a program has ill-effects on either the urban or suburban youngsters involved, it could be discontinued by either board before the close of the 1968-1969 school year. In any event, the program would be designed for a one-year trial period only. The Verona Board of Education and the Newark Board of Education would assess the merits of the program at the end of its trial period.

No official decision on the proposal will be made until the board of education has had an opportunity to weigh the reactions of the citizens of Verona to such a plan. Accordingly, there will be a public hearing for Verona Citizens on the "Proposal for Sharing Educational Opportunities" at the Henry B. Whitehorne Middle School on Monday, May 13, at 8:00 P.M.

Because of the unusual nature of this proposal, at this time we are requesting that there be no comment at this meeting. It is the kind of proposal that needs a little time to think on. The board members who passed this unanimously will not comment on this either. I know it will be hard not to comment at this time, but we feel for a number of reasons it is better not to.

A discussion on various other topics followed, but, as suggested, there was not a single comment on the proposal to share the educational facilities in Verona.

Mimeographed copies of this statement were distributed twice, once after Jaffe's statement was read, and again on May 9, 1968, by the Verona Board of Education.

"Bid to 40 City Pupils," was the banner headline in the May 1 *Newark Evening News*, then the most prominent paper in the area. The story was a condensed version of Jaffe's statement. Comments by Superintendent Mattis included:

> Fourteen suburbs are now taking 425 Boston [*Massachusetts*] children and two more communities will join the plan in the fall; four suburbs are taking 265 Hartford [*Connecticut*] pupils and three more suburbs will join, and one suburb is taking 75 Rochester [*New York*] children.

The Star-Ledger in Newark also reported on Verona's proposal.

On the same day the story hit the papers, May 1, Superintendent Mattis sent all staff members a copy of the district's plan — "A Proposal for Sharing Educational Opportunities."

The last paragraph of Mattis's memo, like Board president Jaffe's announcement, explained that there would not be an official decision on the proposal until the Board could weigh the reaction of Verona's citizens. Mattis's plan was very similar to the statement Jaffe had read at the Board meeting, but had an additional three pages explaining the proposal, as well as reports on the projects in other cities.

Another memo by Superintendent Mattis, on the same date, advised all staff members that the Board of Education had approved the suspension of all classes on Monday, May 20, "so that all Verona staff members may devote the day to an exploration of timely and significant human relations topics." The memo promised an exciting and comprehensive program planned by a committee of the Verona Education Association.

The headline, "Board Proposes Sharing Schools Starting in Fall," and an invitation to all Verona residents to come to a Board meeting at the Henry B. Whitehorne School on May 13, were part of the *Verona-Cedar Grove Times* story on May 2. The article also printed the salient points from Jaffe's statement.

On May 4, a similar story headlined "Verona Proposes Busing of Pupils" appeared in *The New York Times*, noting that out of a population of some 14,600, Verona had only "55 Negro families" and less than "70

Negro pupils" of "2,783 in the school system." The Verona School Board, the paper stated, with the support of Superintendent John Mattis, had drafted the busing proposal in an effort to provide "an educational program and environment which has promise of correcting some of the serious educational deficiencies experienced by some Newark children."

Added to *The Times* article were descriptions of the similar voluntary transfer programs in the Hartford and Boston areas. The article also described how New Jersey State Commissioner of Education Carl L. Marburger had provoked a bitter controversy the previous fall when he had suggested an exchange of students between the poor urban and the more affluent suburban schools. This should have been a cautionary note for the town of Verona.

However, an editorial in the *Newark Evening News* on May 5 commented that the busing proposal "reflects suburbanites' growing readiness to give concrete assistance. . . ." Eleven of the clergy of Verona passed a resolution applauding the proposal by the Verona Board of Education. More importantly, the *Evening News* reported in the same issue that other Essex school heads were also studying the Verona plan. School Superintendent Robert Blanchard of Montclair viewed the proposal "a constructive step." And Robert H. Seltzer, East Orange School Superintendent, thought the proposal "realistic," but needed time to study it further. Other school officials who were not identified viewed the program as "opening new avenues of approach to the ghetto child problem by providing the youngster with opportunities lacking in their present environments."

The *Evening News* also quoted Dr. Thomas Mahan, who had studied the first year of the two-year-old busing program in Hartford, Connecticut. According to Dr. Mahan, there was considerable evidence that children were better achievers in suburban schools. The 268 children in the Hartford exchange program showed an IQ increase of nearly seven points, while the IQs of other children taking the same program — but staying in the Hartford environment — rose only 1.5 points. More than half — 58 percent — of the suburban-based children gained a year or more on their achievement scores in mathematics and reading, versus an increase of only 15 percent in the control group. Dr. Mahan reached the conclusion that the same services made available in city surroundings did not make an appreciable difference on academic performance. Also, he found that children showed no signs of emotional trauma in being bused to suburbs, and that suburban children were unaffected by the Hartford children in their classroom. "If anything," Dr. Mahan said, "our studies show that the classes in which the urban children were placed actually performed slightly better."

The Newark school system seemed to have a multitude of problems, according to various stories in the *Newark Evening News*. The state Board of Education affirmed on May 1 that it was ready to take over the system, as suggested by Governor Hughes, "should the legislature and the City of Newark act favorably." Later that month, black high school students started a boycott, and on May 17, 1,200 of the students held a mass meeting in the Sussex Avenue Armory to air their grievances of unfair and discriminatory practices in the high school system. The Newark Teachers Union condemned actions of both white and black racists, and observed that "extremism can only perpetuate the violence, polarization and the extenuation of differences that have so long torn America."

On May 6, *The Star-Ledger's* editorial spoke of a "Fresh Approach Needed." It briefly described the Verona plan and concluded the article by commending the "experiment" as "worthwhile, even on a short-term projection."

> It is significant in a community sense, too, for it demonstrates
> the real concern of a suburban community for the . . . problems
> of a hard-pressed urban neighbor.

On May 8, the *West Essex Record* headlined its report, "Clergy Backs School Board Decision" and "Racial Problem Solution Hearing Set for Monday." Most of the front page was devoted to the story, repeating the press release of the Board of Education. Jerry Bakst, a Verona resident whose column appeared in the same issue, said of the program, "We will be making a small contribution to the health and well-being of the United States of America. In the last analysis, that is no small thing."

On the same day, *The Star-Ledger* also reported on the upcoming meeting, and quoted the positive results of the Hartford study.

The first public opposition by Verona residents to the Sharing Plan surfaced at the next Verona Borough Council meeting. As reported by the *Newark Evening News*, also on May 8, more than 150 residents came prepared to criticize the Board's proposal. Verona Mayor Walter McKinley explained that the governing body had only been informed of the Sharing Plan on April 29, and could therefore add nothing to the statement released by the Board. The paper quoted Samuel Cameron, identifying him as an administrator in the Hackensack School system and the first Negro to run for the Verona Board of Education. "Public schools are the only medium for children to meet and exchange values," Cameron was reported as saying, "In this process lies America's salvation."

More detailed was the story in the *Verona-Cedar Grove Times*. Citizens who filled the room at the Verona Council meeting were advised to present their views to the Board of Education at the scheduled public meeting. Mayor McKinley announced that the governing body would not take a stand on the Plan, explaining that the Board is an autonomous agency over which the Council had no control. When a recess was called to permit those citizens not interested in other items on the agenda to depart from the meeting, approximately 50 walked out in orderly fashion. The remaining 27 then engaged the Council in questions concerning whether a decision by the Board of Education could be changed, the area of the Board's responsibility, and possible legal recourse in the event the proposal was to be adopted. Borough attorney Emil Mascia stressed the autonomy of the Board of Education, and the Mayor again urged the residents to express their opinions at the public meeting scheduled by the Board. Councilman Samuel E. H. France also advised that one of the recourses of citizens opposed to any kind of Board of Education policy is through use of the ballot at election time. Borough Administrator-Clerk Walter Steinman advised the citizens attending that the statute covering School Board affairs was on file in the Municipal Clerk's office.

On May 9, the *Verona-Cedar Grove Times* reported that the Board had received written assurance from the New Jersey Department of Education that funds from federal, state, and Newark sources would underwrite all costs in the proposed Sharing Educational Opportunities plan. It also reported that the Verona Ministerial Association, composed of leaders of all faiths, endorsed the idea. Through the Association, a group of representative citizens sponsored a full-page advertisement in the May 9 issue of the *Times* supporting the proposal. The membership of the Verona Methodist Church approved the recommended action "wholeheartedly." Another endorsement came from James Hughes, chairman of the recently formed Concerned Citizens of Verona.

Also in that issue of the *Verona-Cedar Grove Times* was a story about

"Human Relations Day," which was set for May 20. The Verona Education Association, with the approval of the Verona Board of Education and the Superintendent of Schools, sponsored an all-day program for Verona teachers to explore their roles as educators in a pluralistic society. Topics by speakers included "The History of the American Negro," "The Problems of Negro Youth," and a film called "A Study of the Boyhoods of Hubert Humphrey and James Baldwin." Benjamin Veal and Samuel Cameron, as New Jersey school principals, were to speak on the problems facing black professionals living in the suburbs.

Mary Hill's letter to the editor in the same issue was one of the first to publicly oppose the project. But Deborah A. Willard, who was attending Vassar College at the time, wrote to the Verona paper that she was surprised to read about the proposal in *The New York Times*. She felt that accepting 40 children was a small but welcome step, and that further programs should be considered. Among other letters supporting the Sharing Plan was one written by Madelin Jensen, who asked that her home town of Cedar Grove should follow Verona. "In the meantime an orchid for the concerned citizens of Verona. . . either upper or lower case C." In contrast, Lorraine Trivett questioned how the ghetto children would feel to come to Verona's nice, clean school with nice playgrounds and then be sent back. She also remembered when Verona's schools were overcrowded, and felt that it could happen again. On the whole, however, most letters were supportive.

An editorial in the *Newark Evening News* of May 9, 1968, lauded youngsters for their meaningful contributions — such as the Verona High School students who planned to furnish an apartment for a Newark family made homeless by one of the recent fires. "Members of the student body for several years have participated in an American Friends sponsored clean-up project in Philadelphia," the article said. In addition, the editorial writer noted, children at Cedar Grove elementary school had collected canned food for the "needy in Newark." It was in both Verona and Cedar Grove, as well as in other communities that the students had been in the "vanguard through the schools and the churches in the various programs of aid for the victims of rioting and burning. They were among those," the paper noted, "who marched and extended 'the hand of friendship' on Palm Sunday."

A full-page advertisement, under the banner heading "Stand Up and Be Counted," endorsed the Sharing Plan and urged that "the reservoir of good will in our town be tapped NOW. Demonstrate your good will by talking to your family, friends and neighbors in support of the board's leadership." The ad requested all to attend the public hearing on Monday, May 13, and it was signed by over 150 families or individuals.

Also on May 9, *The Star-Ledger* briefly discussed the Sharing Plan as well as the public hearing to be held the following Monday night at Verona High School.

More letters to the editor were printed in the *Verona-Cedar Grove Times* on May 16. Under the signature of Boris Weller, the Verona Education Association offered its support. On the other hand, Joyce A. Capria took issue with the endorsing clergy by questioning "whether according to their teachings they are picking the mote from their brother's eye when there is a beam in their own," and suggesting that the lack of family structure in the city, illegitimacy, drug addiction, and crime would provide "an adequate field for the promulgation of Christian doctrine as it was once understood." She continued:

> . . . give the kids the truth. Help them to see that they are responsible for their destinies. . . . Let's give them the satisfaction of accepting responsibilities for themselves and their lives. This "bigot" prays for a successful solution.

A thoughtful letter, signed by James H. Carroll, pointed out that even if all the neighboring communities were to offer similar programs, it would not help every Newark child. He questioned whether this was just a stop-gap measure while Newark was rebuilding its school system, or whether the state of the economy would prevent Newark's support of its own children for some time to come. He expressed his disappointment with some religious leaders who accused the opposition of bigotry and hoped that the elected and appointed leaders would have sufficient faith to trust "the private ballot for the good of the disadvantaged in Newark."

The Newark children — a polite label for Negro children of the slums — have won a tentative welcome to the all-white suburban town of Verona. . . . About two-thirds of the audience of 800 last night applauded the decision. . . . If prejudice can end at the classroom door, Verona feels, there is hope for coming generations, and our society. — *Passaic (NJ) Herald News*

Chapter 7

Meetings and Lawyers

ON WHAT IS presumed to have been the largest-ever gathering of Verona residents, an estimated 1,800 persons, nearly all white, converged on Verona High School on May 13, 1968. Not only was it the largest, but probably also one of the longest meetings ever held. It started at 8:00 p.m., and did not adjourn until a few minutes before one in the morning — five hours later. And at that late hour, the discussions continued outside the school. The crowd not only filled the 700-seat auditorium, but overflowed into the gymnasium and adjacent hallways, where loudspeakers carried the proceedings. Verona police controlled the traffic flow and stood by for possible emergencies. By and large, the proceedings were peaceful, except for minor outbreaks between opposing factions. These were not reported, however, by any of the various newspaper reporters in attendance. Several times Board member John McDonald, who served as chairman of the meeting, had to appeal for order, and did ask the audience to refrain from interrupting speakers.

I had arrived very early and found a seat within the auditorium. Not heard, or at least not reported, were several altercations between members of the audience, as well as a near fist fight between two persons I knew, with anti-Semitic remarks made by one of them.

The complete transcript of the meeting contains 117 pages, which includes the list of all speakers.

The Board of Education, greeted by cheers and jeers after the customary prayer and salute to the flag, opened the meeting. Elmer Gustavson, a Board member, had prayed, "Heavenly Father, we seek Your help and guidance as we exchange ideas on a perplexing and complicated problem of our times."

Chairman McDonald explained briefly the proposal and promised a decision after input was received from attendees, as well as through additional letters sent to the Board by citizens of Verona. In order to regulate the speakers addressing the gathering, numbers were offered. Of the 130 who spoke, the ratio was three to one in favor of the Plan.

David B. Ford, chairman of the newly organized Verona Citizens for a Fair Decision, was the first to speak, presenting a petition requesting a referendum on whether to go ahead with the Sharing Plan. The petition was signed by 1,846 residents who said that they were neither for nor against the Plan, but objected mainly to the suddenness with which it had been thrust upon them. Sixteen other speakers, camouflaging their true intent, also asked for a referendum. Eight of these speakers, early on in the meeting, had opposed the Plan.

Obviously, it must have been difficult for speakers to declare their opposition without being called racists, and some who supported the idea alluded to that possibility. Proponents suggested that the referendum was only a stalling tactic and its supporters were hiding their "fear and bigotry" behind a concern for their right to vote. One speaker questioned whether non-residents should be attending this meeting, and was assured that although residency could not be checked for those in attendance, no one living outside Verona was to be permitted to speak.

Boris Weller, president of the Verona Education Association — which represented the professional teachers, administrators, and staff of the Verona school system — tried to read an Association letter in support of the Plan. But when cries were heard that Weller was not a resident of Verona — he lived in Montclair, the next community to the east — he was not allowed to continue, even though the Verona Education Association was an organization recognized by the Verona Board of Education.

The Reverend Donald Webb, of the Methodist Church, thought that he might be disqualified to speak because he was on the verge of moving.

> Two weeks ago, there were one hundred urgent and pressing reasons why I dreaded leaving Verona in a couple of weeks time; now, there are one hundred and one, and that one is a mighty one, and it is the fact that I can't share in the struggle. And obviously it will be a struggle for this great thing. I think it's clean, it's healthy, it's fine, what you're proposing, and because you believe in little children, you will do it. Because you believe in America, you will do it and because you really believe in God, you will do it!

Robert Hollender supported the Board and added, "I will also say publicly that my wife and I will feed one child, and if necessary, will feed two at one time." Someone in audience yelled, "Take the whole school." Chairman McDonald requested that those who wanted to speak should raise their hands and not hide.

Samuel Cameron quoted Lincoln's "with malice toward none," and expressed his disappointment with the manners of those who had booed speakers.

> . . . I am the man I am today because there have been so many who have helped me to make it thus far, and rather than be discouraged by the things that I saw around me, I was encouraged and determined to do my very best to make the best of my talents and assets.

Peter Zales, one of the signers of the petition for the referendum, said, "No end, however noble and praiseworthy, can justify these means. This proposal was sprung on the people and they should not be denied their right to vote."

Richard Marashlian condemned the Board's motives and said that the Plan would not substantially help the disadvantaged children — jobs for their parents would help more than a few hours in Verona's schools. Peter Petrucelli said that the proposal was in line with a plan of New Jersey Commissioner of Education Dr. Carl Marburger for an urban-suburban exchange of students.

The Reverend John McDermott, of Our Lady of the Lake Church, stated he was "surprised and ashamed that Verona citizens spent so much time and effort getting signatures on a petition for a referendum," when the time spent by the petitioners could have been given to more constructive acts.

> In my eleven years in Verona I have seen no requests for a referendum on any number of questions of major importance in the schools. Each year curriculum changes and additions are made, affecting hundreds of Verona children — no referendum. Each year, foreign exchange students are welcome — no referendum. Each year, new teachers are hired — no referendum. Now the board proposes to welcome forty little children in need of help. My hope is there will be no referendum.

Applause was stopped by the Chairman, to allow the meeting to continue. Father McDermott expressed his hope to have a similar program at the Verona Catholic school.

Henry Bowman stated,

> There've been a great many happy days in my life. I remember a number of them. I can remember the day my son was born. I'd like to say that one of the happiest days of my life was the day I woke up in the morning, got the newspaper, and read that the Verona Board of Education had enough courage to consider a program of this type.

Robert Davis opposed all types of busing. He had heard that Verona's teachers were overworked, that education was based on the slowest student, or close to it. But mostly Davis was concerned with what would happen to the kids after they went to school here for a brief period of time.

I think that maybe just busing and dumping is not a solution, but I think something could be worked out where it would bring the child out of the ghetto, and not just dumping and pulling, dumping and pulling.

Leonard Tucci, who made a point that he had been born and raised in Verona, challenged the endorsements of church groups by questioning whether they spoke only for the Verona congregates, or for outsiders too.

I am one hundred percent, wholeheartedly against this proposal of busing children . . . but if they [*the children*] are going to be helped, they've got to be helped in their own neighborhood first, and I don't think busing them here to Verona is going to help them or help us.

Tucci feared that the ten or twelve miles back and forth would be dangerous to the safety of the children. He also questioned whether the money for the program could not be used to rent a building in their neighborhood and hire a private teacher.

The Reverend Walter M. Moore, of the Presbyterian Church, speaking for himself and his wife, criticized citizens who proposed holding a referendum.

As I have sat here tonight and heard the boos, the disrespect . . . I began to get sick, real sick. . . . According to the books in my library, the sociology books, the psychology books, I could have experienced all those paranoid fears and insecurities that go to make up a bigot. Our home in Columbus, Ohio — and any civil rights leader will tell you what they think of Columbus, Ohio — was on the Mason-Dixon line, right next to the Negro community. My first paper route was entirely Negro customers. The high school that I attended — when there was a Jewish holiday the few of us that were white stood out like a sign along a highway . . . thank God my parents taught me to love my neighbors regardless of color, regardless of religion.

The Reverend Harold Van Horn, also of the Presbyterian Church, was sure that the main question was whether bigotry or brotherhood was to determine the future of the country. Most other local churches were also represented by their clergy.

Walter Wermuth, former high school football coach and a member of the school faculty, pointed out that some children were being bused to Verona already to attend "educable and trainable" classes and there is no criticism of the program.

> After the fires, after the looting, after the flare-ups that have taken the lives of people, after we've become frightened for our very own safety, many of us have turned to our consciences and after much deliberation have concluded that the great fault lies perhaps in ourselves, for ignoring [*in*] our satisfied ignorant complacency, the sordid conditions and inhuman treatment that we have inflicted upon our fellow man. . . . The eyes of many are upon Verona tonight and will be upon Verona in the future. . . . Are we not responsible for the education of those who live in Appalachia and Mississippi and Alabama, as well as those who live in Verona. . . ?

Wermuth hoped he would be able to say to his grandchild, "Yes, child, that happened during my lifetime and we in Verona played a small but important part in making that American dream come true."

He was answered by Frank Lytle who said the ballot box was also part of the American dream and he hoped that there would be a referendum.

Pat D'Entremont told the audience that she helped with preschool children, and, together with her five children ages four to eleven, spent four weeks at a playground in the Newark Central Ward. Even though they were outsiders, her children made good friends and were sorry to leave.

> Our children are the ones who are living in a ghetto. They will grow up into a world where most of the people will be non-white, non-Christian and starving, and it will be a world much smaller than the one we are living in now. I wonder if our children will be able to cope with this situation.

Another teacher and former Borough Council member, John Burguillos, first spoke against the referendum, and then read into the record the statement of the Verona Education Association that Boris Weller had been prevented from reading earlier. Burguillos concluded his statement by quoting his priest from the previous day's services:

> Mr. Gandhi was given a copy of the New Testament and asked
> to read it, and Mr. Gandhi read it and replied to these people,
> "This is a wonderful book. When does it start?"

Charles Pilenger was not convinced that all costs would be covered. He wanted to know why the Board could not mind its own business, and suggested a taxpayers' strike. Ralph Lucatola, a student of law at Rutgers University, had researched the legal question on referendums and came to the conclusion that the Board was not legally bound, but felt they were "honor bound by the spirit of the law of the State of New Jersey to hold a referendum."

Bob Neff explained that he had taught the previous speaker Latin, but did not understand his reasoning.

> I asked my wife last night if we could take one of the children
> in for lunch — we have four already — and she said "there's
> always room for one more," and that's the way we feel about it.

Amy L. Bostwick, one of the prime movers in the Committee for a Fair Decision, explained that even though some of their questions had been answered already, she nonetheless would repeat all 17 questions raised by her organization. She asked for the history of the proposal, the legal statute that authorized the project, where the funds were to come from, and the legal liabilities of all concerned, including the "visiting" homes and taxpayers, etc. More detailed information was requested on the Plan's expenses, including whether the costs were prorated among administration, teachers, facilities, and town administration. Similar detailed answers were expected on the scope and future of the Plan, and on other parts of the Plan that might yet be unannounced. Mrs. Bostwick concluded her speech by complaining that she and her associates had been subjected to a great deal of criticism over the past few days "as to our moral character, our integrity, and what we have in mind for the town of Verona."

Margaret McCloud expressed her pride in Verona and was happy that her children and those of other blacks in the community enjoyed great experiences.

Today I attended a meeting in Newark at which some of the results of the President's Commission were given. One of them that keeps standing out in my mind is that among the twenty cities in the United States cited for having such poor educational facilities, New Jersey has eight of these.

Herb Rappaport wondered why 40 children, ages six to eleven, could evoke such emotional tirades.

. . . Are you aware that last Thursday at noon, one hundred twenty some-odd students out of state were bused to Verona? They resided in this community Thursday, Friday, Saturday and left on Sunday. They ate here, there was an exchange with our youngsters, and I only wish that this gathering could have been present at the high school parking lot when the buses left with these Needham students on Sunday. I wish you could have seen the tears of the Verona youngsters upon the departure of their friends. May I also point out to you that three weeks ago, ninety-six-odd Verona youngsters were bused to Needham, Massachusetts. No referendum was needed, nobody requested approval, it was just done and supported.

Joseph Percevault, who was associated for many years with Henry's Fine Foods — still a privately owned local store, expressed his concern over losing customers because of his speaking up:

. . . With my seven children I need all the customers I can get. If I have to make my livelihood and feed these children by hiding behind a screen when an important issue comes up, I'd rather give it up and sell pencils on the corner. I don't believe I could face myself in the morning if I had a thought on my mind that I thought was important and refused to express it. . . .

Percevault explained that the proposal was not only an economic, social, and educational question, but to him it was mostly a moral question — that of our relationship to our fellow man. Each religion, in slightly different words, states the same sentiments, he noted, and then quoted from the Sunnah — the traditional Moslem law: "No one of you is a believer until he desires for his brother that which he desires for himself."

Peter Petrucelli spoke again, stating that many of the newcomers moved to Verona because of the black problem in the cities where they used to live. Some educators teaching in other cities but living in Verona, he said, were really the bigots who should have stayed in Montclair or Newark to help those people who need it, rather than moving out to Verona.

Adele Sunshine, a mother of five children in the Verona school system and a teacher in the ghetto area in Newark, boasted of Verona to her fellow teachers and was sure that the proposal would be beneficial for all concerned.

> However, as I look at this as an educator, there is another side to this. I went to Newark in September; I intend to stay there as long as I can teach. I went into a ghetto school on Newton Street. . . I call my classroom the dungeon because I have to go down the cellar. I couldn't wear a dress twice in a row because if I sat down I came home filthy, even my underclothes were filthy. The children came to the classroom clean in the morning but if they dropped a piece of paper on the floor, which we swept twenty-five times a day, they couldn't use it again because it was so dirty. Children came in October with colds and one little girl came in a dress, since she had no coat or sweater. . . . Another one told me "All white people hate us and I hate white people," and I told them I'm white and I don't hate you. By the way, I have a retarded class that couldn't understand as much as some of the others.

Sunshine later was transferred to a much cleaner school to teach emotionally disturbed children. When she left, the kids said to her that not all white people hated them and "when I left we were all half in tears."

Mrs. Gilbert Bogard, a Girl Scout leader, quoted their law: "A Girl Scout is a friend to all and a sister to every other Girl Scout." After the fires in Newark, she had requested that the members of her group, who lived in a very privileged area, take a dress that they might have worn the next day, along with canned food, and bring these to the next meeting; these were then sent to the Avon Avenue School. After the Board of

Education's proposal was released, three white group leaders visited the Avon Avenue School, and, Mrs. Bogard continued,

> . . . I cannot tell you the feeling of warmth and excitement that came to us from the teachers and the people in that school; they were just so excited when they found out we were from Verona. . . . We were the Great White Fathers, and I just hope you don't have to go back on your promise or proposal to these people in Newark.

Campbell Care, speaking for his wife and one son, David — "who is working with the underprivileged tonight in the ghetto" — thought that the proposal was the first step from doing nothing to going forward into the future. Carl Bergman commended the Board, but worried about the funding as well as what would happen to the children if Verona schools could not accommodate them. He called for a referendum.

John McMaster, speaking for his family and next-door neighbors, and as a member of the Verona Methodist Church and the Trinity Church of Newark, invited the public to help the next Saturday in their clean-up campaign in Newark's Central Ward.

Jerry DeBenedette explained that he came from the Newark ghetto and that he did not have an educational background, but worked every day of his life. Of his four children, one graduated from Barringer High School, one from Verona High School, and two were still in elementary school. He believed that even though the funds would not come from Verona, he as a taxpayer still would pay.

> I am for the plan if all these educators . . . who cry on the PTA shoulders about all the work they do, and if they're going to donate their time then I'll donate my time. . . . Why can't we have a referendum now?

Kenneth Rosburgh also called for a referendum, and was surprised that Board members had chosen not to speak that evening.

Applauding the Board for this "exciting proposal," Reverend M. Sargent Desmond was

> dismayed and shattered by the timidity and fear of those who

can see nothing in this plan but mountainous hazards and pitfalls. . . and I heartily endorse the frontiersmanship of our board in exploring this proposal and encourage them to bring this plan into reality.

Despite the tempers displayed at the meeting, some minds were changed as a result of the debate that night. Charles Alario came to the meeting opposed to the Plan "whether the children came from [*upscale communities like*] Short Hills, Essex Fells, or Cedar Grove." But after listening, especially to Reverend Webb — who had urged the adoption of the plan "because you really believe in God" — Alario felt a "little ashamed" and decided not to object to the proposition.

Jerry Leopaldi supported the Plan "for the five best reasons in the world — my children." In his lengthy speech, he mentioned that everyone spoke about the children, but not about the parents:

A group of people, primarily Negro, who are entrusting their children to us in Verona, and I think this is a tribute to them, that they would entrust their children to us for several hours of the day, including eating in some of our homes. Now these parents are not shiftless and lazy and so ignorant, because after all, they're willing to share their children with the good people of Verona. . . .

Clem Rockel noted that he was more afraid "of some of the things that I have heard and I have seen here tonight than I am afraid of forty little children."

Bill O'Keefe talked of Essex County as a "microcosm of all the bad and good situations besetting us today as a nation." This was due, he explained, to the population mix ranging from the very rich to the very poor, the black and the white militants, the extremists, and then

the vast middle road, middle income, business-oriented people who are largely represented here tonight . . . it's time for us to go on record as a community of people who care enough to help those in unfortunate circumstances to better themselves through education, to relieve the congested, mean educational facilities of Newark so that these children may have an opportunity to join the mainstream of American life and not to follow their parents into further economic despair or onto the relief rolls.

Fred Lehman presented the analogy of a neighbor's house being on fire, and supplying the few pails of water needed to help put out the flames before they spread. Referring to the opening statement by John McDonald, Steven Sheid wanted to be reassured that Verona's children would not be bused elsewhere, since "I have heard all evening educators talk of an exchange program with the deaf, crippled, retarded, an exchange program between our students and Massachusetts and Verona. . . ."

Heinz Rosenbush had been one of the 1,824 signatories on the petition for a referendum, but at the meeting he withdrew his name, quoting President Franklin Delano Roosevelt's statement, "The only thing we have to fear is fear itself." Rosenbush went on to say he was convinced that the fears expressed during the evening had no bearing on the problems of education. He concluded by paraphrasing the well-known anonymous poem,

> I shall pass through this world but once; if, therefore, there can be any kindness I can show, any good thing I can do, let me not defer it nor neglect it for I shall not pass this way again.

Recalling his youth in the South Bronx, Richard Heaslip spoke about sharing a seat with blacks in a class of 40,

> . . . cheek to cheek on one seat. Some of our entertainment in the evening was taking walks over in the park by Yankee Stadium, up toward Bronx Park, and even through Harlem. We frequently walked across 125th Street, down 2nd and 3rd Avenue, teenagers. There was no fear then because nobody bothered you; there was understanding. I don't know what's happened in the last twenty years, but by God, something has to be done to turn it around. . . .

Calvin Touw, who had helped collect signatures for the referendum, was upset and annoyed by the ministers, who he thought were accusing those who signed the petition of being bigots. As the father of a child being bused due to behavior problems, he spoke of how his son felt like an outsider after not being invited to a birthday party. Touw feared the same thing would happen to the black children.

> . . . The parents' hearts bleed for him because . . . he's left out of these things. Also, programs after school, roller skating, bowling, things the class does. He hears the children talking about them but he doesn't get to participate in them. How do you think they feel about that; they feel kind of often outside. So if this program goes through, whether it's voted on or not, I hope you look thoroughly into keeping these kind of things down as far as possible. . . .

Others had questions concerning the logistics of the proposal. Stephen Demmiss wondered about the legal liability, as well as evaluation procedures and plans for the following year.

Mrs. William B. Spooner, mother of ten children, did not consider herself a bigot:

> . . . I believe that the unity of Verona has been severed by this issue, regrettably, and that the only way it can be healed is to put the proposal to a vote and let the majority speak, and we should remember the old saying, "*vox populi, vox Dei,*" the voice of the people is the voice of God and we should have faith in the people of Verona in doing just as their conscience dictates and keeping the ballot sacred.

Dick Sandler, a Verona resident since birth, did not want to talk about the merits of the proposal, except to say that in order for it to be meaningful, it must also be implemented in every other suburban community in Essex County and every other county surrounding Newark. "It seems clear to me," he said, "that this meeting tonight has by an overwhelming preponderance of the testimony supported your proposal, and therefore I don't see that any referendum is necessary."

Carmine Rando stated that those who were against the referendum should also be against that evening's meeting — that people had wasted their time coming, because it was obvious that the Board was in favor of the proposal. "You are the small people," he said, "and should not assert yourselves; the Board will do your thinking for you." Rando did not agree that it is just as easy to teach 25 children as 21, suggesting that maybe Verona could send its under- and non-achievers to South Orange, or possibly Scarsdale, New York.

Mrs. Donald Zukosky related an experience she had had when she and her husband decided to invite a child from the Baker-Stuyvesant ghetto section of Brooklyn to their home for two weeks. When she asked her children what they would say if the child were black, her seven-year-old daughter said, "Mommy and Daddy, I don't care as long as she has a heart." Then the riots broke out in Newark, and Mrs. Zukosky's daughter was afraid the visitor would not come. But, she did, and the family was so taken with the black child that she was invited again for Christmas.

Mrs. Zukosky closed by expressing her hope that when her son, serving in Vietnam, came home, she could show him the headline proving that Verona had a big enough heart to share its educational system.

Impressed with the turnout, Larry Orlando congratulated the Board and suggested that they have local neighborhood meetings or round-table discussions to raise additional support.

George Wible had previously helped out on a picnic for black children who had never been on the Garden State Parkway or been on a pony before.

> If these kids get up to Verona, I think that they're going to enrich our kids as well. They're going to make our kids stop and think and perhaps they will appreciate a little more what we give them.

Following this, one citizen — who had drawn a low number but had passed up his initial turn because he was worried he might have become too emotional — offered his opinion:

> I know this proposal is not from the Board of Education. . . . I know where it originated. Very few people here tonight know what goes on beyond the curtain, just as the politicians of years ago in the city of Newark repaid a lot of these people with a pint of booze so they'd get the votes, and then they ruined the city and it broke our hearts to leave the city. Believe you me, a lot of these people had to sell their homes for half the price and you can't give them away down there.

He asked the Board to reconsider their proposal, sat down, and then asked to speak again.

> Our old Alma Mater, Barringer High School, the great oldest school in the country, and . . . we turned around only a couple of years back, and we built a country club for these people for ten million; very few people know what's going on down there; they can't read it in the newspapers. This high school is becoming a shambles, Vailsburg High School the same way. My brother was construction superintendent, put up most of the housing projects around there; they bulldozed most of the backyards we played in — six months later, take a look at them. They're worse slums than they ever were. The old backyards we used to play in were picnics compared to what you've got now. I blame the politicians and everybody else for what's going on down there. Please let it not happen here.

Groups that endorsed the Plan with supportive statements at that night's meeting included the Concerned Citizens of Verona, the Verona League of Women Voters, the Rosary Society of Our Lady of the Lake, educators in and out of the Verona school system, and members of the PTA executive boards. Individuals who spoke out in support included merchants, a former Board of Education member, and four former candidates for Mayor and Borough Council. There were numerous other appeals to conscience and to moral values, as well as a few additional speakers against the proposal or just endorsing the referendum. Only the very idealistic — both for and against this controversial proposal — seemed to storm the town gathering to speak from their hearts.

Perhaps the outpouring of support on May 13 lulled the Board into a false sense of security. Or the Board may have misread the tenor of the meeting, because the bulk of those who spoke strongly voiced their support. What the Board did not realize was that all the speakers that night were but a tiny minority of Verona residents. And no one knew what the bulk of the people in the audience really thought.

As the next Board election on February 11, 1969, would show, the majority of the residents did not seem to care one way or another, and did not even vote. But out of the paucity of voters who cast their ballots, the vast majority opposed the Board on its busing proposal.

Two days after the Board meeting, on May 15, an editorial in the *Newark Evening News* expressed admiration for the fact that almost ten percent of Verona's population had jammed the facilities of the high school. The axiom that big crowds mean big opposition seemed to fall, as speaker after speaker — 82 of 115 — endorsed the proposal. "Citizens of Verona have put on a remarkable demonstration of interest in their school board's venturesome proposal . . ." the newspaper stated, adding that most of the speakers were ready to stand up and be counted. This article, too, did not anticipate the silent majority.

Also on May 15, the *West Essex Record* used a news release sent by the Verona Board to show that transporting and educating disadvantaged city children to suburban communities could work smoothly. The Board had quoted the summary and conclusion of the interim report on Hartford's Project Concern. The article also mentioned that the Board had written assurance from the State Department of Education that funds would be provided to cover all costs of Verona's Sharing Educational Opportunities plan.

A newspaper campaign featuring full-page advertisements adorned the *Verona-Cedar Grove Times*. Obviously, the opposition — the Citizens for a Fair Decision — was well financed. One ad asked, "Who Speaks for You?" and complained that not all were able to speak at the May 13 meeting. At the bottom of the page was a mail-in coupon to show support for a town-wide referendum. Also printed in the ad was a coupon stating that the undersigned wanted to endorse the petition for the referendum. A different full-page ad, again paid for by the Citizens for a Fair Decision, asked eight different questions, ranging from why there was a delay in a decision for a referendum when over 25 percent of the voting population had signed the petition, to whether this was the end of the neighborhood school concept. Yet another ad featured an invitation to a "General Membership Meeting" for May 23 at 8:00 p.m. at the F. N. Brown School Auditorium to formalize the organization, solicit additional petitions, gather financial support, and recruit working members.

Another Newark newspaper clipping of that date, with a byline by William Doolittle, discussed the growing concern of New Jersey college officials that black students on the state's four-year college campuses were a rarity.

	ENROLLMENT	NEGROES
Newark College of Engineering	2,570	20
Rutgers, Newark	2,900	60
Rutgers, New Brunswick	6,200	150
Douglass College	2,850	85
Paterson State	3,000	125
Trenton State	(est.) 3,700	150
Montclair State	4,300	80
Newark State	3,200	50
Glassboro State	3,550	150
Jersey City State	2,800	150
Total	35,070	1,020

The three percent enrollment figure was compared to the percentage of blacks in the population — eight percent — with the lowest percentage, less than two percent, in schools in Newark and Montclair. Trenton College refused to officially divulge its numbers. Princeton University admitted 75 blacks to its freshman class, just over five percent of all admitted for the next autumn. When questioned, Spencer Reynolds, Assistant Director of Admissions at Princeton, stated that the black applicants, "particularly those from the inner city school systems," did not appear to be well prepared. He added, "I attribute this to the public schools there."

Princeton and other New Jersey colleges decided to disregard the standard method of evaluation for black candidates for admission. Special programs were instituted at Rutgers, in New Brunswick, where students received a two-week summer pre-training course; at Newark College of Engineering, in Newark, where 18 inner-city youngsters received special tutoring for the first year; at Paterson State, in Wayne, where inner-city youngsters would receive summer tutoring; and at other colleges starting similar programs.

The Star-Ledger pictured Mrs. Oscar Weissendorn, a Verona resident, standing on the tailgate of a station wagon outside Verona High School, addressing those who could not get inside. Even though the story reported that the speakers were approximately eight to one in favor of the Plan, the headline stated "Verona's School Plan Draws Mixed Reaction." All papers agreed that attendance of more than 2,000 was a record crowd for any government public meeting in the suburbs.

The May 16 issue of the *Verona-Cedar Grove Times* ran a photograph depicting the crowded auditorium. It also had the most complete report on the meeting, as well as several side stories: "Board to Offer Reply to All Honest Queries" and "Procedural Action to be Decided Shortly Pending Study of Transcripts." The primary article stated that questions considered to have political implications would not be answered, and that the Board had not yet decided whether its response would be revealed at another hearing, at neighborhood school meetings, or in the form of press releases. The paper also featured the 17-question list posed by the Citizens for a Fair Decision, which had been read at the public hearing by Amy Bostwick. And the editorial in the same issue expressed the hope that the Human Relations Day set for May 20 would draw a large attendance "in a county where no one can say that human relations are not in need of improvement."

Numerous letters pro and con appeared the following week in the *Verona-Cedar Grove Times*. Mary Hill asked for more dialogue and deliberation because the meeting had not afforded sufficient time. John B. Gorman was certain that even though the Board claimed that the program would not be funded by Verona taxpayers, it would cost them anyway, because one or another arm of government would have to pay for it. Sharon N. Leedham supported a referendum to find out the will of the majority. Mr. and Mrs. Henry J. Zebrowski defended Father McDermott, feeling he was entitled to his opinion without incurring the vindictiveness of some of the townspeople. Jean Nugent revised what she called her "ill-considered" support for the referendum. Two outsiders from Newark — Bishop Right Reverend Leland Stark and Sydney Keliner, the New Jersey director of the American Jewish Committee — wrote letters supporting the Verona Board of Education.

"Education Board to Answer 'Honest Questions'" was the headline in the *West Essex Record* on May 22. According to the article, the voluminous transcript of the five-hour May 13 public hearing was expected to be completed the next day. More than 125 citizens had spoken at the hearing, and this newspaper reported the proportion of speakers favoring the Board's proposal as roughly three to one.

In the same issue, editor Jerry Fuchs wrote, "Verona Can Make New Jersey History." After describing the town, its geographical location, and the Sharing Plan, Fuchs stated,

Verona's educational system is excellent. Many local students have gone on to the finest colleges and universities in the nation. Its residents are mainly middle income and owners of one family homes. . . . There are approximately 50 Negro families living in Verona. A large percentage of the Negro men hold their bachelor's and doctor's degree, while earning above average incomes. . . .

Continuing with a discussion of the failure of the Newark school system and the report of the Governor's Select Commission on Civil Disorder, Fuchs concluded,

. . . Suburbia has its stakes in the cities, and self interest demands that communities help find the solutions to urban problems. The cities stand for the life blood of our business, entertainment, shopping and educational world. If they continue to burn, much of the prosperity of our community and the world we live in will burn with them. And when that scene is over, the burning and the rioting will spread to suburbia. That is why it is paramount to find answers now, and Verona is searching.

The scrapbook of Board member Ed Wizda contains handwritten letters, beginning May 4 and continuing throughout that month, from many who supported his stand. Some who wrote had also spoken at the public hearing, including Larry Orlando and Reverend M. Sargent Desmond. Among the correspondence was a letter from Ralph M. North III, who lived in Waukesha, Wisconsin. North ended his letter with, "You must succeed."

Reverend Desmond, of the First Congregational Church, sent a letter to everyone on his mailing list, saying,

When I discovered the traffic approaching the high school, and when I discovered that hundreds of us were to stand and sit in the gym, I feared that I might be ashamed of Verona before the evening was out. I had no idea that so many would stir themselves to express endorsement of the proposal. (Usually we stir ourselves only when we oppose something — so my fears mounted.) I am not ashamed of Verona. Even the initial jeers of a *small* group in the main auditorium do not dim the brightness of the evening. In the gym where I sat there was dignity and respect throughout the evening. I admire the patience and endurance of all who adjusted to the situation and contributed to the total positive impact of the evening. . . . I have confidence in the judgment of our Board of Education. I have renewed confidence in the citizens of Verona. I have confidence in the power of God to use His children in productive and creative tasks of reconciliation and building. May God strengthen us in His service.

The *Newark Evening News* reported on May 23 that more than 350 teachers, school administrators, and clergy participated in the seven-hour Human Relations Day that had been sponsored three days earlier by the Verona Education Association and the Board of Education. That the overcrowded and poorly equipped inner-city schools "help to perpetuate underachievement" was the message of one speaker, to which must be added the poverty and general living conditions in the ghetto. Several Verona residents remarked on the fact that unless they were overeducated, black professionals had difficulties obtaining teaching positions. The people of Verona were lauded for their support of the proposed sharing program, but were also warned that this gesture should not absolve them from further responsibilities. Some of the topics discussed were ghetto population, post-war immigration, racial understanding, and a return to the fundamental task of educating students rather than promoting a race for college admission. The only Essex County Superintendent attending was Verona's John Mattis. It was noted that not one county or municipal lawmaker was present.

On May 23, Joseph R. Thomas, managing editor of *The Advocate*, quoted Joseph White, a young black man whose column, "Cocoa Background," had appeared in the *Newark Sunday News*. The question of how white suburbanites could help the black community had been answered by Joseph White, according to Thomas. The answer lay on their own doorsteps, the young man had said, stating that middle-class suburban attitudes needed to overcome prejudice. Thomas, a Verona resident, lauded the Board of Education for its effort, but added his dismay as a Catholic

> . . . at the opposition which has come from some Catholics . . .
> especially . . . because of the vitality of the apostolic move-
> ments in Verona and because the Church in Verona — as repre-
> sented by its priests, by its Sisters and by the leaders of the
> parish societies — has never left any doubt about its stand on
> racism. What appears to be reasonable arguments against the
> proposal take on an air of unreasonableness in the face of
> assurances that what is proposed is a one-year trial with profes-
> sional evaluation along the way. They also take on an air of
> unreasonableness when amateur psychologists and sociologists
> predict dire psychological and sociological consequences in
> advance of testing. And they take on an air of unreasonableness
> when some Catholics with children in public school let it be
> known that if the proposal is adopted they will transfer their
> children to parochial school.

Letters to the editor continued to flood the *Verona-Cedar Grove Times*. On May 23, Mrs. R. Kiernan, Jr., declared that all her questions had been answered through the public meetings, and hoped that in years to come Verona would not be known as the community that rejected 40 little children. Mrs. Nicholas Liberato stated that she would be happy to permit the children to experience teaching at the same level and same quality as her own children, which would help her community to grow socially, men-tally, physically, and spiritually. Yet, she first wanted the people to speak in a referendum.

On May 28, during the regular meeting of the Verona Board of Edu-cation, Hilda Jaffe announced that the Board would reach its decision on the proposal at a special public meeting on Tuesday, June 11. Jaffe com-mented on the considerable correspondence received by the Board as a whole and by individual members, and stated that the letters would not be answered individually, but would instead be addressed collectively by the Board. After briefly outlining the proposal again, Jaffe devoted some time to answering the most frequently asked question: How did the proposal originate?

She explained that during March, members of the Verona Board of Education had requested information from Franklyn Titus, Newark's Superintendent of Schools. Titus verified the estimate that approximately 10,000 children lacked proper classroom space, and that there were no immediate plans for expansion. And based on his information, as well as studies of the similar programs in Hartford, Boston, and Rochester, the Verona Board was proposing to offer a few seats in the Verona elementary schools.

Another question raised was whether the Sharing Plan was authorized by law. Jaffe quoted from statutes under which this proposal was deemed to be legal.

> Any person not resident in a school district, if eligible except for residence, may be admitted to the schools of the district with the consent of the Board of Education upon such terms, and with or without payment of tuition, as the board may prescribe.

Another provision stated,

> the Board of Education of any school district having the necessary accommodations may receive, or may be required to receive by order of the state board, pupils from another district not having sufficient accommodations at rates of tuition fixed as in the article provided.

And other questions were answered. In no case would a Newark child be put in a classroom if that class size would rise above 25, and in no case would more than 40 children be accepted. Further, there was no plan — nor would any plan ever be considered — to send Verona children to Newark. The Newark children would represent a cross-section of abilities, and children with emotional or special education problems would not be selected.

During the open question-and-answer time, Anthony Ditri introduced himself as the legal counsel for the Verona Citizens for a Fair Decision. He prefaced his speech by stating that it had been prepared prior to that evening's explanation by the Board. The members of the organization, he said, were mostly concerned because they had insufficient information and because there had been silence on the Board's part.

> The Verona Citizens for a Fair Decision have steadfastly maintained they are not against this proposal, but [*the decision*] should be made by all of the people because of its far-reaching effect.

Ditri presented a new petition signed by over 2,300 citizens, and also discussed the statute for obtaining a special election. He pointed out that the petition, signed by roughly 25 percent of the voters, contained more than sufficient signatures needed for a special election.

The Board asked Ditri if the organization would withdraw its request if the Board answered all the group's questions. Ditri replied that he had no authority to make such a decision, and that all he could ask was that the issue would be put on a ballot for the group to decide.

A few other questions were posed by those attending, followed by questions on food, football, and extra-curricular activities, which temporarily replaced the Newark topic. More questions were raised as to what would happen after the one-year trial period, whether additional children would be started the following year, and if the 40 children would stay from first to fifth grade.

Richard Marashlian, who had spoken at the public hearing on May 13, made a lengthy statement. He first indicated that he was impressed by the candor and amount of information given, but then said that time was too short for a decision to be made, and that it would be difficult for the Board to weigh the reaction of the residents. He also spoke about the public meeting.

> When [*we*] came in there were people clapping and there were boos. As the speakers began I saw some interesting techniques. There were those who were afraid, and there were clergy. Were they speaking for all their flock? Were the teachers speaking for all the organization? The best of all were the endorsements. With all of those, I certainly hope that you did not fall for this. I saw certain members who are active in organizations and know how to make an audience react. The Madison Avenue advertising men know how to do this. I personally feel that this

meeting was stacked. If there were the slightest doubt that this meeting was stacked, how would I decide if the citizens were for or against? I don't envy your position. . . . Bearing in mind all this difference, if I were in your position, I would hate to make a decision, and I would let the people decide it in a referendum.

Jaffe replied that the ultimate decision would stay with the Board. Emil Tomecek, another Board member, explained that he was torn because he was interested in promoting policies that would provide educational programs for all, especially the lower 75 percent — including children from out of town — but that "the school system belongs to you and not to me."

One man even accused the Board of advocating forced integration, which had nothing to do with underprivileged children.

Questions were also raised on costs, and whether the individual Board members would be polled. The meeting adjourned after 11:00 p.m.

According to the *Newark Evening News* of May 29, the majority of the 150 residents who had attended the Board meeting the previous evening favored a referendum. The account went on to say that Tomecek sided in part with supporters of the referendum when he said that the Board could have avoided much of the speculation surrounding the proposal by settling many of the unresolved problems before introducing its ideas to the public.

"Verona School Decision Due" and "Board to Announce on Newark" were front-page headlines in the *West Essex Record* of May 29. By this account, June 11 was the date set by the Verona Board of Education to make public its decision on whether to implement the sharing proposal. A mailing and a press release would be prepared in order to answer all questions.

"Out-of-Towners Accepted; Bias Loses in Jersey Suburb" was the heading in *Education News*. The brief article reported on "1,600 attending" the public meeting, and stated that the vast majority of the speakers supported the proposal.

On June 5, the *Newark Evening News* disclosed that the leader of the Plan's opponents, David B. Ford, was a teacher in a Newark public school, which was 91 percent black. He had been the first speaker at the May 13 public hearing, and as chairman of the Verona Citizens for a Fair Decision had presented the petition asking for a town referendum.

. . . Speakers at various hearings on the busing plan who favor the board's position have termed the referendum move a stalling motion inspired by "fear and bigotry." Ford, however, has contended that his group simply objects to the manner in which the busing proposal was presented.

. . . Ford has recently been unavailable for comment on the matter. . . . According to the Board of Education's Department of Personnel, Ford is a provisional elementary school teacher. Last week Ford was invited to have a conference on the Verona busing situation with Simeon Moss, Acting Assistant Superintendent of schools, at which the position of the referendum seekers was discussed.

Ironically, there has been no resistance in Verona to previously arranged student busing from Newark into the town. Only last week the Newark Board voted to pay $3,357 in tuition to the Verona Board for seven children. In the previous year, 16 Newark youngsters were educated by the Verona school system. Conversely, there has never been any significant opposition in the suburbs to sending suburban children to Newark's Bruce Street School for the Deaf, located in the Central Ward. Presently there are no Verona children at Bruce Street among the 70 out-of-city pupils. . . .

The May 30 issue of the *Verona-Cedar Grove Times* carried a full account of the Board meeting, noting the more than 200 in the audience and nearly all supporting the petition for a referendum. The article stated that on a number of occasions, Board president Jaffe had to rap for order and remind the audience that this was a Board meeting. And, according to the *Times*, Peter Petrucelli criticized both the Sharing Plan and the Human Relations Day, which had been held on May 20. He questioned the cost of that program, and wondered why it could not have been held at night or on a Saturday to avoid closing the schools in order for teachers to attend. The explanation given was that the program had been sponsored by the Verona Education Association, and that it had been deemed worthwhile by the Superintendent of Schools.

Most of those engaged in local politics carefully stayed out of the controversy. None except Harriet Dolin, who was running in the June primary for a Democratic nomination, made any public statement other than that citizens have recourse at the ballot box. In Dolin's press release of May 28, she endorsed the Board of Education's proposal and stated,

> Verona does not exist in a vacuum, yet many of our citizens live as if it does. The thought of change is like a spear piercing a hole in their vacuum vessel. They don't know what the rush of air will be like; they only know one response, panic. . . . It was appalling to witness the furor created by the Board of Education's desire to give forty children "a taste of honey." It was as if a sprinkle of pepper could ruin the dinner instead of bringing out its richness and goodness. . . .

The local paper also reported that 168 residents had attended a meeting of the Verona Citizens for a Fair Decision at the F. N. Brown School auditorium and heard David Ford, acting chairman of the group, emphasize that "the petition for referendum is neither a position for nor against the board's proposal but only for a fair, informed decision by all Verona voters." Plans were presented at the meeting to establish a board of governors, consisting of two members of each of the four school districts. The article noted that they would work as a non-profit organization, and that they had already rented a post office box. The new organization's finances were not reported. Its statement, which was created by those present at the meeting, read that the question was not that of 40 children, but of concern that the integrity of community-run education by the will of the people was at stake.

"Moral Basis Cited for 'Plan,' Board Mails Answers," was the major headline on page one of the *Verona-Cedar Grove Times* on June 6, 1968. The questions posed, and the Board's responses, had been mailed to 4,000 families. The proposal was once again explained and 34 questions answered, including the Plan's origin, legal basis, scope, similar programs, financing, tuition costs, selection of children, benefits, and methods of evaluation. The Board stated that the Plan should be implemented as soon as possible, and reaffirmed that the ultimate policy decision was its sole responsibility.

The Sharing Plan provided for a maximum of 40 children for one year. The informational sheet listed all the communities having similar programs — Hartford, Boston, Rochester, and Los Angeles — as well as one in Chicago, which was still in the planning stages. In great detail, the Board explained the primary sources for funding, which would come from Title III of the Federal Elementary and Secondary Education Act. Any continuance would depend upon federal funds. Newark funds would pay the balance of tuition and all transportation costs. A supplementary teacher would be paid from Title I funds of the FESEA.

Because the Hartford program had similarities to the Verona plan, an article by John J. Daly Jr., news editor of the *Catholic Transcript,* was reprinted in the local paper, describing the program.

> Each school day for the past two years, chartered buses have driven down the two-lane roads of five affluent suburban towns in north-central Connecticut carrying cheerful children from Hartford's predominantly Negro ghetto. These elementary school youngsters have been the front-line troops in a controversial regional assault on racial imbalance in inner-city schools. They have been attending classes with white children in modern suburban schools, where both their progress and their stumbles have been watched closely by a team of educational researchers.
>
> Though the program was to end after two years, efforts have been made by Hartford educators, businessmen and newspapers to continue, even though it may cost Hartford as much as $300,000 above normal costs. This had been the brainchild of the Connecticut State Department of Education, and the 260 transported pupils were under the watchful eyes of experts from Harvard, Brandeis and the University of Connecticut. The transported pupils, their parents and the suburban teachers were in favor, while the biggest obstacle has been the indecision of the suburban parents "who invariably turn out by the hundreds for long, loud meetings of the local school board." This was especially because of a current campaign to increase the cooperating towns to 16, and to increase the student numbers from

260 to 700. Advocates had a reasonably strong hand — aside from that of the humanitarian aspect — state and federal interest, careful record keeping, "class balance" (two to three city children in each suburban class), cost-free participation aside from desk space (one town — Farmington — made money last year on tuition and other charges), one extra teacher and an aide for each 25 pupils bused, and strong preliminary evidence that everyone benefits. There was no serious organized opposition, and even the staid Connecticut Education Association had encouraged the suburbs to participate, "an unusual step for a professional teachers organization."

According to Daly, the tentative conclusion after the first year showed results "not miraculous, but encouraging." The differences were statistically significant across the full range of grades. Bused children scored significantly higher in intelligence and achievement compared to three control groups. The 91 youngsters remaining in the ghetto who received similar supportive help (versus the transported group of 19) scored higher in only eight intelligence measures, but none in achievement. But aside from these impersonal results and statistics, there were dozens of moving personal experiences connected with the project.

Again, there were numerous letters to the editor of the local paper, ranging from Lois P. Butt, who praised Emil Tomecek and regretted that the rest of the Board was not like him, to John Farrell's doubts about the Plan.

The Council for Inter-Religious Activity, in a strongly worded press release, made an appeal to Verona citizens to look beyond peripheral questions to the obvious moral basis for the Sharing Plan proposal.

Ever since Cain asked, "Am I my brother's keeper?", there has been universal recognition of the theory that religion has a social dimension. Indeed, the religious act — the act of worship itself — is a social act, expressing the unity of the assembled people.

The statement stressed that all of the community's Christian and Jewish

clergymen, individually and collectively through their ministerial association — as well as some associated groups — such as the Rosary Society
and the Christian Family Movement of Our Lady of the Lake Church —
supported the proposal.

> We here in Verona now have an opportunity to prove that our
> beliefs do govern our social acts by making it possible for our
> Board of Education to bring 40 disadvantaged Newark children
> into the classrooms. . . .

Referring to education as the

> key to liberation from poverty . . . we see a moral obligation to
> undertake this program because we cannot hold ourselves aloof
> from the crisis in which the Newark school system finds itself.

And while the opponents could offer some valid political argument,
the Council argued, the Board's proposal should not be judged on whether it had political merit, but whether sharing was the right thing to
do.

In his letter to the editor of the *Verona-Cedar Grove Times*, Reverend
M. Sargent Desmond, the spiritual leader of the Congregational Church,
stressed that his endorsing the Plan should not be construed as meaning
that the First Congregational Church of Verona, on the whole, had approved the program. Hrant H. Yousoufian, who had run for a vacant seat
on the Board a few months earlier and lost, was on a business trip in Australia. He not only endorsed the Plan from far away, but censured those
who opposed it.

> Like so much of the "educational scene" in Verona, the pre-
> sent problem placed before us seems to have aroused some of
> the negative emotions which seem to work against the common
> good and interest of our people. Encouraged by my family, I
> feel compelled to add my voice to those who support busing
> Newark children to Verona.

A. G. Calvanese and John Farrell, in separate letters to the local paper, supported a referendum. Robert C. J. Krasner, of the University of

Maryland School of Medicine — who attended and taught in the Verona school system and also taught in Newark — described the experimental studies sponsored by the Department of Social-Psychiatry, which demonstrated that children exposed to better social and educational conditions fared considerably better than those who stagnated in ghetto areas.

> The Verona school system prepared me very well for my further education in college and medical school. I, for one, would certainly not deny the same beneficial opportunity to another. . . .

David Landsberger, a student at Carnegie-Mellon University, had changed his mind about Verona being a small, narrow-minded town, and was now proud of his hometown.

The public meeting of the Verona Board of Education on June 11, 1968, was recorded and transcribed by Brooks Sound Service in Trenton. After the usual opening ceremonies, and the prayer asking for guidance on the decision in this most important matter, Assistant Superintendent Thomas J. Sellitto, who acted as Board secretary, read the resolution for consideration:

> Whereas, at a regular Public Meeting on April 30, 1968, the Verona Board of Education unanimously offered for public consideration a proposal for sharing educational opportunities in Verona for one year with up to 40 children from a Newark public elementary school and
>
> Whereas, at a special Public Hearing on May 13, 1968, many citizens of Verona, and representatives of local groups availed themselves of the chance to voice their reactions to the proposal, and
>
> Whereas, many citizens have communicated their views in person, by letter, by telegram and by telephone to the Board and/or to individual Board members, and
>
> Whereas, the Board has duly considered these comments offered by citizens of Verona,
>
> NOW, THEREFORE, BE IT RESOLVED, that the Verona Board of Education endorses the concept underlined in the proposal of April 30,1968, for sharing educational opportunities in Verona.

The resolution was moved by John McDonald and seconded by Elmer Gustavson. Emil Tomecek raised the question, as a point of order, whether the Board's policy on students from outside the district needed to be changed first. Board president Hilda Jaffe, quoting the Superintendent's opinion, answered that the resolution was a concept, and if the agreement were acted upon, the policy needed to be changed.

Each member, in alphabetical order, was then given time to comment. McDonald explained that after he had read the Governor's Select Commission on Civil Disorder's report, he had agreed to a study to ascertain if there was any way in which Verona's school system could aid the youngsters of the neighboring community in achieving the quality education to which each child is entitled. He believed that Verona's educational system was capable of meeting and resolving any problems if the proposal were accepted, and was greatly encouraged by the statements of Verona's citizens and organizations that supported the Sharing Plan. "I will not attempt to speak for any of the other members," he said, "but for myself, my contact with the public has been most encouraging. It has been substantially in favor of the proposal." After distribution of the flyer asking the residents who supported the referendum to contact the Board members — whose names, addresses, and phone numbers had been included in the flyer — McDonald had tallied the responses, day by day, for a total of 16 calls and six pieces of correspondence supporting the referendum. There were more calls favoring the proposal.

John McDonald went on to say,

> This board is charged with the responsibility of making decisions such as that. . . . To present this matter on a referendum, solely because it relates to children from Newark, is to me a shirking of responsibility which I agreed to accept when I was sworn in as a member of this Board of Education in February 1967. . . .

One question asked was what the people of Verona owed Newark. McDonald answered,

> There is a great community of interest between Verona and Newark, which is our county seat. Our public transportation system centers in Newark; our communication network center

is in Newark. A great number of our citizens earn their livelihood in Newark; many of our citizens have lived in Newark
most of their lives and many of them have deep investments in
family, business and other factors in the city of Newark. Verona
does have a community of interest with Newark. We cannot
ignore the problems of Newark. We are constantly reminded of
them. . . .

For those who did not want the program instituted until all questions
were answered, he quoted a phrase used in discussions relating to opening
the second front in France during World War II: "Don't wait until the last
button is sewed upon the last vest to begin the operation."

Jaffe requested that demonstrations be kept short to save time.

Those of you who were rude enough, and I use that word, to
interrupt the speaker, I must remind you that this is a meeting
of a public body, that you are within your rights as a citizen, but
not within your rights to interrupt or disrupt the meeting. I must
ask you to behave properly. . . . Again I ask, if you wish to
approve or disapprove, that you please confine yourselves to a
very short period at the end of each speech. Thank you.

Gustavson spoke next regarding his mixed feelings about the proposal.
He thought that the concept was good, but foresaw problems, and then
quoted from a letter whose authorship he did not want to reveal:

I do not require of you any guarantee that this proposal will be
100 percent effective, nor that there will be no problems, nor
that these children will not return to a detrimental environment.
I understand that such guarantees are impossible. Do you, could
you, guarantee that every Verona child will have no problems
or that every Verona child will not go home to an unsympa-
thetic environment?

Tomecek quoted statistics on Newark's educational problems.

Newark is 10,000 pupil stations short. Some of its pupils are on
split sessions. A significant number of its pupils are functioning

far below applicable grade level norms. For example, for Grade 3 in 1966, the Newark reading median was 1.9, while the national norm was 3.2.

After visiting three of Newark's schools, Tomecek's impression was of having too many substitute teachers, crowded classrooms, busing to other schools within Newark, split sessions, and overlapping sessions — all problems that he was sure needed to be solved in Newark with state and federal assistance. Tomecek asked interested Verona people to organize and adopt early grades of Newark schools, much as had been done in Montclair, with its "one-on-one" volunteer-staffed tutoring program. Originally, Mr Tomecek said, he had accepted and supported the proposal as a charitable gesture, but "the main goal seems to have been the meeting of unrealistic time schedules rather than promoting acceptability of the proposal by holding numerous open meetings, where required by law to take place." One open meeting, according to Tomecek, was not sufficient. Many discerning questions, he added, had not been answered. He went on to say that the school system belonged to the people of Verona, and began to request a referendum. At that moment, Jaffe again had to ask the gathering to preserve order. Tomecek concluded that he supported a referendum, and would thus vote against the proposal.

Edward P. Wizda denied that this was a crash program, and said that Verona had studied similar programs in other areas. Ever since the publication of the proposal, he said, the majority of letters in the local paper were in favor, with 275 showing their support in a one-page advertisement. He had received five telegrams and more than 60 letters for the proposal, versus only one letter against and six for a referendum — and the vast majority during the public meeting favored the Plan, which, to Wizda, indicated a positive reaction by the public to the proposal. He went on to say,

> As a parent, I am particularly convinced we must take this step. I have three children in the public schools of Verona, one of whom is in the first grade, and I feel that their lives can be enriched if they have opportunities to know children of different background.

Board president Hilda Jaffe spoke last.

> Public reaction is not easy to weigh. Do you count signatures on letters or signatures on petitions? Do you count membership rolls in recognized organizations? Do you count telephone calls in which the callers repeat a pat argument that is printed out for them, or those with original reasons for or against something? When the issue seems to be changed from education to democracy, is that really [a] reaction to the original proposal? For myself, I must weigh the total impact of public sentiment. Numbers, pro and con, are not valid in themselves. The weight of ideas, the strength of acceptance and of rejection are more important.

Jaffe's impressions were that since the Board had answered questions, acceptance had increased, that the most recent letters and phone calls had been positive and definite. "People in Verona are in favor of the proposal and expect the Board to go ahead with it." She quoted Tomecek's previous statement, "At best, the city schools are old and overcrowded with insufficient teachers and materials," and added,

> Even for children with strong motivation and family support, the schools cannot offer much dynamic help, but for children with ghetto problems, education doesn't seem worth the effort, and so they lag behind and eventually drop out. Do we want to lose another generation?

Jaffe spoke of the experiences of the other communities sponsoring similar projects, and quoted the president of the Board of Education of West Hartford, Connecticut, that it "seems to break the kids out of the mold of their inner-city society and to help them develop self-motivation. They are generally trying now to the limit of their capability." And she referred to his comment that there were no greater discipline or behavior problems with the city children than there were with their own normal suburban children.

In discussing the requests for a referendum, Jaffe explained that the state Constitution of New Jersey

> specifically removes public schools from the whims of the populace by vesting control policy in the hands of a continuing lay

school board. Only money decisions, budgets and bond issues, are made directly by the voters. . . . Elected School Board members are responsible for making all policy decisions. To hand over this responsibility to others would be to deny the democratic process. . . .

She concluded,

To stand by encouragingly in the suburbs, to offer a hand, this to me is not charity; it is the very height of self-preservation. We and our children will have to live with the fruits of the present urban crisis. To those who ask "Why Verona?" I answer, "Why not Verona?"

Thomas J. Sellitto called the roll. The resolution carried four to one, with only Tomecek voting no.

Once again, nearly all Board members expressed their opinion that according to what they had heard and what they had read, they were sure that the majority of Verona was solidly behind their plan.

A second resolution was introduced:

Whereas, the Verona Board of Education has endorsed the concept underlying the proposal of April 30, 1968, for sharing educational opportunities in Verona

THEREFORE, BE IT RESOLVED that the Verona Superintendent of Schools and the Secretary of the Verona Board, with aid of counsel, enter immediately into negotiations with the Newark Superintendent of Schools and the Secretary of the Newark Board, to prepare a contract for implementing the aforementioned proposal for sharing educational opportunities, such contract to be acted upon by the Verona Board of Education at a Public Meeting.

It is agreed that the following items be part of any negotiation and/or considerations by the Verona Board and the Newark Board before final acceptance:

1. Complete authority of the Verona Board in the administration of the program.

2. The length of the contract: 1 year.

3. Financing of proposal from completely outside sources, federal, state and Newark.

4. Method of arriving at cost of proposal, such as: pupil tuition, supplemental assistance, research, etc.

5. Available number of spaces without exceeding class size standards and with provision for normal pupil population growth.

6. The number of students: up to 40.

7. The method of selection of children.

8. The selection of schools: Newark's responsibility with Verona's approval.

9. Provision for periodic review and right of either board to terminate contract in 30 days.

10. Insurance necessary to protect the Verona Board and local cooperating citizens.

11. Transportation to be the responsibility of the Newark Board of Education.

12. Method of payments to be made to the Verona Board of Education.

13. Plan for supplemental assistance.

14. Research, goals and methods.

15. Such other items as the Verona Board of Education may consider proper for inclusion in the contract.

The resolution was moved by Gustavson and seconded by Wizda. Tomecek and Jaffe were the only Board members who discussed this resolution.

Tomecek felt there were questions on items 2, 5, 7, and 8, which he thought should be answered, and which had never been explored to his and other citizens' satisfaction. For instance, he did not think that there was any space available in two of the schools. He also questioned the criteria for selecting the children. Tomecek had heard that gifted children were wanted, or at least normal children, but he suggested that kids be picked who really needed the help, kids who were on half-session in overcrowded classrooms. Tomecek objected to the generalities in the motion and was sure that it was the Board's job to determine those answers long before getting into contract negotiations.

Jaffe explained in detail specific parts of the resolution. She wanted to make sure that it was understood that the Verona Board had the last word on the resolution, not the administration. And to answer Tomecek, she added, "it means stipulations and criteria can be made by the Verona Board that are *not* subject to negotiations." The Verona Board is the complete authority of the program, she stated. The children would be subject to the rules and jurisdiction of the Verona School District, and this would include all policies by which all students and staff members in Verona were governed. The money must come from outside sources and be available for one year, the length of the contract. Most funding would come from federal grants, which would not carry over from one year to another. The program would be constantly evaluated with reports from all people involved. There would not be any hasty decisions as to continuance of the proposal.

Jaffe addressed those who were concerned with local children who have learning problems by saying,

> . . . a large percentage of the children have learning problems of one kind or another, and I feel that the inclusion of children from outside with somewhat different problems will be of benefit all through the classrooms, and that our teachers, in recognizing slightly different reasons for learning problems, will, in effect, be given greater insight into working with Verona children within the classrooms.

The 30-day determination clause was important, since that made it feasible to terminate the contract if any drawbacks or financial problems occurred. The desirable class size was 25, but provisions had to be made for families moving in with children during the school year; therefore, it was not certain that every available seat would be filled with Newark children. Jaffe concluded by explaining the terms "random selection" and "normal" children. Children with great problems would be excluded, such as those attending Special Education classes, or those who were handicapped. The children would come from a disadvantaged area, but they would still fit into the range of classes and ability in Verona.

Again, with Tomecek voting against, the resolution carried by a vote of four to one.

Twenty-three speakers, of whom three were unidentified, addressed the Board. The first had just purchased his house. He had worked for three years in four of Newark's schools, and he felt that there would be a language barrier, that the children in Newark used off-color language and "you should see what these children actually think, and how they actually talk, and hear what they call the white people in the schools."

Mr. Cawthorne offered to invite a priest who had formerly been located in Newark to address the Board on the problems they could expect. He stated that they had had to rewrite the readers for the first and second grades because, "The children didn't understand. They never knew about going to visit grandmothers and grandfathers; they just didn't know anything about it. . . ." Jaffe told Cawthorne that they would be happy if the priest would contact the Board.

Anthony Zangari warned the Board that they should not forget the 2,300 who signed the petition for a referendum. He felt that the middle-class had been largely ignored because they had been silent. The mistrust would be lessened, he said, if the Board had listened to the request for a referendum, and he warned that future proposals coming from the Board would also be resented.

Counsel Anthony F. Ditri, speaking for the Verona Citizens for a Fair Decision, advised the Board that while his group respected the decision that had been made, he was

> . . . very saddened to see this community divided as it is, but I think its division in some respect must go on and the responsibility must fall upon the members of this board . . . because there was absolutely no indication, no philosophy, no inkling of your particular thinking with regard to this proposal.

He assured the Board that no member of the Citizens for a Fair Decision would ever participate in becoming "a wall of rejection to these children."

Former high school football coach Walter Wermuth supported the action of the Board, but thought that Tomecek's suggestion to adopt schools in Newark was a wonderful idea. Wermuth hoped that Tomecek would act as initiator of a committee, and Wermuth added that he would be happy to help stir up interest in instituting tutoring programs.

Tomecek thanked Wermuth and told him that he could not be the head of such a committee, but that as a citizen he would be more than glad to help get such a project going.

Ralph Lucatola did not think that the vote that had just been taken would end the conflict, and aside from the fact that he felt the legal process would entail a referendum, the Board would also have to answer to voters during the next election. Richard Marashlian felt that the only one to be congratulated was Tomecek. Originally, Marashlian had commended the Board for their motives, but as time went on he had begun to feel that the Board "had already decided, that it was predetermined, and then you decided to sell the idea." While he did not see any real harm in bringing in these 40 children, his resentment was on the way it was put over, the method in which it was sold, which he felt was with high-pressure methods.

David Jordan did not think that the Board had acted out of courage, but rather out of fear of not doing enough for the disadvantaged people.

> In Mrs. Jaffe's words, it is a matter of self-preservation, and perhaps most important of all, the board apparently does not have the courage of its convictions, for it will not place the issue before the citizens of Verona in a referendum, for they fear it will be defeated by an overwhelming majority. So much for the courage of the board and its interest in the democratic process, but what of civil rights? . . . Since the Board of Education is not courageous, nor does it want to adhere to democratic principles and ignores the civil rights of our citizens, what may we expect of them? Education? What kind of educational standard can we expect be set by people who listen to fewer than 200 people in favor of the program, ignore 2,300 people asking for a referendum, and then by some magical formula, decide that the community is in favor of the plan?

Jaffe had announced at the beginning of the evening that the public meeting would close at 9:45 p.m. Even though there were some objections that this was an arbitrary time, the meeting was adjourned. Again, the majority of speakers that evening seemed to have complimented the Board on their decision.

"Verona Opens School Doors to Newark Ghetto Children," proclaimed the *Passaic Herald News* on June 12, while "Verona OKs Busing," was the headline in the *Newark Evening News* the same day. The *Passaic Herald News* stated,

> The Newark children — a polite label for Negro children of the slums — have won a tentative welcome to the all-white suburban town of Verona. . . . About two-thirds of the audience of 800 last night applauded the decision. . . . If prejudice can end at the classroom door, Verona feels, there is hope for coming generations, and our society.

The *Newark Evening News* provided a much more factual report. The *Courier News* of Plainfield also reported that Verona had approved the measure.

On Thursday, June 13, *The New York Times* reported that the Verona Board had decided to accept "Pupils From Slums." Despite a petition by 2,300 residents calling for a public referendum, *The Times* wrote,

> the Board of Education of this virtually all-white suburban community voted 4 to 1 last night to open its elementary schools to as many as 40 youngsters from Newark. . . . Although restricted in scale, the program will represent a pioneering educational move in New Jersey.

According to the June 13 *West Essex Tribune*, a representative of the educational task force of the Coalition for Concern in the nearby town of Livingston, Frank Witkus, had recently addressed that community's Board of Education to explain the Verona plan in detail. Livingston Board president Judy Zients announced that an Administrative Council Committee had been organized to explore what Livingston could do to help, and said that an appointment had been made with Newark school officials. Columnist Barbara Mackey (Bakst) also described in her article the Livingston meeting and reported in a different vein that the Livingston group already had nine volunteers tutoring children at the Waverly School.

On June 13, the *Verona-Cedar Grove Times* reported the Verona Board of Education's approval of the Sharing Educational Opportunities plan. According to this account, an estimated 400 citizens attended the Board session, which was held in the high school — as compared to approximately 1,800 who had attended the public meeting on May 13. This time, too, it was reported, the supporters of the Sharing Plan seemed to outnumber those who opposed it. Emil Tomecek, the lone objector to both resolutions, won standing applause from about 50 persons. By contrast, approximately 150 citizens rose to applaud Edward P. Wizda's statement that the Board was elected to make educational decisions and not to act as "crowd pleasers." The paper quoted from the speeches of each Board member, and also from those citizens who spoke either for or against the proposal.

Former Board member Edward F. Fritche, in a letter to the *Verona-Cedar Grove Times* editor, agreed that the Board was within its right to approve the proposal without a vote under a public referendum. Pat D'Entremont saw leadership in the action of the Board, and J. Malcolm Simon and Diane C. Simon were appalled at the time, money, and manpower being expended by the Verona Citizens for a Fair Decision in their efforts to thwart the worthwhile proposal.

Unfortunately, Anthony Ditri, counsel for the Verona Citizens for a Fair Decision, was correct in his prediction that the Board's action would divide the community. It did so not only at that time, but for years to come.

Among the many letters received by Edward Wizda is one by Joseph Percevault, the gentleman employed by Henry's Fine Foods, dated June 6, 1968. In this handwritten letter, Percevault enumerated a few facts:

1. After my talk at the Open Hearing I lost 3 known customers.

2. I received 14 phone calls all in favor of my talk and the board's proposal.

3. I received 2 notes at home; complimentary.

4. I have 50 to 100 new customers at the store who make it a point to introduce themselves and favor my talk and the board's proposal.

5. Of those I speak to at the store, at least 500 to 800 in the last few weeks, a great majority believe some or much good can come from the 40 students brought to Verona.

6. I find that those who oppose the board's proposal are either very old and worried about a tax increase, or they are very new

to Verona and the suburbs and would hate to see a minority group likewise make the "next steps on the ladder" to Verona; almost like the children's game of "King of the Mountain."

Percevault did not envy Wizda's position and the pressure brought upon him; he further felt that Wizda's sense of responsibility, though clouded by noise and petitions, was an important step for freedom and democracy. He ended the letter with, "May God be with you in your decision."

Of the 62 messages Wizda received, only six wrote asking for a referendum. Louise B. Ritcher, who was employed as the school nurse, not only endorsed the project, but volunteered to cooperate to make it successful. Another letter writer, while neither endorsing nor opposing the proposal, was worried that Verona would get mixed up in the "dirty politics of Newark" and with Newark teachers' "union tendencies, and . . . the strikes, etc., they promoted in Newark."

The balance of the letters in favor of the Plan — as well as those who spoke at the various meetings — cut across all the economic ranges in the community, from rich to poor. Support also came from nearly every ethnic group, and certainly there was support from all religious groups — or at least from their leadership. No wonder Board members were under the impression that the town was solidly behind them.

On June 18, the *Newark Evening News* reported that the Paterson, New Jersey, Diocese, which covered three counties and had 77 elementary schools, was studying a busing plan to bring up to 50 black children from the city to a Catholic elementary school in a suburb. Father Simonet said that the Council had already surveyed three schools in Wayne, Pompton Lakes, and Upper Morris County as possible areas, and added that local pastors would have to give their consent before their schools could become part of such a program. Pupils who were transported, he said, would be scholarship students. Father Simonet agreed that he might find opposition: "A lot of people don't want to send their kids out to the suburbs. They see them as an armed hostile camp." The report's last paragraph cited Verona's approval of its Sharing Plan.

It seemed that Verona had begun the process, and now other communities and School Boards were thinking along the same lines, including places like Chicago and San Francisco.

. . . The Board of Education has violated the trust put in them by the citizens of this community. They have resorted to the scare tactics of the radical extremists, ignored a mandate from 30 percent of the citizens they "represent" and capitulated to the demands of less than 5 percent of the community. — Richard Meehan

Chapter 8

Agreeing to Disagree

A COPY OF THE signed agreement between the Board of Education of the City of Newark and the Board of Education of the Borough of Verona is attached to the minutes of the Verona Board meeting of June 25, 1968. In this document, Verona agreed to take up to 40 children, subject to 21 very specific conditions including:

- neither board would commit itself beyond the 1968-1969 school year;
- each board could withdraw on 30 days' notice;
- Verona had complete authority in the administration of the program;

- children were eligible regardless of race, color, or creed and would be selected at random, provided they were of appropriate age and free from emotional or special education problems;
- the addition of Newark pupils could not cause any class in Verona to exceed 25 students;
- the parents of "transported" children had to give written permission;
- the Newark Board would be responsible for the transportation;
- under no circumstance would Verona children be bused;
- a supplemental teacher who was an employee of the Newark Board of Education and accepted by Verona would be assigned to Verona, to provide necessary instructional and guidance services for the children of the project.

In addition, the program would be completely financed from federal, state, and Newark sources, and Verona was to receive $1,014.85 per pupil, the estimated per-pupil cost at that time. To this was added the cost of milk, field trips, and insurance — including liability coverage for the parents who would take the Newark children into their homes for lunch, as no food was to be provided by Verona's elementary schools. Five percent was added to achieve true costs, not including that of transportation. And finally, any testing program for the participating children would be agreed upon by the two Boards, but would remain under the jurisdiction of Verona, and any costs for special testing programs would be paid for by the Newark Board, which could also include research and evaluation, including consultant services of up to $3,000. In addition, the agreement was contingent upon approval by all parties by August 1.

A motion to execute this agreement was moved by John McDonald and seconded by Edward Wizda. It was passed three votes to two, with Elmer Gustavson abstaining and Emil Tomecek dissenting.

Thomas Sellitto, as Board secretary, read the agreement and explained that counsel for both Boards had negotiated the contract, and that every point asked for by the Verona School Board had been included.

Gustavson explained that he thought this to be a good proposal, but he was not sure that it was really an agreement as yet, because only the previous night had they met to agree on the language. Tomecek complained that this was only the second in a series of four resolutions. The first, according to Tomecek, was

> characterized by unrealistic time schedules and an almost com-
> plete disregard for the importance of broad community accep-
> tance of the proposal. Since I did not accept the first resolution,
> I reject tonight's resolution because I do not believe in the idea
> that the "end justifies the means."

Tomecek also objected to having seen the contract for the first time at 6:30 the previous evening, then having to meet with the Board at 8:00 p.m., believing it to be "completely unrealistic to ask a person to read, digest, understand, evaluate, criticize, correct and accept such a document in one three-hour sitting." Yet, even though he had voted against the Plan, he reiterated his interest in getting children from Newark, but so far there was no firm written commitment on available spaces and no guidelines on the selection of the pupils.

In the ensuing discussion, it was pointed out that all members of the Board had been aware of the general outline of the proposal since March, that no children would be accepted if there was no available space, and that most guidelines had been set two weeks prior to the meeting. The resolution, in other words, was not something that had suddenly turned up the previous evening. Tomecek was accused of pandering to the opposition's stand: "I am in favor of it, but I don't like it."

But Tomecek continued to complain that he heard mostly generalities, and Board president Hilda Jaffe reminded him that the proposal had been agreed upon originally by all five Board members and supported by the Superintendent and Assistant Superintendent, who had helped to develop the proposal. The current agreement, she said, was very similar to the one that had been developed previously.

During the open discussion period there was some criticism of Tomecek. But Carmine Rando, who had also spoken at the first public meeting, called Tomecek "the most progressive of all the Board members here tonight," and accused the Board of not having the highest ideals. Others questioned the vagueness of selecting the children "at random" or the exact meaning of the word "appropriate." David B. Ford, chairman of the Citizens for a Fair Decision, also wanted definitions of "random selec-tion," "normal child," and "special educational problems or emotional difficulties." In addition, he questioned what recourse residents might have and whether there might be a referendum. Wizda explained that "random" meant that they did not want to be accused of taking the cream of the crop.

Marshall A. Butler, who would later run for a Board position, questioned the members on the evaluation of the program's effectiveness, and noted that the agreement did not stipulate a control group for comparison purposes. Arthur E. Benson also wanted a control group as part of the agreement, and feared that without such a group, any result of testing would be invalidated.

Questions also were voiced concerning what might happen if the state were to take over the Newark school system. Joyce McEvoy questioned the remedial help a Newark child might require. It was explained that this was one of the reasons for a supplemental teacher, paid for by Newark, and that it could not be assumed that all of the children would need help.

Anthony J. D'Agosto questioned if there was an age limitation on a fifth grader. Could he be assured that a 13-year-old would not be in fifth grade? McDonald replied that the children needed to be at the same age level as those in Verona, and explained that the agreement could not be specific, such as,

> the child will be eight years old, one hundred and thirty pounds, black hair, blue eyes. We don't know what will develop until we sit down and work out who the forty children will be.

Superintendent John Mattis also pointed out that each participating School Board could withdraw any student, and a 14-year-old in third grade would not be in the proper age bracket.

The June meeting had been covered by a reporter from the Verona paper, and an article appeared on June 27. Only about 55 citizens had attended this meeting, but 30 "diehard" opponents to the Plan remained until after 11:30 p.m. to question various aspects of the Sharing Plan. In the July 2 letters to the editor section of the paper, visitors Janet N. and H. M. Kassler, of Lexington, Massachusetts, wrote that their town was one of the 16 communities in the greater Boston area participating in the METCO program that provided an integrated suburban education for Boston students, nearly all black, without costing the participating communities a single penny. It was already their third year of participation, and

Lexington expected to have 90 METCO students in Grades 2, 3, 4, and at all high school levels the upcoming year. A total of 850 students were to be bused to various communities. The Kasslers wrote:

> The newly elected presidents of the sophomore and senior class at Lexington High School are Negro METCO students. We in the white community feel that the children from the urban area come to us for an education, but they bring with them an equally important education for our children. We feel that education through direct contact — face-to-face — is the best way to dissolve fearful prejudices.

But Richard Meehan, whose letter appeared in the same issue, expressed his preference for a referendum.

> I personally feel that the Board of Education has violated the trust put in them by the citizens of this community. They have resorted to the scare tactics of the radical extremists, ignored a mandate from 30 percent of the citizens they "represent" and capitulated to the demands of less than 5 percent of the community.

Mary Hill's letter on the same day agreed that every person in Verona wanted to help the children of Newark to obtain an education that would enable them to become self-respecting, self-supporting adults, but did not think that the Verona Sharing Plan met those qualifications. She added,

> For the sake of the children of Newark, money available to help them must be spent with wisdom and careful planning. One touch of Verona for forty pupils at a cost of $1,250 per pupil is not the answer.

The *Asbury Park [New Jersey] Sunday Press* of July 7 headlined its story, "Voluntary School Busing Showing a Slight Trend." Instead of being forced by court or legislative action, the article read, some education officials were beginning a trend toward voluntary involvement. Even though it might upset the traditional neighborhood school concept, there was a growing feeling that a moral obligation existed "to pursue such means no matter how painful, to spread their cultural wealth." Verona was cited as an example, and while it was speculated that this gesture could not ease Newark's problem to any great extent, it seemed it could be a significant prod for other suburbs. Chicago was also cited, as the Catholic Archdiocese had announced that some 350 elementary school children would be bused in the fall from their parishes in the city slum areas to 19 Catholic schools in outlying Chicago and suburbs.

Emil Tomecek made the headlines in the *Passaic Herald News* of July 18, when the paper reported that he favored the sharing idea but felt that the Board was moving too rapidly.

> As far as our own proposal is concerned, I had accepted the proposal for sharing educational opportunity as a charitable gesture whereby, while steps are being taken to solve Newark's educational problems in Newark, we would provide a small number of Newark children with the immediate opportunity of coming to Verona's uncrowded elementary classes for a full day rather than attending a crowded Newark classroom for a half day.

His substitute plan had suggested that through an effort of the teachers' organization, more children could be helped through a tutoring program every Saturday in Newark.

Before the Sharing Plan proposal, the meetings of the Board of Education had never been attended by more than a handful of residents. But after the Plan had surfaced, the gatherings had to be moved to larger quarters. The regular meeting of the Board on Tuesday, August 27, 1968, was held at the cafeteria of the Whitehorne Middle School; 75 citizens and 2 press representatives attended.

After the opening prayer, Board president Hilda Jaffe announced that there would be two portions open to public discussion; the first would be limited to 30 minutes, immediately after the report of the Superintendent. Questions during this period had to relate to that report. Subsequently, at the end of the meeting, an hour-long question-and-answer session would be held for any other pertinent matters.

Board secretary Thomas Sellitto explained that on the previous Thursday, at approximately 12:00 noon, the Board had been served with an official complaint and order "to show cause," signed by five citizens, regarding the sharing of educational opportunities. It was answerable in court before Judge Samuel A. Larner the following Friday at 9:30 a.m. A resolution was thus introduced authorizing the Board's attorney, George Buermann, to prepare the answering papers. All voted for the resolution except Emil Tomecek, who abstained because he said he had learned about the motion only ten minutes before, and that he would need further time to evaluate it. Tomecek was told that the complaint had been received only five days before, and that a response was needed in three days. Interestingly, the fees for the Board of Education on this court case (as well as that of the subsequent appeal) were paid for by all the taxpayers of Verona. This meant that the opponents of the Plan paid not only for the complainants, but partially for the defense as well.

After the resolution had passed, authorizing the attorney to proceed, Superintendent Mattis followed with his complete report, which had been distributed to the people in attendance. He explained that the criteria used for the selection of a Newark school were location in a disadvantaged area, overcrowded conditions, lack of physical facilities, and response from receptive parents. Children needed to be transported to Verona within a 45-minute period. Three Newark schools had been designated as appropriate, and from those three, the Hawthorne Avenue School had been selected, because it appeared "that this school district would receive the most positive benefit from the Verona plan." On July 15, the two superintendents had met, and a tentative number of 38 possible spaces was offered in the four elementary schools of Verona. "It was emphasized," Superintendent Mattis said, "that numbers could not be considered final until enrollments for the new year are firm."

Mattis then outlined the steps that had been taken earlier that month to develop an implementation plan for the program. On Friday, August 2, 13 people, including parents from the Hawthorne Avenue School, met in Newark's Board of Education building to discuss the process of selecting children. A committee from Newark, who had asked to see the Verona schools, visited on Tuesday afternoon, August 6. The group toured the community, went through several of the schools, and, at the conclusion of the visit, met for a social period at the home of Superintendent Mattis. On Friday, August 16, Mattis met with a representative of the Division of Educational Studies of the Educational Testing Service in Princeton, New Jersey, to discuss methods for evaluating the Sharing Plan. The ETS proposal was to be submitted to both Boards for approval.

On Monday, August 19, another meeting was held, again in Newark, and a group of participants and alternates were drawn from volunteers at the Hawthorne Avenue School. In this way, the selection avoided unintentional bias in the choice of children to participate and would ensure a fair cross section of students, so that comparisons could be made later in the evaluation process. The parents of the children selected had been contacted, and a well-qualified and experienced teacher had been chosen. Superintendent Mattis closed by saying, "This is what happened and that is what has had to be done to implement a program that is to begin in September."

After the Superintendent completed his report, the Board opened the meeting for its first public discussion period. Richard Marashlian, who had spoken against the Plan at the hearing on May 13, wanted to know more about the testing procedures — how soon they would start and whether the results would be made public. A definitive answer could not be given, because the procedures had not yet been set up. Marashlian then accused the Board of hesitation, and added,

> I am sure you wouldn't deny the citizens what they are seeking. If you had started this program with the idea of measuring the help, definite and specific tests should be set aside to measure the performance of these youngsters.

Mr. G. M. Bailey spoke, saying that he assumed that the disadvantaged children would need a great deal of remedial work and wondered whether there would be sufficient time, or if the buses would have to wait. Again it was explained that an additional teacher was provided, paid for by Newark. In response to a question by Mr. A. A. Steinitz, John McDonald explained that the opposing group had requested a temporary restraining order. Judge Samuel Larner only granted the order, "to show cause"; and this required the Board to show why an order declaring this contract *ultra vires* (beyond the legal power or authority of a corporation or corporate officer) should not be issued,

> Which means we have to show that the Board of Education is acting within its legal responsibility or acting within the scope of its authority. . . . We are proceeding with the project because we have not been restrained or ordered not to go forward.

Later, Steinitz requested the names of the plaintiff and signers. According to Board attorney Buermann, the signers were Amy Bostwick, Sydney W. and Robert Dickinson, Edward Newkirk, Fred Mahn, and the Citizens for a Fair Decision.

Marashlian reminded the Board that at one of the previous meetings, the idea of offering tutors in a school in the ghetto area had been expressed. He wanted to know if there had been any response. Tomecek admitted his fault in not meeting with those who had volunteered, saying, "Don't make any conclusions. This is entirely separate from Board of Education business." Jaffe pointed out that Tomecek had made this suggestion at the June 11 meeting, and the question had not been discussed since. The action would be purely voluntary, and she suggested that those who were interested in helping should call tutoring organizations already in place. Marashlian requested that the Board instruct the Verona Educators Association and others who had voluntarily lauded such programs to prove their intentions. "I would like to see how many members of the Verona Educators have actually volunteered to teach in the ghetto," he said.

Richard Heaslip said he hoped that the Newark children would be treated properly, without harassment.

> I hope Verona shows its colors. I think it is so important for these forty kids. I would hope that all kids in the schools treat them . . . just like they are another classmate.

Richard Meehan, a member of the Citizens for a Fair Decision, said that as far as he was concerned these children would be accepted into the community. It was the method the Verona School Board had used that he objected to.

On August 28 and 31, the lead stories in the *Newark Evening News* were "Verona Group in Court To Hold School Busing" and "Will Fight Verona Ruling." The first story described the Verona Board's plans for the arrival of the Newark children, despite the court case and the concern of several residents that those who opposed the Plan might "make the visiting Newark students feel unwanted." On August 29, the local Verona

weekly carried the headline: VERONA BOARD MUST ANSWER, SHOW CAUSE." But on the 31st, the *Newark Evening News* reported that Judge Larner had refused to issue a temporary restraining order. The attorney for the undaunted Verona Citizens for Fair Decision was reported to have said, "He is only one judge."

The climate of the times — riots, discrimination, the demand for integrated schools, and busing — had combined to create an atmosphere of distrust.

Chapter 9

The New Jersey Department of Education

ORIGINALLY, IT WAS assumed by its proponents that the Verona Sharing Plan was a purely local issue. In retrospect, this was not correct. The climate of the times — riots, discrimination, the demand for integrated schools, and busing — had combined to create an atmosphere of distrust. Any study of New Jersey's educational system would find coming to the forefront, again and again, a strong desire for local control. Dr. Carl L. Marburger, who had been appointed the State Commissioner of Education just a year before the Verona Sharing Plan was presented, did not in 1968 endear himself to those who wanted nothing more than local control of their schools. He spoke often of busing and integration, and reaction to the tenor of the state's Department of Education since his appointment could easily have been foreseen by those who participated in county and state educational affairs.

The evolution of the public school system in New Jersey had commenced with a new state Constitution in 1844; 22 years later, the first State Board of Education was authorized. Ten years after that, in 1876, a changed Constitution charged the state with maintaining and supporting a "thorough and efficient" educational system, which is still the catch phrase today.

Over the years, the issue of who appointed whom, and the personnel who sat on the Board, changed several times. In the early years of the 20th century, the office of the Commissioner of Education was created, and the Education Department was charged with additional responsibilities, such as setting minimum standards in the curriculum, overseeing local bookkeeping, and hearing controversies. State aid to local schools was funded even during the Great Depression of the 1930s.

The Department was reorganized once again in 1945. In the Sixties, the Department of Education was part of the Executive Branch. The 12 members of the State Board of Education were appointed by the Governor; they served without pay, only reimbursed for expenses. Together with the Commissioner of Education, this Board set the general policy on all elementary and secondary educational matters. The Board was charged "with general supervision and control of public education," and had to plan and recommend steps for "unified continuous and efficient development of public education."

The Commissioner, as the chief executive and administrative officer of the State Board of Education, was appointed by the Governor for a five-year term. The Commissioner had to work with the Board, and also was in charge of several assistants, a budget office, and all other employees of that Department. In addition to a myriad of other duties, he had to oversee a minimum curriculum, instructional guidance for teachers and Superintendents, inspection of buildings, inspections of accounts, and special services — such as education for adults and disabled students.

In April 1967, Dr. Marburger was nominated by Governor Richard J. Hughes to be the next Commissioner of Education. Confirmed by the New Jersey Senate later the same month, he took office on July 5 of that year.

Carl L. Marburger was born in Detroit, Michigan in 1921, had attended public schools in Detroit, and received his Bachelor's, Master's, and Doctorate degrees from Wayne State University in Michigan. He served in the U.S. Army during World War II and the Korean War, then returned to Michigan as a science teacher and, later, as a principal.

In 1964, Dr. Marburger worked as a special consultant to the U.S. Office of Economic Opportunity, developing guidelines for education for the Economic Opportunity Act of 1964. Head Start, the popular preschool program that continues today, was one of the programs he helped create. In 1966, Dr. Marburger joined the Bureau of Indian Affairs of the U.S. Department of the Interior as Assistant Commissioner of Education. He also authored numerous articles in professional journals, many of them dealing with education programs for disadvantaged youth. In September 1967, President Lyndon B. Johnson named him to serve on the National Advisory Council on Education Professions Development.

Kenneth David Pack, in his 1974 doctoral dissertation at the Graduate School of Rutgers University, presented a thesis entitled *The New Jersey Department of Education; The Marburger Years: A Case Study of Bureaucratic Innovation, Planning and the Politics of Education at the State Level.* It details "stormy, controversial years" because "Marburger's concept of the role of the state in education was one of change and innovation."

Dr. Pack states that Dr. Marburger gained national stature through his efforts to upgrade education in New Jersey, which were not always successful. But, because of this, he also collected many New Jersey enemies.

Pack also stressed that the New Jersey education system was of interest because of the conservative "tenor of the state . . . , especially in education where a strong tradition of local control holds sway." Pack noted that some of the key issues were racial balance, equal educational opportunity, community control, and accountability. And a strong-willed Commissioner of Education such as Marburger raised a "major fear" of increased power of the state agency, especially when coupled with the needed but worrisome state funding of local education. Pack explains,

> There is little doubt that there has long been a cloudiness surrounding the boundaries of state and local responsibilities. The basic authority for control of the LEA [*Local Education Authority*] rests with the local school board. In most cases the

board was, to all intents and purposes responsible to no one. . . .

Dr. Pack then neatly summed up some of the achievements of the Marburger years:

> The Department has changed its role and functions. The leadership service concept has been installed. The new service intermediate units are functioning and two more will follow. The state has educational goals where none existed before. A testing program has been established on a statewide basis, in spite of strong opposition, and data on educational performance will be available. Students have been included in the education decision-making process for the first time, and their rights as citizens have been officially recognized. Along with the students, large numbers of parents and citizens have become involved in, and aware of, state and local education processes and decisions. New groups have been brought into the politics of education in the state, and a more broadly-based coalition is forming for the future. The state Board of Education has emerged from a "rubber stamp" role to one of leadership and policy making, and the style of conducting the business of education in the state has altered. Decisions are made more openly, conflicts are more visible and the entire political alignment has undergone a process of change, and probably will continue to do so.

Those were the pluses — but less positive consequences of the Marburger years included stronger anti-integration forces; a weakening relationship between teachers and the state Department; and antagonistic legislators who had become alarmed by the power that rested with the Department of Education.

Verona is not mentioned in Dr. Pack's dissertation, though the name of Marburger and his imagined role certainly inflamed the opponents of the Sharing Plan. If there was leadership, according to Dr. Pack, it certainly did not show up in open strong support for the experiment that was to start in Verona.

A limited number of other school systems gingerly discussed following in the footsteps of Verona, but not a single one did. Surely the state in general, and Dr. Marburger specifically, could have used their influence to tilt worried and reluctant local Boards into also sharing their facilities, even in such a limited manner. Verona's Board had hoped that similar efforts elsewhere in New Jersey would take the pressure off them and show that their efforts were not unique. But that never happened, and this was likely one of the reasons the program endured for only one year. To this date, there is sentiment that Dr. Marburger was intent on destroying the local control of School Boards in order to integrate either along county or regional lines, and to create vast school districts in New Jersey.

But this worry did not start with Dr. Marburger's tenure. Quoted in the book by Dr. Pack is a discussion of the politics of education on the state level (by Bailey, Frost, Marsh, and Wood) prior to Dr. Marburger's taking office.

> Localism is not confined to the rural hinterland of the northeast. Some business and professional men in New Jersey, largely centered in New Jersey suburbs, have been against taxation for school aid increases, not so much from any general anti-tax attitude as from a very real localism. They do not want to support schools in South Jersey or anywhere away from home, and know that this is what increases in state aid would mean under present formulae. They may or may not rebel against high or higher property taxes at home, they at least know where the money is spent. This local chauvinism is roundly supported by North Jersey spokesman, the *Newark News.*

In January 1967, Dr. Marburger formed a state committee, "to study the next steps of regionalization and consolidation of school districts." Its findings, which became known as the Mancuso Report after the committee's chairwoman, Ruth H. Mancuso, were released in April 1969, and must have added fuel to the growing anti-Marburger feeling. The report, which among other recommendations called for legislative action to reduce the number of school districts by reorganizing at the county level, was not issued until the Sharing Plan in Verona was dead. But just the formation of such a committee in 1967 — which many felt had an incendiary purpose — was a sufficient worry.

Dr. Marburger originally had been nominated by a Democratic

Governor. To the surprise of many, the next Governor, William T. Cahill, a Republican, renominated Dr. Marburger. But even though the Governor and many others supported him, this was the first time in the history of New Jersey that a cabinet nomination was voted down on the Senate floor. A factor in his defeat, among others, according to Dr. Pack, was that most people remembered Marburger as the "busing" Commissioner; in addition, Marburger had accused some Senators of "blatant racism" in making him a scapegoat. Yet Pack notes that,

> Although many of his rulings in desegregation issues did lead to busing, in the only ruling Marburger handed down on the issue of busing for racial balance, he ruled that Trenton did not have to continue a compulsory busing plan because it was counterproductive.

Speeches by some Senators indicated that, indeed, the racial question and school regionalization underlay the defeat, with one, Senator DeRose, predicting that future studies of busing would show that children who are forced to attend school with children of different economic backgrounds would suffer "personality problems which will manifest themselves in later years." In other words, anti-busing sentiment did indeed provide the bulk of the nay-votes.

Dr. Marburger wrote about his memories of the Verona Sharing Plan in a letter to the author dated December 17, 1996:

> I do remember my delight at Verona's attempts to right some of the racial injustices of the time. I was under tremendous pressure from the legislature to do nothing about racial balance, particularly since I had infuriated some of them by placing 80 other districts under the Commissioner's jurisdiction with directions to address, in their own way, the segregation which existed. Most complied, but I had to take state funds from one district for their refusal to deal with the issue.
>
> The whole racial balance issue was probably most responsible for the failure of the legislature to reconfirm me for a

second term. I can still hear one suburban senator telling his colleagues, "If you want your children to sit next to children who have poor clothes, need food and who will drag your children's performance down, then vote for Marburger."

I felt that I failed confirmation for all of the right reasons.

The Newark Board minutes, in general, do not record actual discussions . . . they are simply records of votes on decisions made by various committees, boards, and consultants, without any explanations of why and how these decisions were made.

Chapter 10

Newark Board of Education Minutes

NLY AFTER READING the minutes of the Newark Board of Education does one realize the complexity of such a huge school system. The Newark Board minutes, in general, do not record actual discussions; rather, they are simply records of votes on decisions made by various committees, boards, and consultants, without any explanations of why and how these decisions were made. Long lists of appointees or transfers are confirmed; expenditures are approved; a special construction account is listed separately. Bids are approved or rejected, salaries increased or adjusted, final payments usually approved. Rarely do the minutes narrate discussions, or show disagreements or dissent. Those who address the Board are taped and their statements are not copied into the minutes.

It certainly was not easy to obtain the Newark minutes; in actuality, it took me a few years. In the beginning I was stonewalled. The excuse I was given was that the state was investigating the school system, and most of the minutes had been removed. Only after the state took over in 1995 (nearly 30 years after such an action had been proposed) was I told that the Newark Library had a copy. This was true, except that the year I needed was "temporarily" lost in the basement files.

Though the minutes held no lengthy discussions of the Verona project, nor for that matter any project, they do reveal other relevant happenings.

In April 1968, the members of the Newark Board of Education were Mrs. Churchman, Dr. Garrett, Mr. Malanga, Mr. Gerard McCune, Mr. Moran, Mr. Stolowski, Dr. Harold Ashby, Mr. Cervase, and Mr. Krim.

The April 23 meeting recommended the establishment of two neighborhood Community Relations Offices, to be opened initially two nights per week. The only financial obligation would be the hiring of a clerk-stenographer for six hours a week to help the Director of Community Relations. Specifically, the office would assist people who have problems but lacked specific knowledge of where to go for assistance, interpret policies and programs of the Board of Education, assist Community Action programs, act as liaison between PTA groups and the Board, and assist people who had school problems but who could not come to the Board during the day. All members of the Board voted for it except Mr. Moran, who agreed with the basic philosophy, but not with the implementation.

On May 28, 1968, the minutes state the number of students registered by schools as of March 29, 1968: 53 elementary schools, 8 senior high schools, 5 junior high schools and 14 special schools, with a total enrollment of 75,486. Hawthorne School had 1,423 students; only ten elementary schools had a larger enrollment, including South Eighth Street School, which had 2,036 students, and the Quitman Street School, which had 1,984.

The average daily enrollment in the Newark schools was 75,177, versus the average daily attendance, which was 63,648 — 11,529 children missing each day, or 144 per school. The minutes list a breakdown in attendance, by percent:

	<u>1968</u>	<u>1967</u>
Senior High (9-12)	80.2	85.5
Junior High (7-9)	79.6	84.2
Elementary (1-8)	87.3	89.7
Kindergarten	84.0	85.2
Special	73.8	79.2

The sharp decline in 1968 is noteworthy, as is the attendance percentage of younger children compared to that of secondary students. The fact is that the older the children were, the less they attended school. There is no mention in the Newark Board's minutes of a discussion of these figures, however.

Not all of the Newark schools offered playgrounds. The largest percentage of activity meetings were for athletics; arts and crafts was a poor second. There was scant interest in dancing, dramatics, music, and hobbies.

A tuition payment of $3,357 was made to the Verona Board of Education marked "Essex Mountain Sanatorium." The children of Newark citizens working and living at the Sanatorium, which was a county institution, apparently attended Verona Schools — a fact not addressed at all during the Verona-Newark Sharing Plan discussions. Naturally, the color of those children was not disclosed in the minutes, but it is interesting that during all the heated debates in Verona, out-of-town children — including some from Newark — were already attending Verona schools.

A special meeting of the Newark School Board, which was held on June 13 at the Board Room at 31 Green Street, was called for the purpose of awarding a contract for swimming pools and to consider any other matters that might come before the Board.

Matter Number 24, which came before the Board that day, read, "From the Board of Education of the Borough of Verona, New Jersey, enclosing Resolution on Concept of Proposal for Sharing Educational Opportunities in Verona for one year with 40 children from a Newark Public elementary school." According to the minutes, the resolution would be introduced later in the meeting, after the Board addressed other business.

This particular meeting must have lasted several hours. The Board addressed committee reports on numerous requests, expenditure approvals, resignations, leaves of absence, transfers, reassignments, provisional appointments, and more. Also on the agenda were the Summer

Remedial and Development Program, Project Head Start, and the appointments of school medical staff, as well as bids for cafeteria food.

The Committee on Building, Grounds, and Supplies also had a list of appointments, payments for work completed, changes in position, and additional bids. Included were alterations to the Hawthorne Avenue School, which included a base bid of $56,000 by Pellecchia Construction Co., and bids for plumbing, heating and ventilating, and a new roof. Other schools had interior or exterior painting contracts, auditorium window and curtain contracts, and recharging of fire extinguishers. Approval was given for the purchase of a number of properties. School business in Newark is big business.

The Committee for Instruction dealt with such projects as teachers for a day camp in Fairfield, New Jersey, swimming instructors, special summer programs, Head Start, food service workers, and much more.

Finally, the resolution on Verona was introduced:

> Agreement by and between the Board of Education of the City of Newark acting herein by Harold J. Ashby, its president, and the Board of Education of the Borough of Verona, acting herein by Hilda Jaffe, its President, and attested by Thomas J. Sellitto, its Secretary.
>
> Witnesseth that whereas the Verona Board of Education has submitted a plan and proposal for receiving up to forty children in Grades 1 though 5 from a Newark elementary school to elementary schools in Verona as more particularly set out in a "Proposal for Sharing Educational Opportunities," which is marked Attachment I, and which is specifically made a part of the Agreement; and
>
> Whereas the Board of Education of the City of Newark and the Board of Education of the Borough of Verona are desirous of cooperation and implementing Verona's Proposal for Sharing Educational Opportunities for the school year 1968-1969, and subject to the following specific conditions:
>
> 1. Participating boards of Education are in no way committed to the plan or any contractual arrangements beyond the 1968-1969 school year.
> 2. The right to withdraw from the project is a privilege

maintained by each participating Board of Education. Intention of withdrawal must be presented thirty days prior to the actual date of withdrawal.

3. The Verona Board of Education shall have complete authority in the administration of the program.

4. Participation in the program by co-operating boards of education in no way indicates an official interest in a regional suburban-urban educational system.

5. The children to be invited to fill available pupil stations in the Verona schools shall be selected at random from a school which would be identified as appropriate and jointly agreed upon by the Newark and Verona Superintendents of School.

6. The children selected from a Newark school shall be children of appropriate age now functioning in regular classroom situations free from emotional or special education problems.

7. Each participating Board of Education reserves the right to withdraw from the program any student, who, in the judgment of its Superintendent of Schools, poses a problem which cannot be solved in any other way.

8. All children, regardless of race, color, or creed, will be eligible to participate.

9. In no instance will the addition of Newark pupils cause the Verona Board of Education to exceed the number stated in its policy on class size, specifically twenty-five pupils per class.

10. Each parent or guardian of "transported" children from the City of Newark must give written permission allowing his child to attend the Verona Public Schools.

11. The Newark Board of Education shall be responsible for the transportation of participating children between Newark and Verona.

12. Transportation shall be arranged to insure that travel time is made as efficient and effective as possible.

13. Busing of Verona pupils under this program will not be allowed under any circumstances.

14. The supplemental teacher shall be an employee of

the Newark Board of Education agreed upon by the Verona Superintendent of Schools. The Newark Board of Education shall assign said teacher to the Verona Board of Education to provide the necessary instructional and guidance services for the children of the project.

15. The supplemental teacher will be under the direction of the Verona Board of Education.

16. The program shall be financed completely from federal, state and Newark sources.

17. The Verona Board of Education will receive $1,014.85 per pupil from the Newark Board of Education. The cost per pupil is based on the following:

(A) It is the amount secured when the estimated number of elementary school children who will be attending the Verona elementary school during the 1968-1969 school year is divided into the amount budgeted for the elementary schools of Verona for the 1968-1969 school year.

(B) The computation is further defined by the following factors:

(1) Per-pupil costs for the Newark children shall include costs for milk, field trips, student accident insurance and liability insurance for parents who take the Newark children into their homes for lunch.

(2) An indirect cost allowance of 5 percent will be added to average estimated costs to insure that true actual per-pupil costs are achieved.

(3) Food service (#900) costs will not be included in the amount budgeted by Verona for the 1968-1969 school year as no food services are provided for children from Kindergarten through Grade 5.

(4) Transportation (#500) costs will not be included in the amount budgeted by Verona for

the 1968-1969 school year as the transportation costs for project students will be paid by the City of Newark.

The aforesaid costs per pupil shall be adjusted at the expiration of the 1968-1969 school year according to the actual number of elementary school children and the actual amount expended for the elementary schools of Verona for the 1968-1969 school year, which amount shall be further adjusted by an indirect cost allowance of 5 percent.

18. One-half of the total estimated cost will be due and payable September 15, 1968, one-quarter thereof on February 1, 1969, and the actual cost adjusted, less the payments received, will be due and payable on the completion of the 1968-1969 audit of the Verona Board of Education.

19. Any special testing program for participating children shall be kept as normal as possible and such testing program shall be approved by the superintendents of schools of the participating communities.

20. The cost of the special testing program, research and evaluation, including consultant service up to $3,000, will be borne by the Newark Board of Education and the administration thereof shall be carried out under the jurisdiction of the Verona Board of Education in cooperation with the Newark Board of Education.

21. The within agreement shall be contingent upon approval and execution by the respective parties hereto on or before August 1, 1968, unless such time be extended by mutual agreement.

Attached was the equivalent Proposal for Sharing Educational Opportunities, which had been issued at the public meeting of April 30, 1968, by the Verona Board of Education.

Mr. Krim moved that the agreement with the Verona Board of Education be approved. The motion was seconded by Stolowski, approved by a roll call vote, and adopted unanimously.

The organizational meeting for the following school year was held on July 1, 1968, in the Board Room of the Administration Building. Newark Mayor Hugh J. Addonizio had reappointed for three more years those members whose terms had expired. Dr. Ashby was re-elected as president, Gerard McCune was elected as vice president.

Two meetings later, on July 23, a letter written by State Commissioner of Education Carl L. Marburger, was referred to the Board's Committee on Finance and Budgets. It contained the formula for arriving at costs and the method of payment described in items 17 and 18 of the proposed contract between the Newark and Verona Boards of Education. No further information on the letter was given in the minutes.

Also at the July 23 meeting, David Campbell, Chairman of the Committee of Better Education, requested permission for three speakers, each from a different school, to address the board. One of the speakers was Marguarita Bush, the chairman of the PTA, representing the Hawthorne Avenue School.

The Board again approved the tuition of $3,816 to the Verona Board of Education for the attendance of Newark children from the Essex Mountain Sanatorium. The neighboring town of Cedar Grove was paid $18,829.75 for the Essex County Overbrook Hospital Center School. Our Lady of Grace School in Morristown and the Mountainside Board of Education also received payments. Several bids were invited, including one for new boilers to be installed at the Hawthorne Avenue School under the rehabilitation program.

It was requested that permission be granted to advertise for bids for bus transportation to and from Verona Schools.

The Committee for Instruction informed the Board that a total grant of $495,917 had been made to the Newark Board of Education to implement what was referred to as P.L. 89-10 E.S.E.a. of 1965, Title III- Supplementary Education Centers "Newark Greater Cities Project" #68-6750. Various programs were enumerated, such as "A Design for Community Involvement," "An Expanded Program for Early Childhood Education," "A Prototype for Change in Secondary Education," and "Sharing Educational Opportunities (Newark-Verona Interchange)." A short description of the program was included in the minutes.

Also listed under the heading, "Teacher-Newark-Verona Plan, Title I, P.L. 89-10," was the following:

> That in concurrence with the Superintendent of the Verona Public Schools, Hawthorne Avenue School be identified as the school from which children will be invited to fill available pupil stations in the Verona program. These children shall be selected at random with the approval of the parents. They shall be of appropriate age, now enrolled in Hawthorne Avenue School, free from emotional or special education problems.
>
> That, beginning August 1, 1968, a teacher be assigned for the Verona Plan, at regular salary plus $75. per month.

A sole bid, one to install new boilers at the Hawthorne School under the rehabilitation program, was rejected because the cost was deemed excessive.

A rather revealing discussion, one of the few noted in the minutes, came when a resolution was introduced to engage five persons to write an African American History curriculum. Mr. Moran said that before a motion was made on this item, he would like to move that a Spanish-American History curriculum be established in recognition of contributions of Spanish, Puerto Rican, Mexican, and other Spanish-speaking groups to American history. This was approved, with only Mr. Stolowski voting against it. Mr. Cervase, Mrs. Churchman, and Mr. McCune abstained. The motion on African-American history was moved by Mr. Krim. Mr. Stolowski was noted as saying that if history were to be taught in schools, then all world history should be included. He went on to say that he had no objection to the teaching of foreign languages, but that only American history should be taught in the schools. He voted against the motion. Dr. Garrett said he would agree with Mr. Stolowski if all groups were equal, but they were not, and he could find no black person in history with whom he could relate. He went on to say that teaching Polish-American history or that of any other group was fine, and he did not care what it was called, as long as black history was included.

Mrs. Churchman said that courses in African American history were needed to give children of African origin something to view with pride, and that she also felt it was well for white people to know that black people had done something. Dr. Ashby said that this would be a special course given in the high schools, and that the administration had been asked to include all groups in the teaching of social studies. During the roll call, all voted for the motion except Mr. Stolowski.

Once again, the Newark Board of Education in August made a payment to Verona for the Sanatorium students. A bid by the S & E Transportation Co., Inc. in Hillside, New Jersey, for bus transportation from Hawthorne Avenue School to Verona was rejected.

Maurice Lutzke, principal of the Hawthorne Avenue School, was granted a one-year leave of absence for rest and recreation. He had been appointed on February 1, 1937. Later in the evening, Woodrow Davis, a project coordinator at the Funding Office, was assigned as acting principal of the Hawthorne Avenue School. The acting principals were given an additional $100 per month above the base rate of pay.

At that time, Board Rule 308.2, which regarded homework, stated, "No pupil of a grade lower than the fifth shall be required to prepare any lessons out of school." At the following meeting, a vote would be taken on a new rule:

> Teachers shall provide homework for children in all grades. Meaningful relationship shall exist between the assigned homework and the daily lesson. The superintendent shall prescribe the allocation of time for homework at each grade level.

The New Jersey Department of Education had advised that sufficient funds were available to establish a breakfast program in one additional elementary school. Under the Child Nutrition Act of 1966, the maximum subsidy to be paid from federal funds could not exceed 15 cents per breakfast. During the previous year, at the Warren Street School, the cost of a breakfast amounted to 7.45 cents per breakfast, which included breakfasts served to adults who participated in the program. Breakfasts served to adult staff were without charge. The total cost was in excess of $12,000 and the income, including the federal subsidy, was over $8,000. The Board picked up the difference. A total of 59,024 breakfasts were served to children.

The Superintendent recommended that Ruby Dixon, teacher at

Alexander Street School, be assigned as Project Teacher in the Newark-Verona Plan at her regular salary plus $75 per month, effective August 19, 1968. This was approved by a unanimous vote.

Elementary schools were divided into five districts that could be more closely supervised by assistant or deputy superintendents. It was felt that the smaller staffs would be more attuned to the educational needs of the new districts, there would be greater community participation, and it would be easier to institute new and innovative programming. The Hawthorne School, along with seven other schools and two annexes, was placed into the Southern District, which had an enrollment of 11,616 pupils. Mr. Cervase thought the proposal had merits, even though additional personnel were needed, but he also feared that the proposal was decentralization in disguise. He was the only one who voted against it.

At the next regular meeting, on September 30, 1968, an increase in summer school attendance was reported. Attendance in Grade 3, for instance, jumped from 2,879 in 1967 to 3,171 in 1968. Both average daily enrollment and daily attendance increased in that age group. Hawthorne Avenue School decreased by 20 students overall, but the report does not break student/school attendance down by age groups.

Buses delivered the children to Verona in early September 1968, but nothing further was mentioned in the minutes. The only time Verona appeared again was in the October 29, 1968, minutes, when Katherine Howser, of Newark, was hired as bus attendant at Hawthorne School with a salary of $18.50 per day, effective October 15, on a per diem assignment: PL 89-10 E.S.E. Title III, Greater Newark Cities Project Component #3, Newark-Verona Interchange — a very long name for a relatively short-term project.

From the very beginning, Board members were well aware of possible political fallout. They knew that the proposed project must be completely legal, and must not cost the Verona taxpayers a single penny.

Chapter 11

Verona Board Members, Candidates, and Staff

W HO WERE THE elected Verona Board members and school officials? Who were the leaders of the groups opposing the Board? What were their backgrounds? What made each dare to confront a community?

I found common threads among the male members of the Verona School Board who initially passed the Sharing Plan. Many were children from immigrant families, which had little money, but a tradition of self-reliance and education. Quite a few were able to advance through the liberating opportunity of the G.I. Bill of Rights, which furthered their education and helped them reach their goals. With very few exceptions, the players in this drama did not mind recalling the past, and freely talked about their experiences. Board member John McDonald and Superintendent John E. Mattis died prior to the writing of this book. The widows of both men recalled those turbulent days, but neither of their husbands left any papers pertaining to the Sharing Plan.

Edward P. Wizda — Board Member

Ed Wizda remembers how it feels to be poor and to hunger for an education. His father died when he was only five years old. Of Slovak heritage, Ed's father, a coal miner, lived and worked in a town owned and operated by the coal company. After his father's death, the family survived on the rent paid by a boarder. Ed's brother went into the mines when he was barely a teenager. His older sister also joined the work force at an early age. During those days, when warm summer weather decreased the demand for coal to a minimum, the mine closed down. All food had to be purchased at the company store; the store offered credit until the fall, when the mine opened again. Then the money went right back to the company store.

The first of his family to be able to attend high school, Wizda obtained high marks. After his service in the U.S. Army, he enrolled at Pennsylvania State University under the G.I. Bill. His first job as a teacher was at the Clifford High School in East Orange, New Jersey, where at that time blacks were roughly 10 to 15 percent of the student body. Ed taught Spanish; and he took his third- and fourth-year students to the Spanish theater. Even today, years later, Wizda still spends many evenings in one or another of New York's theaters. But teaching was not enough for Ed; he wanted to offer his services to the community. He became a candidate for the Verona Board of Education, and won.

It is Ed Wizda's impression that John McDonald started the discussion on the Newark project. McDonald, a strong voice in the Catholic lay movement, had read the reports issued after the riots, especially of the shortcomings in the Newark school system. It was McDonald who told the Verona School Board about the conditions of education in Newark. The Board members met privately — there being no Sunshine Law yet, requiring public disclosure of proceedings — and discussed the pros and cons of starting a sharing program. Once they listened to an invited speaker who told them of the Hartford, Connecticut, program.

During all these weeks of meetings, not one of the Board members revealed these private and ongoing discussions. Ed Wizda recalls that Emil Tomecek, who eventually would be the one member of the Board speaking against the Sharing program, went along at first. Emil Tomecek was in support of the "underachiever," an anti-elite; he had once suggested that one of the students in the Distributive Education curriculum — in which students receive on-the-job training as well as classroom instruction — should be a speaker at commencement exercises.

Ed Wizda feels that there may have been other meetings to which he was not privy. Surely, he speculates, there must have been feelers, contacts, meetings, and negotiations with Newark educators, state officials, and others. He remembers that the Board hoped other school systems would join Verona in their project. Yet, during the occasional meetings of the various county School Boards, the Verona group felt like pariahs — nobody wanted to be near them.

At the seemingly unending meetings concerning the Sharing Plan, Wizda listened carefully. He did not feel anger at the objectors — perhaps more a feeling of frustration with the way they acted. His next-door neighbors stopped talking to him — at least as long as he was on the Board. But his family supported him, including his children. And he never heard of any complaint that his children suffered — mostly, he thought, because their friends were like-minded. He remembers other families who became embroiled in the town's struggle, especially a pair of sisters, one who was a strong advocate for the Sharing Plan, the other who fought it.

Wizda feels that Marshall Butler, who ran as a candidate for the opposition, gave only lukewarm support to the anti-sharing group after his election. As time went by, many of the anti-sharing folk seemed to behave like an anti-educational group, and Butler, an educator himself, did not feel right about that.

Ed Wizda's greatest regret was the termination of the program. He remembers that Tomecek and Butler voted to stop it after the first year, and he could not understand why John McDonald, the member who had started it in the first place, voted for its discontinuation. Wizda did not care that he expected to lose the next election, and that the opponents would then have the votes to stop the program. In the meantime, the children would have had another year of good education. This would have been the best for them, and would have brought more credence to the test results. And, perhaps, some of the voters would have changed their minds by then.

It is possible, Ed Wizda admits, that the Sharing program politicized the town. But it was only the forerunner of things to come — Vietnam, censorship, anti-education feelings. He has no regrets. He served for eight years on the Board, and is proud of his tenure. His service gave him an opportunity to act on his beliefs.

There is another monument to his strong sense of education — his children: a doctor, an engineer, and an attorney.

Elmer Gustavson — Board Member

Elmer Gustavson, who died in 1998, never lost touch after he retired from the Board of Education. He helped young Newark school children with math and reading skills, managed the hotline of the Essex County Extension Agents' office, worked at the Newark International Airport arrival building as a Travelers Aide, and assisted senior citizens both at a senior care program and as a board member of the Iris Garden in Montclair. What time was left he spent in his own garden.

Elmer Gustavson's Swedish grandfather, a coal miner, had arrived in the United States some time around 1890. His father, a house painter, raised his family on the south side of Montclair, near the West Orange border. This section of Montclair, characterized by its two-family houses, was not one of the upscale areas of town.

Elmer's grandfather, a very handy man, was a carpenter and a plumber, and his services were used in the building of Upsala College in East Orange. The family just about made ends meet. Self-reliance was the principle of that family; education, while it was important, did not come first. But Elmer remembered his father's dictum: "I do not want you to climb ladders and swing a paint brush." In school, and especially in track, he remembers his friendly relationship with the blacks living in the area.

Elmer Gustavson joined the Marine Corps, and after his discharge, with the help of the G.I. Bill, he went to Upsala, the same college his grandfather had helped build. Later, he did graduate work at New York University. He sold group insurance in various locations, and in 1957 finally moved to Verona. He regularly attended Board of Education meetings, when David Aikman was president and Bernice Tode was vice president.

When a vacancy occurred on the Board, Gustavson was appointed. When his term was up, he ran for the position and won. At that time, there were few controversies, no opposition candidate, and relatively few people voted.

Elmer Gustavson also recalled how John McDonald first brought up the report that Newark was some 10,000 student stations short. During one of the Board's discussions, someone asked whether a small token effort, a gesture, would help. Hilda Jaffe, president of the Board, picked up the momentum. The group became an *ad hoc* committee to pursue the question. From the beginning, Gustavson wondered if this plan might become a political problem and was worried about inflammatory reactions. But the first outpouring of public support somewhat mollified his anxiety.

From the very beginning, Board members were well aware of possible political fallout. They knew that the proposed project must be completely legal, and must not cost the Verona taxpayers a single penny. It was Gustavson's recollection that John McDonald and Hilda Jaffe had negotiated with Newark, the state, and other officials, because he himself did not remember participating.

After the project was introduced, his home was deluged with phone calls. He remembers some dirty looks, but no other abuse. Nor did his children seem to suffer. But endless hours of meetings took their toll; after the completion of his second term, he would not run the following year.

Gustavson was also rather surprised that McDonald voted against the continuation of the Sharing program, and could only assume that McDonald, too, was aghast at the fragmentation of the community. While Gustavson felt the project definitely was worthwhile, he was not sure that if another opportunity had arisen he would have voted for it again.

Soon afterward, the Republican Party of Verona asked him to run for local office, even though he had voted for the Sharing Plan. They obviously thought he could win. But Elmer Gustavson declined; his family, home, and garden came first.

His children went through the Verona school system. One became a commercial illustrator and partner in a bicycle shop, the other, he said, is a "computer person" who wanted his dad, Elmer Gustavson, to get with it and stop using pens and typewriters.

Emil Tomecek — Board Member

Emil Tomecek's voice is as vigorous as it was some 30 years ago. He states his opinions just as strongly as ever, and he has not changed his mind on the educational problems of yesteryear — which he believes still exist today.

Emil is of Czech ancestry. His grandfather was a blacksmith in the old country, and, according to tradition, he passed his trade knowledge on to his son. After Emil's father arrived in Chicago, he continued to work as a blacksmith. It was also in Chicago that his father fell in love and married. But blacksmithing soon ceased to be a thriving trade, so he opened a grocery store — only to fall victim to the Depression. His father then worked in an iron factory, and was unfortunately disabled when he was hit by a car.

Emil Tomecek was the youngest child in the family. His brother and sister had to work to support the rest. After taking commercial courses, his sister worked as a secretary. The money coming in enabled him to attend high school and junior college.

At that time, every potential soldier received a number, which determined the sequence of his call-up in the Draft, requiring one year of service. Tomecek, in gratitude for his brother working and supporting the family, took his brother's lower Draft number. In the spring of 1941, he was called into the Infantry. A few months later, he applied for a three-year enlistment, and at his request he was transferred to the Air Force. For further training, his unit was sent to the Bendix Corporation in East Orange. There, at one of the socials arranged for the soldiers, Emil Tomecek met his future wife. New Jersey thus became his new home.

After his discharge, and with the help of the G.I. Bill, Tomecek went to night school at the New Jersey Institute of Technology. Because he worked all day, it took him ten years to obtain his first degree. After taking a year off from his studies, he went back to night school, and in another five years, he obtained his Master's degree. In addition to his own financial contributions and the G.I. Bill, he was helped by a scholarship and the Bell Laboratories Educational Plan.

While he was working as a mechanical engineer, in his spare time Tomecek taught undergraduate students and tutored others who needed help. But he was always interested in sports, especially in soccer. One of his fellow soccer players suggested Verona as a possible home, and in 1946, Emil Tomecek and his wife moved there, where his son was born.

Tomecek was asked by the PTA to help in a bicycle inspection program for the kids. It was at that time he noticed the gaps in the sidewalk along Linden Avenue where children walked to school. For over a year, he attended every town Council meeting, requesting sidewalks, and finally he was rewarded with a new sidewalk ordinance. He was told that this was the first such action in Verona in 50 years. Part of the ordinance was a requirement that the Board of Education build a new sidewalk across the street from the F. N. Brown School. That was how Tomecek started to attend School Board meetings.

He was not overly enthusiastic with what he perceived as trends, and decided to run for the Board of Education himself. During his campaign, he stressed that his main interest was in helping those kids who were not top students. Once elected, he often visited the high school and claims that the top students, sometimes as few as four or six, had classes with the better teachers, while the average kids were in classes of 25 or more. This convinced him that the Verona school system was mainly interested in promoting the elite, with little emphasis on the below-average children. No attention was paid to the slow learners. It was his suggestion that the school start summer classes for those children who had learning problems or otherwise could not make the grade.

When the Sharing Plan was first discussed at one of the Board's executive meetings, which were then private, Emil Tomecek reasoned that if Verona could not help its below-average children, why add the kids from Newark, who certainly seemed to have the same or worse problems. Emil visited one Newark school and came away convinced that students in that city certainly deserved the same attention that the Verona children needed. But he thought it would be better if Newark could handle it itself.

He listened carefully to the suggested program, which he remembered being proposed by Hilda Jaffe. He also listened to a speaker who told the Board about the Hartford project. As a result of his visit to the Newark school, he was in total agreement that Newark school children needed help. But from the very beginning, Emil Tomecek assured me, he voiced objections for the simple reason that charity should begin at home, and Newark's schoolchildren should be helped in Newark.

On the Verona School Board, Tomecek always thought of himself as an outsider; he was not invited, and therefore never participated, in any of the meetings with Newark or the state. To this day, he feels that all together, in principle, the Sharing Plan may have been a good idea, but that it was not sold properly either to him or to the citizens of Verona.

Once the project became a fact and the Board approved it in public, with Tomecek being the only dissenting voice, he was very adamant in insisting that the visiting children should be treated properly, and that there should not be any demonstrations against them. He also made a point that if any of the parents of the children wanted to move to Verona to avail themselves of the better school system, no one should object.

He had his share of nasty letters and phone calls, and once an egg was thrown at his house. He was not happy when his son was told in school that his father should not be on the Board of Education.

Emil Tomecek stated that he did not work with the opposition parents' group. And although he is listed as a speaker at one of their meetings, he had little contact with their leaders, nor did he ever meet with their attorney. Even though Marshall Butler came onto the Board in opposition to the Sharing Plan, Tomecek was not happy with him either, since Butler did not advocate for below-average kids. As a matter of fact, Tomecek felt that the group opposed to the Sharing program was less interested in education and more in social issues.

Emil Tomecek decided not to run again for the Board of Education. Nobody should have the impression, he stressed, that he did not like good students. As a matter of fact, he himself graduated with the highest average in his undergraduate class at NJIT. Rather, he wants to be remembered as the Board member who cared most for the less gifted children.

Hilda Jaffe — Board President

Hilda Jaffe grew up in Williamsburg, a part of Brooklyn, where her parents were storekeepers. She went through the public school system in Brooklyn and later commuted to City College, all the time helping out in her parents' store. Even after she married, she worked, eventually serving as office manager in a doctor's office.

During one summer, she was a counselor in a summer camp in the Philadelphia area. Always an avid reader, Hilda subscribed to *The New York Times*. Her future husband, who also worked at that camp, found both the newspaper subscription and Hilda to his liking. They married, and after her husband received his Doctorate and a job in New Jersey, they moved to Rutherford. Six years later, at the recommendation of a fellow worker, they purchased a home in Verona.

Both were active in the PTA during the time their two children were growing up. As a member of the local League of Women Voters, Hilda worked on its "Know Your Town" series of studies, which was printed in the *Verona-Cedar Grove Times*. The Jaffes felt that they should continue to work for the betterment of the Verona school system, and after discussing who should be in the forefront, it was decided that Hilda, who had somewhat more time available, should run for the Board of Education. Hilda served a total of three terms. It is her opinion that this is just long enough to learn what it is all about. After that comes a period when most volunteers peak and it is time to bow out, which she did.

Initially serving as a Board member, Jaffe later was elected vice president and eventually president. Hilda also became active in county and state educational groups.

There being no Sunshine Law in the Sixties, Hilda Jaffe recalls that many topics were discussed during private meetings. It was after John McDonald called the Governor's report on the 1967 riots in Newark to the attention of the other Board members that the idea for sharing slowly evolved. All Board members were involved. She recalled that Emil Tomecek, who later opposed the Plan, was fairly quiet during these meetings, but did not voice any opposition.

From the very beginning, Superintendent Mattis was a strong supporter of the idea. It was he who met with the Newark School Superintendent, and after receiving a good reception, he next started to discuss the Plan with state officials. His assistant, Tom Sellitto, did what he had to do, but was somewhat more cautious about the Plan. After the introduction of the program, according to Jaffe, and especially because so many supporters spoke up initially, all the Board members were surprised at the depth of the opposition. And except for Emil Tomecek, she recalled, the Board did not waver.

The Jaffe household received numerous phone calls — some of them hate calls. Especially disturbing, she remembered, were the silent calls, when the phone rang but nobody spoke. The phone company was not able to trace them. Some neighbors stopped talking to the family. But there also were messages of support. Both Jaffe children, then in college, voiced their enthusiasm for the Sharing Plan.

Over the years, Hilda Jaffe had become quite active in the New Jersey

School Board Association, representing Verona at the county and state levels. She chaired a number of committees — one of which considered the tenure of Superintendents, and another discussed ethics. One year she even chaired the state convention.

These activities at the county and state levels were the reason for all kinds of rumors in Verona at the time of the Sharing Plan meetings. For instance, it was proposed that Dr. Carl Marburger, the Commissioner of the New Jersey Department of Education, was behind the plot, and put Hilda Jaffe up to introducing the Sharing Plan. The president of the Cedar Grove Board of Education had called Hilda to voice the same suspicion — and was worried that Cedar Grove might be the next to be asked. The Mancuso Report and Marburger's politics at the state level raised doubts and fears of regionalization.

One of the few outsiders who was friendly, Hilda remembered, was the president of the Bloomfield Board of Education, who was quite helpful in facilitating the first meetings with the Newark officials. Another official, Mildred B. Garvin of East Orange, by then a state legislator, encouraged the Verona Board.

The Newark children came to Verona and there were no incidents. The host parents were really the ones who shielded the kids. Hilda Jaffe noted that the Laning Avenue School PTA invited and welcomed the Newark mothers to their usual opening meeting, but other parents at Lanning Avenue apparently asked the Board not to send them any of the black children from Newark, because the only blacks living in Verona were in their school district, and black children were already part of the student body.

According to Jaffe, it was only after the next school election, when the opposition candidate won and the school budget was defeated again, that the Board became disheartened. It was really the budget defeat that bothered them, because that was unusual in Verona. Ed Wizda and Hilda Jaffe decided that they would vote to continue the Sharing program for another year, and the two opposition members voted to cancel the project. It was now up to John McDonald, the man whose impetus had been the original driving force. McDonald feared that continuance would badly damage the school district, and, taking a judicious view, he cast the deciding vote against the Sharing Plan for the good of the school system of Verona.

Hilda felt that Marshall Butler, while he was in opposition to the

Sharing Plan, and perhaps was suspicious of the motives and decisions of the other Board members in the beginning, was in all other respects a valuable member of the Board.

In retrospect, Hilda Jaffe said she would do it again. There was only one serious error — from the very start, the contract and agreements with Newark, the state, and the local Board should have been for two years. Then the change in the Board's makeup would have had less impact, and the tests of the Newark children would have been more meaningful.

The political climate in Verona was changing at that time. Vietnam was in the limelight; the celebration of Earth Day was declared subversive; the high school principal resigned. Hilda Jaffe, who had years earlier decided not to extend her stay on the Board, made it official and announced that she would not again be a candidate for office.

To some, Hilda Jaffe was the most hated person in town. And after all these years, there is still pain.

〜・〜

Marshall Butler — Board Member

Younger than the other members of the Board, Marshall Butler, who replaced Elmer Gustavson in the 1969 election, was born and raised in Montclair. His parents encouraged their children to further their education. Butler's father worked in the engineering department of Western Electric and his mother had a degree in nursing.

Butler attended Newark State Teachers College, which was located on Broadway in Newark. He obtained his degree in industrial education and taught for six years at Bloomfield High School, followed by three years at Montclair State College. He married a Bloomfield girl whom he had met at college. She, too, is a teacher, and has taught in East Orange. After Butler's teaching stint, he started his administrative career at Montclair State, where he remained for 30 years. He finally retired in 1992 as the Registrar.

The Butlers kept busy, raising their family of four girls and one boy. For a while, they sought larger quarters, and even thought of building a new home for their growing family. Eventually, they decided to just make do and concentrate on raising their children. Now, with all their children grown up, they are happy with that decision. Marshall was not at all involved in local politics or school affairs; he coached track at the high school and taught graphic arts and drafting while locally participating in PTA affairs, especially in their recreational activities. He also coached the girls' softball league and for many years was a member of the Verona Recreation Department.

The Sharing Plan came as a total surprise to Marshall Butler. He had no idea what was going to happen; there was a lot of fear in Verona that this was the precursor to losing control of local schools, and that eventually Verona students would be bused to Newark in a reciprocal plan. Dr. Carl Marburger's formation of a committee to study district reorganization — which eventually released the 1969 Mancuso Report — also fueled the fear of regionalization and added to the unease. "Not In My Backyard" (NIMBY) was the general attitude in the town.

Butler was not part of the crowd that organized the opposition. He thinks the leadership was a group of friends. He does not remember how he was asked to run for the Board, or who did the asking. His primary feeling was that the Board of Education had acted without getting the community involved, and that there was a lack of communication between the Board and the residents. However, in his opinion, the outcome would not have been different even if the Board had been more open.

Other questions, according to Butler, had also been raised: how would the Newark youngsters cope once they were removed from their usual environment? And he felt that this was not truly a representative sampling of Newark children, since those parents who volunteered their sons and daughters obviously were interested in furthering their education and probably were effective even in their own school system in seeing that their children would work harder.

Marshall Butler had always felt very good about the Verona educational system — it was one of the reasons he and his wife moved to Verona. And when he ran for the vacant seat on the Board of Education and won, he wanted to assure that the educational process would continue as it had been, or even improve. He was not close to any of the sitting Board members and knew very little about them or their motives. But due to his and Emil Tomecek's shared interest in opening communications, which was Marshall's platform, at least in the beginning he worked most-ly with fellow member Tomecek.

Butler did not enjoy long meetings, where every word was questioned by those attending. His primary motives were twofold: to open communi-cations and to keep educating. His supporters originally told him that he could be his own person, but after a while Butler felt that their previous platform — communications with the electorate — was not truly the primary aim of that group anymore. They tried to tell him what to say and how he should vote on various other unrelated issues.

Once, his life was even threatened. In a face-to-face confrontation with a previous supporter, Butler was told, "We'll get you." He does not remember any other intimidating phone calls or messages, nor was his family threatened. His original supporters were not happy; there had been a definite change in their attitude. Although he kept his promise to keep them informed, he felt they were really more interested in someone who would do their bidding. They soon claimed that they had not gotten from him what they had wanted.

Though Butler appreciated the hard work done by Superintendent Mattis, in his opinion Mattis did not display a strong leadership role. Butler also felt that two members of the Board — Hilda Jaffe and Emil Tomecek — were too involved in day-to-day operations. Marshall Butler, unlike some of the others, had a completely different perspective on the role of a Board member. He did not think that the Board should get involved in hands-on situations, visiting schools and classes. But that's exactly what his original supporters wanted from him.

He was eventually elected president of the Board, and is especially proud of his successful efforts to have the Board of Education work closely with the Mayor and Council, especially on finances and taxes. At the end of his term, he decided to run again. Now, he feels that he was naive in those days, when he assumed that he did not have to campaign for the office, feeling his record would stand for itself. He trusted that the people interested in education would know what he had done for the school system.

His opponent, Dr. Richard Mascera — with the help of Butler's former allies — campaigned from house to house, and Butler lost the election. His ego was bruised. He felt later that his original supporters probably used him for their own agenda. Nevertheless, he always felt he was working for the whole community, not for a small select group.

Marshall Butler finally convinced himself that his family, career, and other interests were more important — as well as the satisfaction he derives from doing what he thinks is right. The issues that defeated him were never resolved. Today, Marshall Butler feels closer to the group that initially opposed him. He realizes that both he and his original opponents

— those who supported the Sharing Plan — were primarily interested in good education. As a matter of fact, a few years later, when one of the Board members died, Butler was asked to fill that vacancy until the next election. It was at that time he realized that there were many who appreciated his efforts.

Even though he feels one must be courageous at times, Butler still thinks that the Sharing Plan was ill-conceived, incomplete (he agrees that the proposal should have been written for more than one year), and a public relations disaster. He does not think it helped the Newark children at all. Verona was divided, and it took a number of years before Board meetings became reasonable and constructive again.

Marshall Butler is proud of his record as a Board member, but he is not happy with the circumstances that propelled him into the limelight.

Bill Hartke — Candidate for School Board

"I do hope that this will not open old wounds," Bill Hartke said in his interview for this book. Hartke wanted to be sure that this message was part of his story. There was still pain apparent when I listened to Eileen and Bill Hartke relate what had befallen their family in 1969.

He remembers hearing about the Sharing Plan in very general terms and, as such, he thought that it would not be a bad idea. Why not take lower grade kids from overcrowded Newark schools to join classes in Verona — which had less than 25 children? After all, he reasoned, those children, too, deserve a better education. However — and Bill is quite adamant about this — under no circumstances would he have sanctioned busing Verona children to Newark's overcrowded and understaffed schools.

Bill Hartke was born in Williamsport, Pennsylvania, attended Columbia High in Maplewood, New Jersey, and received his degree at the University of Vermont. That is also where his met Eileen Deacon, his wife-to-be, who grew up in Montclair. Hartke was a member of the National Guard, serving part of the time on active duty. He has remained a member of the active Reserves. For a couple of years, he was a plant manager for the Borden Company in Watertown, New York, and later changed his job to industrial sales.

The young couple lived in Bloomfield, New Jersey, and befriended their neighbors, the Heaslips. When their third child was born, they decided it was time for a house — and found it on Morningside Avenue in Verona. Their friends and neighbors, Richard and Marie Heaslip, also moved to the same town.

At parties and other social gatherings, the Sharing Plan was often discussed, and Hartke freely stated his convictions. There was a meeting at Hartke's house attended by, among others, John McDonald, Father John McDermott, Jerry Bakst, Ed Barz, and Dick Heaslip — all supporters of the Sharing Plan. The school situation was discussed, and Bill Hartke was extensively questioned on his beliefs. Bill understands that there was another meeting at which, he was told, Father McDermott declared that Bill Hartke would be the perfect candidate to run at the next Board of Education election. Bill was willing to run, but wanted his friend, Dick Heaslip, to be his campaign manager. He thought it would be a good combination — he was the salesman and Dick was the good organizer. Heaslip agreed.

Bill is still proud that he received the highest number of votes received up to that date for a School Board position. Yet, even with such support, he still lost to his opponent, Marshall Butler, by a landslide. It was an ugly campaign, filled with hatred, innuendoes and rumors; Hartke could not believe how much racial hatred there was in the usually staid, quiet town. One of the rumors he heard was that Hilda Jaffe had started this program primarily as a stepping stone, to earn an appointment to the state Board of Education. People were screaming at him, insulting him, calling him stupid. Quite a number clearly seemed to be bigots.

Even some of those who couched their opposition in intelligent verbiage used body language that showed hatred. Some suggested, Hartke said, that if blacks wanted their children to join Verona schools, they should move to Verona and buy a house. No doubt there were some in the opposition who had legitimate questions not inspired by bigotry, Bill Hartke believes. Certainly not all Veronans opposed to the Sharing Plan were racists.

Bill and Eileen remember the eggs that were once thrown at their house, the nasty phone calls they received, and, worst of all, how their kids were hassled. Even Karen Cassel, their daughter, who is now married and again living in Verona, recalls how sad she was when other kids told her they hated her father. It was especially bad the day after the election, when some of her first-grader classmates told her how happy they were that her father had lost. But through it all, she was so proud of her father, because he stood up for what he believed in.

As soon as Bill Hartke learned that he had lost, he went to Marshall Butler's house to congratulate him. Bill thought this was the honorable and gentlemanly thing to do. The two shook hands, and Herb Brau, who was at the Butler's house, exclaimed in his booming voice,"There is a man!" It was not many years later that Bill and Marshall Butler worked together to elect Herb Brau to the Board of Education.

Bill Hartke is sure that he ran a good, clean campaign. He always stuck strictly to issues, and even if he thought of a few invectives, he kept those to himself. In his opinion, nobody who supported the Sharing Plan could have won that election; there was just too much anti-black feeling in town. But not once did Hartke regret having been the candidate. He feels that in everybody's life there is one time when it is important to speak up and be counted.

Thomas J. Sellitto — Assistant Superintendent of Schools

After 37 years in education, Tom Sellitto has never forgotten the strife of the Sharing Plan controversy.

Sellitto is, and has always been, an Essex County resident. He was born, raised, and educated in East Orange. He studied at Montclair State College, where he received his Bachelor's degree in business and accounting, and his Master's degree in supervision. His family members are all natives of Essex County, though his grandparents originally came from Italy. Of his parents' four children, three were girls. His father was a painter by profession. Tom's wife also came from East Orange; he met her through a friend while they were in college. Partially retired, Tom now teaches at Seton Hall University in South Orange, New Jersey.

Both the East Orange schools and Montclair State, then as well as now, have a fair share of black students. Sellitto always had a friendly relationship with everyone, regardless of color.

Tom Sellitto was always interested in sports. After college, Sellitto sent out his resumes. Of the three job offers, only the one from Verona included coaching football. So Verona it was, in 1956 — teaching accounting, business law, economics, and, naturally, coaching the football team. Five years later, he also became a resident of Verona. Eventually, his job changed to

Assistant Superintendent of Schools, and after Mattis left, he was appointed to the top job. Tom Sellitto well remembers the Sharing Plan from its very first mention.

Tom Sellitto and Board member John McDonald were both part of the Corsilla Movement, a renewal movement of the Catholic church. He describes McDonald as a "real Christian" who was willing to do anything for anybody. It would take a John McDonald, who had no children, but who loved to help children, to initiate the plan. And it would take somebody like Hilda Jaffe to immediately join John McDonald. Between the two of them, they nurtured the idea from germination to fruition.

Initially, all Board members were heavily in favor of the Plan, and they asked the Superintendent and his assistant to query Newark on their position. The two men went to meet with Newark Superintendent Franklyn Titus, their Newark counterpart. After this meeting, their basic agreement with Titus, though not yet reduced to writing, was much further developed than was generally known. But it was up to Verona's Board to check and sign the final written agreement. (Tom Sellitto still wonders whether the payments received from Newark really covered all the expenses.)

But it was only after the opposition was able to garner a couple of thousand signatures, and after the huge opposition crowd came to the high school meeting, that, according to Sellitto, two of the Board members changed their opinions. Emil Tomecek openly supported the opposition, while Elmer Gustavson, worried about community support, started to waffle.

Tom Sellitto himself did what he was asked to do as an employee. He thought that the basic idea was good, but from the start he worried what the fallout would do to the school system and to the educational process in Verona. Sellitto remembered his days in East Orange, and knew very well that black students could use help, but wondered whether the Sharing Plan would be the ideal way to do it.

Sellitto recalls that Superintendent John E. Mattis, the man in the forefront, was threatened by innumerable phone calls. When it got to the point that his wife needed medical help, they decided to leave Verona. Mattis had been like a father to Sellitto. Even after he moved, Mattis, who had a wonderful second career in New Hampshire, talked at least once a month with Tom Sellitto.

Edwin Willard, the high school principal who was beloved by many, refused to buckle down to threats, and also left Verona.

According to Tom Sellitto, there are people in town who do not talk to others since "that time," and some of these people who are still angry are even related.

When questioned on the relatively small percentage of voters participating at the crucial election of 1969, Sellitto rightly points out that for a school election this was a huge turnout, and that similar large numbers voted for the next couple of years. But it is interesting to note that the perception of some of the opposition candidates changed once they were elected and in office. As long as they were candidates, they were suspicious of the Board, but once they joined and realized that education was the only goal, they became supportive and good members of the Board. It is also interesting that not one of the original Board members tried to run for reelection.

The Sharing Plan was a success; it did help the Newark children who came to the Verona schools. The testing of the children showed their great improvement. Sellitto agrees that from the start the experiment should have been for two years. However, for Verona it was not worth the effort; it temporarily destroyed the tenor of the town. Even many supporters changed their mind after they saw what it did to the community.

Tom Sellitto points out that, even at that time, all the states surrounding New Jersey had county school systems. To this date, New Jersey has over 600 school districts, as opposed to the 21 they would have if the state were to have county districts. In Verona's immediate area, there are five districts, five Boards of Education, five Superintendents, five offices, and many times the expenses of running these offices. The two neighboring communities of Cedar Grove and Verona are very much alike; they have a similar population mix, and usually a fairly close relationship. But when they recently tried to merge the two school systems, they were not able to come up with a plan that would find sufficient support, even though such a plan would be financially and educationally beneficial for both communities. The regionalization that had supposedly spurred the opposition to the Sharing Plan would not have been a factor if there had been an Essex County school district, in lieu of each town fending for itself. Even now, years later, regionalization is still a non-issue, even though financially it might be more advantageous.

There is no doubt that the members of the Board of Education were surprised at the unexpected vehement reaction the Sharing Plan elicited. Originally, they thought they would have close to 100 percent support —

never realizing the undercurrent, the venom, the anger. Tom Sellitto will never forget that large meeting at the high school — the outpouring of hatred and enmity.

The "Walk for Understanding" in Newark, New Jersey, April 7, 1968.
Photo courtesy of the Buckley family

The "Walk for Understanding" in Newark, New Jersey, April 7, 1968. Pictured left to right: Verona residents George Hectus, Ann Buckley (pushing carriage), John McDonald (wearing hat), and Mickey McDonald (in sunglasses).   *Photo courtesy of the Buckley family*

The Forest Avenue Elementary School in Verona, New Jersey, built in 1927.

Verona's Brookdale Avenue Elementary School, built in 1927.

The Frederic N. Brown Elementary School in Verona, built in 1931.

The Laning Avenue School, Verona, New Jersey, built in 1918, additions in 1955 and 1966.

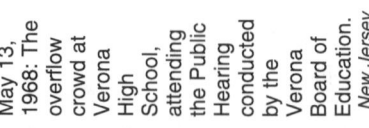

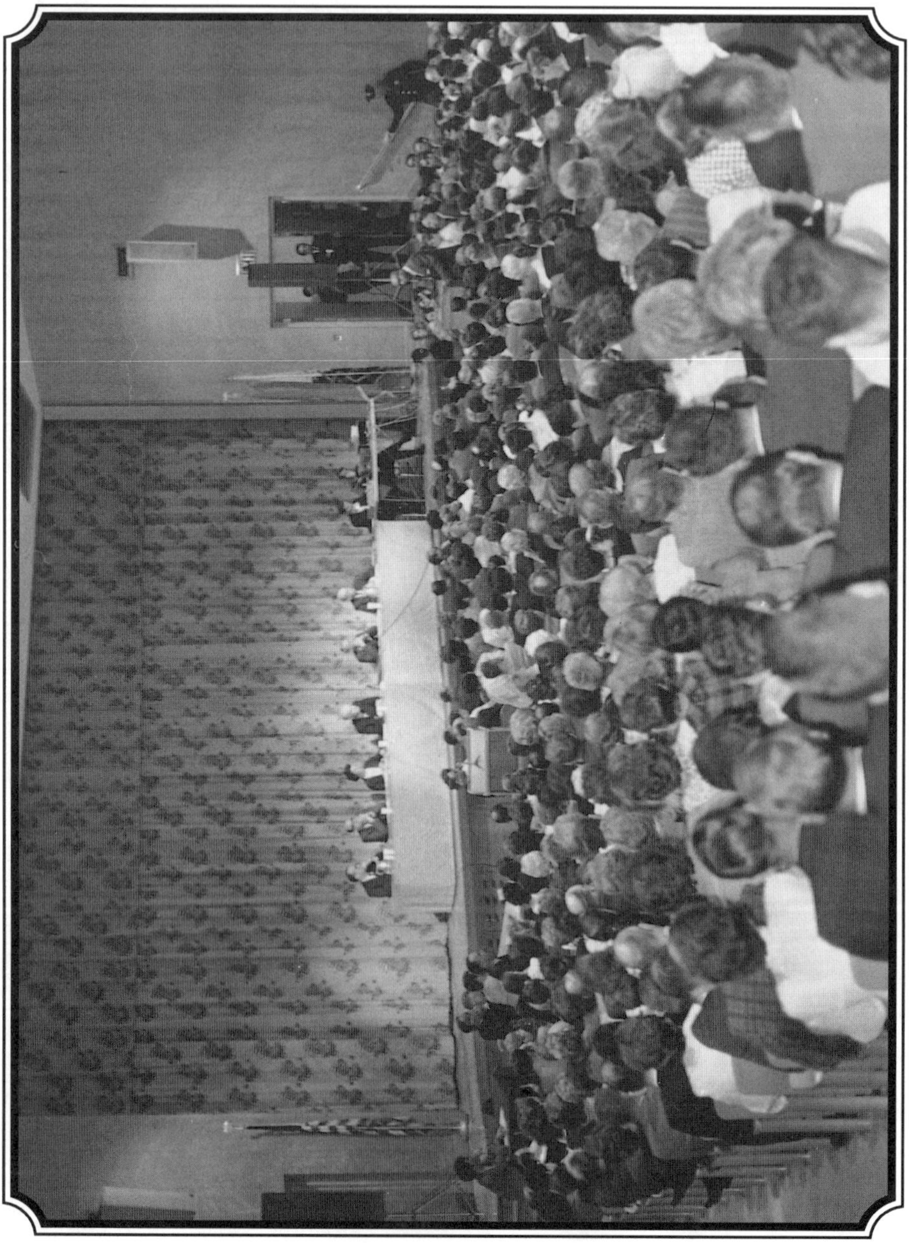

May 13, 1968: The overflow crowd at Verona High School, attending the Public Hearing conducted by the Verona Board of Education. *New Jersey Newsphotos*

Mrs. Oscar Weissendorn, a Verona resident, stands on the tailgate of a station wagon outside Verona High School on May 13, 1968, to address those who could not get inside to the public hearing conducted by the Verona Board of Education. *New Jersey Newsphotos*

The Hawthorne Avenue School in Newark, New Jersey, as it looks today. Built in 1897, the school was enlarged in 1900, 1908, and 1914.

The Hawthorne Avenue School outdoor "playground."

The Hawthorne Avenue School auditorium.

The basement cafeteria of the Hawthorne Avenue School.

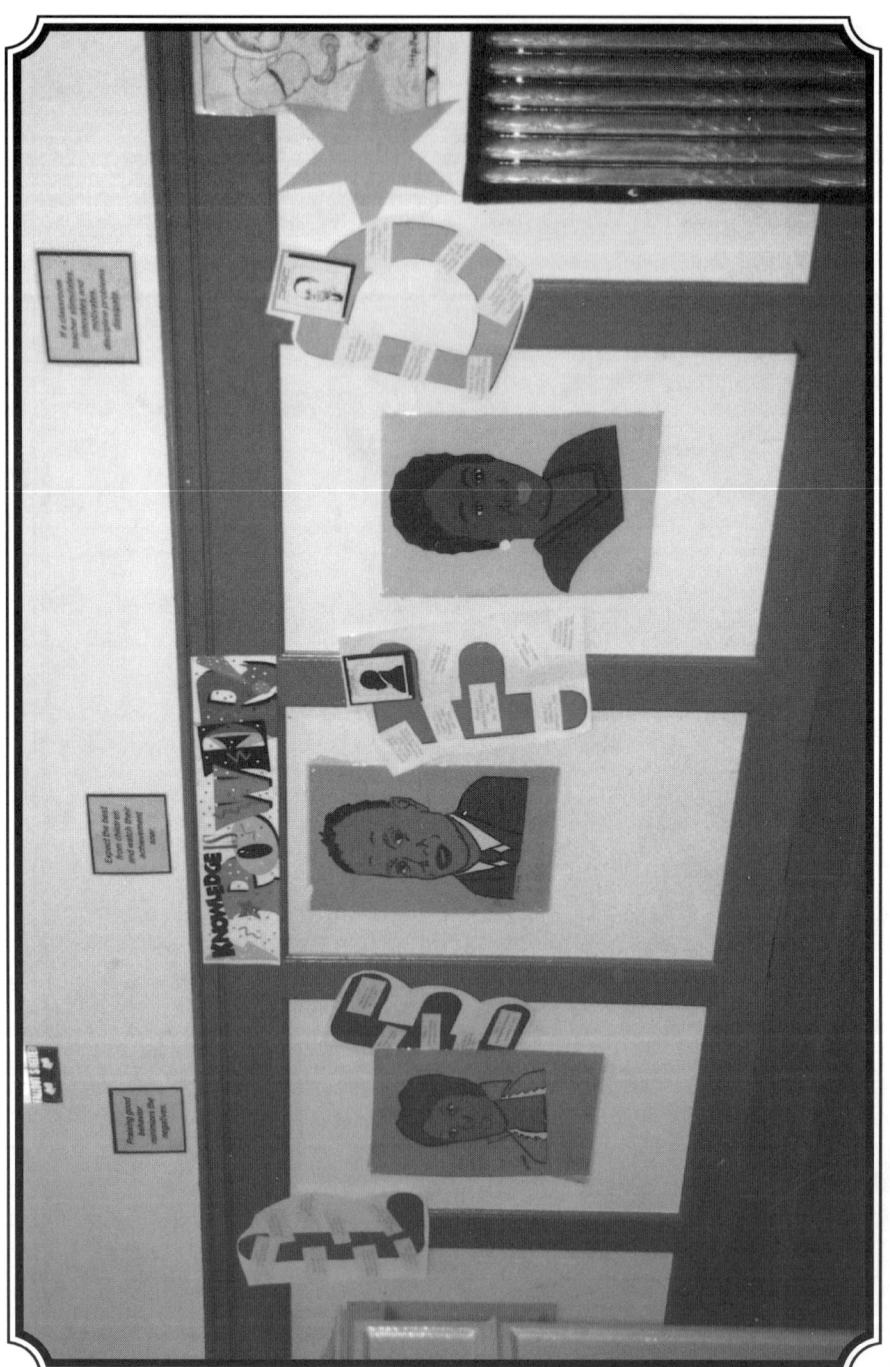

The pictorials near the front entrance of Hawthorne Avenue School.

At the Frederic N. Brown School in Verona, Newark children board the bus for the return trip home on September 4, 1968.   *New Jersey Newsphotos*

Photo courtesy of Nancy Edelhausser

The 1968-1969 first-grade class of Nancy Edelhausser at Frederic N. Brown School in Verona.

The third-grade class of Laning Avenue School, 1968-1969. Craig Boone is standing in the middle of the second row. The other black children pictured were all the children of Verona residents. Like all other youngsters, Craig was dressed in his best suit when the Sharing Plan started, and when this photo was taken. (Note that the photographer misspelled the school name on the sign.)

Donald Boyer (left) and Mark Waldstein.

Photo courtesy of Eugene Waldstein

Opposite page: Russ Nugent's fourth grade class at Forest Avenue School, 1968-1969. Front row, left to right: Chip Bauer and Lynn Nuzman. Second row, left to right: Jimmy Cheatle, Brian Lawless, Susan Janett, Lindsey Emmons, Mary Fitzpatrick, and Lynn Paulsen. Third row, left to right: Eugene Oliphant, Monica Evans, Richard Milford, Richard O'Neill, Janet Finkelstein, Jim Callander, Betsy Fehrs, and Robert Berman. Fourth row, left to right: Mr. Russ Nugent (teacher), Ruth Jamieson, Jim Hiteshew, Carolyn Davis, Jeremiah Kelly, Jean Gillen, David Gamble, and Michaelle Ger___ (name missing). *Photo courtesy of Russ Nugent*

Left to right: Rachel Waldstein, Donald Boyer, and Mark Waldstein.

Photo by Sally Foster

Students attending Verona's summer program in 1969.

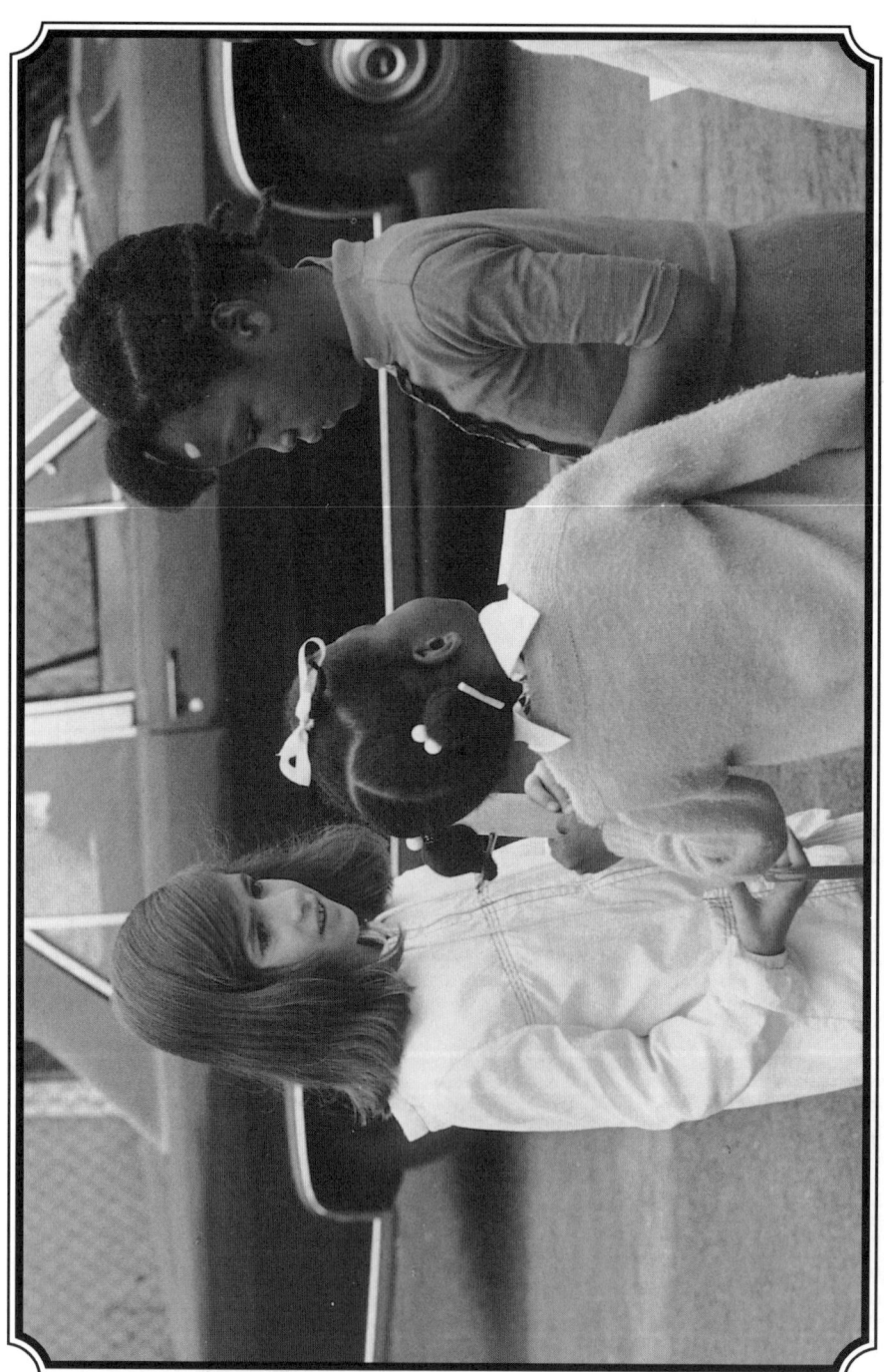

New Jersey Newsphotos

Above and opposite: two of the photos printed in the June 29 issue of Newark's *Star-Ledger.*

June 24, 1969: John LaVigne, principal of Frederic N. Brown School in Verona, escorts Newark children to their home-bound bus — for the last time — as school vacation begins. Because of the opposition to the town's busing plan, the program was not implemented the next year.

New Jersey Newsphotos

. . . What really upset the members was their perception that the state planned to regionalize the school system. . . . the Central Ward in Newark was to be the center of the pie and the rest of Essex County would be divided up; and, according to the new guidelines, all the schools were to be thoroughly mixed.

Chapter 12

Speakers for
the Opposition

AVID B. FORD, chairman of the Verona Citizens for a Fair Decision, heatedly denies that he or his group were racists or bigots, and makes his points convincingly.

Ford was born in Essex County and has lived there all his life. His father, a factory foreman, was born in East Orange and grew up in Newark. His Scottish-born mother went to work as a nurse after Ford and his sister were out of school. Since his parents were strong believers in good education, Ford went to parochial elementary school and then to prep school. Studying originally for the priesthood, he switched to medicine and obtained his degree in psychology. A part of his education was obtained at night, and during the day he held various jobs, including assistant vice president at a bank and manager of a loan company. He found that teaching offered him the most spare time to pursue his evening studies. He received a Master's degree in teaching and another in administration.

David Ford was teaching in Newark in 1968. When the Newark Board of Education learned he was the acting chairman of the Fair Decision group, which was in opposition to the Sharing Plan, he was asked to discuss the situation with Newark Superintendent Franklyn Titus. Ford had taught in Newark for two and a half years, and nearly all of his students were black. He maintains this did not present a problem to him. He is sure that neither the children nor most of the blacks living in Newark received a fair shake in either education, housing, or employment.

Verona Borough Councilman Jim Orr suggested that Ford should attend an upcoming Council meeting, and for the first time Ford met those residents objecting to Verona's Sharing Plan. The Council informed those attending that they had to plead their case with the Board of Education. David Ford objected to the idea that those who met with him initially were immediately branded as racists. Ford had gone to school for nine years with Father John McDermott's brother, and was outraged that the Father considered the group members, now including Ford himself, to be bigots.

A meeting of the new group was called and held at the Public Library. Ford remembers Sydney and Robert Dickinson, Lou Leffler, the Bostwicks, and Dick Meehan participating. David Ford simply wanted to find out what this was all about. He claims that it was his "big mouth" that got him elected acting chairman. He wanted to make sure that it did not become a political issue, even though he was approached for the position by Bob Davis, a Republican.

The information the group received does not seem to jibe with reality. According to Ford, his group had been informed early on that the Sharing Plan was a done deal, that all agreements had been signed, and that the teacher to accompany the children had been picked, though the minutes of the school boards of Newark and Verona show this to be untrue.

But what really upset the members was their perception that the state planned to regionalize the school system. Their impression was that the Central Ward in Newark was to be the center of the pie and the rest of Essex County would be divided up; and, according to the new guidelines, all the schools were to be thoroughly mixed.

The clergy, which played a leading part during that time, inflamed Ford's group with their statements. Father John McDermott, who had marched in Selma, Alabama, called the request for a referendum "murder at the ballot box." The Episcopalian minister compared a refusal to bring 40 Newark children to Verona to leaving 40 miners underground. It was the clergy, more than the Board of Education, that was perceived as the enemy. Certainly Emil Tomecek looked like an ally, and Hilda Jaffe, ever conscientious and hard working, was the one to be held accountable.

Even though a majority of the speakers at the various hearings — especially at the first meeting at the high school — spoke in favor of the Sharing Plan, neither the newspapers nor the Board ever tied the speakers — who seemed to speak for themselves or for their families — to the petition signers. And yet 2,000 signatures had appeared on the petition for a referendum. The media and the Board misinterpreted the signals of the populace.

David Ford is very emphatic that at no time did his group oppose the busing of the children. On the contrary, the Fair Decision group kept a lid on the growing unrest in town. The group offered an opportunity to become active for those residents who had moved to Verona to escape the blacks, and also to the many Veronans who felt that the town should solve its own problems first. The Fair Decision group did not want to polarize Verona any more than it already was. The group pleaded with the Board to clarify whether its motive was charity, or a beginning toward regionalization. Without further testing the kids who were bused to Verona, a charitable motive could have been accepted by nearly everyone in town. Certainly, David Ford stressed, he does not oppose black aspirations, and he did oppose those who brought in hate literature. The only issue he opposed was regionalization.

At election time, the Fair Decision group was not sure about Emil Tomecek. Deciding that their candidate should not be an active member of their group, they settled on Marshall Butler, an educator, who agreed in general with their principles. During those embattled days, most of Ford's friends firmly supported the Board of Education's actions. Finally, David Ford decided to stop getting involved — involvement meant responsibilities. He had always resented being branded as a bigot.

Kenneth and Amy Bostwick contend that the Sharing Plan was not about education at all, but only about money. Newark was broke, Mr. Bostwick asserted, and in order to get state and federal money, Newark's Board was interested in busing their children to other communities, with Newark being in charge. It was even rumored that a couple of Newark ladies found rooms full of new books that had never been opened, and that these books had been ordered only so buyers could get commissions.

According to Mr. Bostwick, it was Hilda Jaffe who not only had the idea for the Sharing Plan, but also connections to Trenton. Trenton had connections with Newark, and that helped to get the Sharing Plan going. Newark, he asserted, used subsidy money to inveigle Montclair to bus children, but Montclair had told them to get lost. Mr. Bostwick claims that the ultimate plan was really to bus suburban children to Newark.

Race was never the issue, Mr. Bostwick claimed. The clergy and others accused the group of bigotry, he said, but it was certainly not race — only money — that was at the root of the commotion.

On May 28, 1968, Hrant Yousoufian, who was away on a business trip in Melbourne, Australia, wrote to the *Verona-Cedar Grove Times* that his wife and teenage daughter had notified him of the Sharing Plan and that he was gratified so many had come to support this Plan at the public meeting. He wrote further, "It is disquieting to learn that a significant number of our fellow citizens have chosen to align themselves against the institution of the busing proposal." The next five paragraphs all started with, "It is disquieting" and each paragraph stated a reason why it was a good plan.

And, yet, now Hrant Yousoufian gives convincing reasons why he felt he had to change his mind.

Of Armenian background, Hrant Yousoufian's family fled Turkey to the safe haven of America; they arrived when his mother was pregnant with Hrant. His father, well educated and the editor of an Armenian newspaper, died when Hrant was only five years old. His mother then remarried. Yousoufian grew up in Brooklyn and started his studies at the Polytechnic Institute, but then had to join the Army. After his discharge, he completed his education with the help of the G.I. Bill.

While under General George S. Patton's command, Hrant landed in France, crossed the Rhine, and continued on to Germany. Later he met and fell in love with a distant cousin, who had been born and raised in France. They were married and she came to the United States as a war bride. After he started to work in the Industrial Village in Cedar Grove in 1958, the family moved to Verona.

Originally it was Yousoufian's impression that the Sharing Plan called for bringing gifted children to Verona in order to help them further their education. When he found out that this was not the case, he, too, became convinced that the Plan was a ruse — an excuse, a forerunner of busing throughout the state. He never objected to bringing black children to Verona, but feared that eventually his children would be bused outside Verona, to who knew where.

Education was important to Hrant Yousoufian. The year prior to the introduction of the Sharing Plan, he decided to run for the Board of Education. One of the rumors that had surfaced during the campaign was that he would propose to cut out musical education to save money. While he and his wife had privately discussed this and similar ideas concerning ways to save taxpayer dollars, they had come to the conclusion that this economy was not good for education. And yet the rumors persisted.

The League of Women Voters held a candidate forum and Yousoufian adhered to the request to stick to the issues. Unfortunately, others did not follow the rules. Personalities were discussed, and Hrant Yousoufian lost the election.

Earlier, Yousoufian had joined the Verona Taxpayers League, eventually becoming its spokesperson. When the town proposed a noise ordinance that would have permitted a decibel level that he thought too high, he was able, through the help of charts, to convince the town fathers to change their minds. But Yousoufian was not always successful. When the location of the town swimming pool was being debated, Hrant and the members of the Taxpayers League suggested that the proposed piece of property was desirable for development and could bring in valuable ratables. His group studied other properties available, and proposed an alternate location. However, this time the elected officials did not agree.

It was the contention of the Taxpayers League that good education depends on good teachers, and not necessarily on the pay for teachers. The League proposed merit increases for excellence, because they felt that more pay to all the teachers did not necessarily improve teaching standards. When the Board asserted that smaller classes would improve teaching, the League countered with the argument that smaller classes would be quite costly, and perhaps no better. Yousoufian also believed that the Board tried to demonstrate the proficiency of the student body at its best by boasting of the top students without evaluating the total system.

He was not impressed with the Board nor with the Superintendent, and that is why he decided to become a candidate. In retrospect, he felt that Emil Tomecek had done a good job, and that Elmer Gustavson had done a fair job.

In 1969, Hrant Yousoufian's employer moved him to Spain. Upon his family's return, he tried to find a suitable home in Verona, but settled instead in Montclair.

The Verona schools had given his children a good education. His son is in real estate, one daughter lives in France, and the second daughter works for a large European corporation.

Richard Meehan is a Verona native; his parents moved to Verona in 1921. Meehan attended public school at Verona's Lady of the Lake, and then went to Immaculate Conception in Montclair. After his four-year stint in the Navy, he pursued his education further, again with the help of the G.I. Bill, at St. Peter's College in Jersey City, New Jersey.

Meehan's wife grew up close by in North Caldwell, and the two settled in Verona. In time, they raised a family of seven children. In 1968, Dick was working hard and had little time to follow local politics. At that time they already had four children, the oldest only five years old. None were yet in school, and Meehan was not following Board of Education policies. One evening, while Dick was mowing his lawn, his neighbor invited him to attend a meeting to be held at the library. For the first time, Richard Meehan learned about the Sharing Plan. He had mixed emotions. He could not fathom why the Board of Education would be taking this action, and could only assume that it was a step to integrate the white suburbs.

Meehan agreed that an elected Board of Education was entitled to set policy, but thought that the Sharing Plan was outside the realm of educational policy. He felt people should have been polled, possibly even under a non-binding referendum, and if a majority responded, the Board could have gone ahead. He acknowledged that more citizens at the public meeting spoke in favor of the Sharing Plan, but assumed that the Board knew that the vocal Veronans had an agenda, and that a silent majority was not in favor of the project.

While the town was engaged in rancorous discussions, Meehan reported that the membership of his Catholic Church in Verona was torn apart. The hierarchy and some church members supported the Sharing Plan, but the majority were opposed. When Dick told the leaders where he stood, he was threatened with hell and damnation. Meehan was a member of the CFM — the Christian Family Movement. While this group endorsed the Plan, Meehan felt that the majority of its members were against the idea. He remembers that even before the Fair Decision group was officially organized, Meehan and others in CFM asked for a meeting with Verona's clergy. The meeting did not last long, because one of the clergymen accused them of being racists, bigots, and liars. Meehan did not think this was the way to cement relationships and build bridges.

But Dick Meehan noted that even though the grown-ups fought each other, no one bothered the black children. They came and left in peace. There had been little doubt in his mind that a year in Verona would help those kids; they all came from motivated families, after all. On the other hand, Meehan did not think that a second year would have been beneficial for the town of Verona.

Meehan remembers that in 1969 there was a relatively good turnout at the polls for the Board of Education election, but it was the activists who voted. Butler was elected, but in the long run, according to Dick Meehan, Butler did not come through with what the group had been promised. Primarily, the group wanted the Board to get the curriculum back to basics. Discussions on contracts between students and teachers, or the pass/fail method, were superfluous. More important to the group was the total structure of education. Dick Meehan did not approve of kids getting up when they felt like it and wandering to the back of the classrooms.

Meehan ran for the Verona School Board in 1970 and won, only to lose in the following election to Frank Nunziata.

The split in the Catholic Church did not heal for more than ten years, and Dick Meehan never did make peace with Father McDermott. It was not only the Sharing Plan, he said, but other issues on which they could not agree. Other group members still remember how they were talked to. Dick Meehan had vituperative phone calls from people who never identified themselves, visitors who yelled wildly at him, and a few Veronans did not talk to him for years.

Anthony Ditri, the attorney for Verona Citizens for a Fair Decision, grew up in a tenement house on Bloomfield Avenue in Bloomfield, New Jersey, near the Belleville line. His Italian-born father came to the United States as a small boy, and for most of his life operated a forklift for Lehn & Fink, manufacturers of cosmetics and chemicals. His mother, who had been born in America, kept herself busy raising the three children.

Ditri went through the Bloomfield school system, received a scholarship for athletics, and graduated from Providence College, Rhode Island. During World War II, he served in the 7th Air Force in the South Pacific. His brother, a member of a famous Ranger Battalion, was killed in Italy. After Tony was discharged, he taught at Boys Town, a Catholic orphanage, during the day. At night he attended John Marshall College, thanks to the G.I. Bill. He met his future wife when she visited friends in Bloomfield. For a time after their marriage, they lived at her home in Newark. Ditri, by then a lawyer, worked for Sam Rosenblatt, a Montclair attorney. A podiatrist, Bob Corso, who worked in the same building, had purchased a home on Linden Avenue, and he introduced Ditri to Verona.

The Ditri family built their beautiful brick home in Verona in 1955, and have lived there ever since. Their three children went through the Verona school system. Both of his daughters are pharmacists; his son, who lives in Virginia, works for a food company. Ditri served two terms on the Verona Borough Council. He feels that his proudest achievement was the building of the Verona pool. The pool had once been a political issue, suggested by the Democratic candidates and derided by the Republicans. Ditri, a Republican, said that he had always been more interested in the pool as a facility that would be beneficial for all of the residents.

Tony Ditri related that one day Chief of Police Edgar Coffin informed him that the people who were objecting to the busing proposal were in urgent need of legal advice. A number of attorneys, the chief said, had already refused to accept what was shaping up as a controversial case. He had not been pleased himself with the way he felt the Board of Education had sprung the Sharing Plan on the populace, and he had very strong feelings that everyone should have legal representation. After listening carefully to the objectors, Ditri decided to take on the case.

Ditri had his own misgivings about the prospects of a legal suit, but he kept them to himself. To win a case against children, specifically poor

black children, would not be easy. Most of the judges, in Ditri's opinion, were very liberal and would side with the children. It was the trend. But he did not relay these worries to his clients; his chief concern was to find proper legal answers to the questions asked, whether or not children were involved. Furthermore, he was assured by the Veronans who retained him that they had nothing against the children *per se*. For them, too, it was strictly a question of legality.

When questioned about the high costs of this legal undertaking, Tony Ditri told me of the *pro bono* aid he received from other attorneys, especially those versed in appellate cases. Ditri was paid very little — mostly expense reimbursements — and felt he was volunteering his services for something that had to be done.

Ditri indicates there was a lot of strife in the Catholic Church, of which he is a member. Father McDermott was perceived as one of the architects of the Sharing Plan idea. Tony felt that the religious leaders of all denominations should have started a dialogue with their parishioners, discussing the Plan openly, instead of taking sides. Only after the townspeople were aware of the specifics of the Plan, had discussed it, and had accepted it, should it have been introduced by the Board of Education.

To this day, Anthony Ditri thinks that if the preparations for, and introduction of, the Sharing Plan had been handled properly, Veronans would have accepted it without any fuss or qualm.

The Verona educational sharing plan, which enters its fourth week . . . has proven a delight to teachers, parents and . . . children being bused from Newark's hard-core poverty area. . . . The children . . . "adjusted quickly, . . . were accepted by their Verona classmates," and "settled into regular classroom routines."

Chapter 13

They Are Here!

THE PLAINTIFFS WERE Amy Bostwick, Sydney W. Dickinson, Robert Dickinson, Edward Newkirk, Fred Mahn, and the Verona Citizens for Fair Decision, a New Jersey Corporation. The defendant was the Verona Board of Education. The civil action complaint was filed on August 1, 1968, by Anthony F. Ditri. Attached to the legal papers were the Verona Board of Education's Proposal to Share; the statement published by the Verona Board of Education, dated May 9; the undated answers distributed by the Board to questions posed by the citizens; and a copy of the agreement between the Newark and Verona Boards of Education.

The papers maintained that all of the plaintiffs were legal voters of Verona, and that their children attended the schools of Verona. The complaint spelled out in detail how the plaintiffs learned about the proposed Sharing Plan, and described how they presented a petition for a town-wide referendum, which was to be considered together with all other views and statements by the Board. Paragraph seven of the complaint stated that a total of 1,846 names were listed on the petition for a town-wide referendum, which was presented on May 13. Paragraph nine stated that on May 28, an additional 500 names, and a further addition with 70 legal voters' names, were added to this list.

Further, the pleading stated that according to New Jersey Statutes Annotated 18A:14-3, special elections may be held when the Board of Education desires it, or "whenever 50 of such legal voters shall by petition so request. . . ." Because the defendant adopted the resolution and thereafter executed a formal contract for sharing education opportunities, they "refused the plaintiffs their lawful rights to a special election or referendum pursuant to N.J.S.A. 18A:14-3." The Verona plaintiffs also alleged that if the contract were to be implemented, they would be without a remedy, "thereupon . . . denied their rights . . . and . . . suffering irreparable injury, harm and loss." The plaintiffs demanded that the Board be ordered to hold an election "for the purpose of voting for or against the proposal for 'Sharing Educational Opportunities'." They also demanded a restraining order to enjoin the Board from proceeding in the implementation of the contract.

The plaintiffs had asked the Board of Education whether the proposal was authorized by law, and the Board's answer was attached. The Board had pointed out that under the statutes, any person not a resident "may be admitted with the consent of the Board upon such terms, and with or without payment of tuition as the Board may prescribe." Because it is the Board's responsibility to provide a thorough and efficient school system, the plaintiffs allege that the action

> in contracting with the Board of Education of the City of Newark is *ultra vires* and outside the scope, responsibilities and duties to provide a thorough and efficient school system within the district it comprises.

Attached to these papers was an affidavit, signed by the five plaintiffs, and notarized. This statement reiterated that the plaintiffs were legal residents, taxpayers, and parents of children in grades one through five; outlined the way they found out about the proposal; stated that they had all attended the public meetings; and said that they had been active in presenting and in obtaining over 2,000 signatures on petitions. The Sharing program, as the Board stated, aimed to correct some deficiencies experienced by the Newark children, and also provide the opportunity for research and evaluation that might serve other children. However, the plaintiffs alleged, neither of these purposes related to the function and responsibility of the local Board. "The defendant has gone beyond its lawful authority insofar as this proposal and contract are concerned."

The plaintiffs claimed they had been denied the right of the ballot, and because the next school session was rapidly approaching, they were without a remedy to determine their rights, "and will sustain immediate irreparable loss and injury if said contract is implemented without adjudication of our contentions and rights."

The defendant was ordered to show cause before the Superior Court of New Jersey in Newark on August 30, at 9:30 a.m., why it should not be restrained and enjoined. This order was served by Richard L. Gennaro, Special Deputy Sheriff of the County of Essex, and delivered to Thomas Sellitto, the Verona Board of Education secretary.

On September 9, George Buermann, Esq., appearing for Keer, Booth, Buermann & Bate, Esqs., attorneys for the Verona Board of Education, appeared and Judge Samuel A. Larner ruled:

> . . . the Court having considered the affidavits and briefs submitted by the parties and having heard the argument of counsel, and the Court having found that the plaintiffs were not required to exhaust their administrative remedies; It is, on this 9th day of September, 1968, ORDERED that the application of plaintiffs for an injunction or stay of defendant's contract of July 1, 1968, is hereby denied, and that the matter proceed as in plenary action and that defendant be required to answer the complaint of the plaintiffs in this cause within 20 days of the date hereof.

The Board's answer was filed on September 26 by Buermann. In the barely two-page answer, the Board admitted the factual allegations, but denied that it was at fault.

In its defense, the Board charged:

> that neither the individual plaintiffs nor the corporate plaintiff
> have the requisite interest or standing to prosecute the alleged
> cause of action [*and stated*] that the corporate plaintiff, Verona
> Citizens for Fair Decisions, was not duly authorized to institute
> the within cause of action and such action is outside the scope
> of its powers and authority.

Metropolitan New Jersey school problems were discussed in the September 3 issue of *The New York Times*. Included were Bergen, Hudson, Middlesex, and Monmouth counties. The report covering Essex County noted that its problems were as diverse as were the districts, but "nowhere else in Essex, however, are the difficulties so great as in Newark," where the Governor's report had declared, "the educational breakdown in Newark's schools is a crisis."

The Governor's Commission had concluded that the state should "take over the administration of the Newark school system" temporarily. However, the paper reported that the state had not acted on the recommendation, and that the Newark school system, "where 75 percent of the 76,000 students are Negro," would begin the school year with what amounted to an "emergency program and a cut-to-the-bone budget." The Newark Board of Education, the paper added, has said that the city would be short "10,000 pupil stations."

The *Times* further noted that the city of Orange was entering its school year "having seemingly settled a financial issue with racial overtones . . . approving construction of a new $4.2 million high school." The paper added that under the controversial Sharing Plan in "virtually all-white" Verona, 38 mostly first and second grade Negro students would be brought from Newark's Hawthorne Avenue School that fall, and Verona Superintendent John B. Mattis was quoted as saying, "I look forward to it."

The *Newark Evening News* of September 4, under the twin headings, "Bused to Verona," and "36 Kids Begin Learn-In," wrote:

> Thirty-six freshly starched children who ordinarily would have
> registered today in Grades 3 to 5 at the overcrowded Hawthorne

Avenue School in Newark, boarded a school bus there and rode instead to Verona to attend classes in the borough's four elementary schools.

Despite press reports, the students actually numbered 37. Although 38 had been accepted for the program, one fewer actually participated. The children, after registering, attended regular classes until 11:45, when they adjourned for lunch at various private homes. A dry run, without publicity, had been held the previous day in order to alleviate confusion, to give the youngsters a chance to meet their respective teachers and principals. Forest Avenue received 14 children, and eight each went to Laning Avenue and Frederic N. Brown schools, and six to Brookdale Avenue school. A photograph pictured Pamela Davis, one of the Newark children, at lunch with her hosts, Stephen and Stephanie Klabenesh. Pamela and Stephanie now were classmates.

"Had Fun in Verona School" was the headline the next day in the same newspaper.

> Pamela Davis, 8, of . . . Newark, summed up the feeling yesterday afternoon of students, school administrators and parents involved in the first day of the Verona-Newark busing project: "We had a lot of fun."

She had liked her teacher and was excited about making new friends. Her mother, the paper added, had been "a little apprehensive" about sending her daughter to Verona because of the resistance to the project. But after the orientation session, Pamela was anxious to return for the first day of school.

Ruby Dixon, the Newark teacher who was accompanying and assisting the visiting students, said that Verona students and parents were very receptive. Board president Hilda Jaffe was pleased that this opening day was much like any other opening day. "During each summer many new families move into Verona," she said in the interview. "When school opens, therefore, we welcome a new group of students in our classes, and the children from Newark were simply part of this year's group."

Robert J. Braun, who subsequently wrote additional articles on Verona, together with Ted Serrill, noted in *The* (Newark) *Star-Ledger* of September 5, 1968, the calm welcome the ghetto students had received in Verona.

There were no incidents in Verona and according to the principal of the F. N. Brown Elementary School, everybody enjoyed it. One youngster said it is a long way from Newark and another questioned whether Verona ever had riots. When reassured he said, "That's really good — because I sure don't like riots." According to one first grade teacher, "the children do not recognize differences."

"Verona Testing Ground for 'Involvement'" was the headline of another *Star-Ledger* article by Robert J. Braun. He explained that some of the larger cities in New Jersey no longer had a sufficient revenue base to support their schools adequately and they had turned to the state; but the power of New Jersey's Legislature was based in the suburbs:

> Legislators from urban areas are convinced the suburban and rural legislators do not have sufficient knowledge of these problems. . . . Observers in the cities and in the State Department of Education think that if suburban residents can be convinced that urban problems are also their problems, they would open up some of their schools to inner-city children. However, many suburban parents fear that this would also mean that their children will be bused into the city.

Braun added that in spite of "the silence on the question," the sharing proposal between suburban and inner city schools was "very much alive."

> . . . Superintendents from the suburbs and administrators in Trenton are hoping the [*Verona*] program is successful and is repeated. They are hoping that what could not be done by suggestions from Education Commissioner Marburger may be accomplished through the collective will of suburban citizens.

Braun also wrote that observers were watching and worried about the next school election in Verona, because the make-up of a new Board would determine the "Verona Plan."

Ruby Dixon, several children, and Superintendent John Mattis were pictured next to the bus in the September 5 issue of the *Verona-Cedar Grove Times*. Dixon and one little boy were smiling, the other kids looked like they were not quite sure whether this was a happy occasion. The accompanying story also reported on the "dry run" the day before, when the bus had arrived approximately at 1:45 p.m. and, after the initial greetings, everyone was taken on a tour.

All the presidents of the school Parent Teacher Associations and the elementary school principals involved in the experiment attended a meeting on September 6. The minutes state that the principals in each school were responsible for all home-away-from-home Newark children, and PTA presidents were asked to cooperate with the principals in arranging for host families and alternates. Host families needed to have their guest's name and grade, home address, and special information concerning health and diet, as well as emergency phone numbers — *i.e.*, the Board office number, or the Rescue Squad number.

Each host family was to be advised that they were fully protected by insurance against the child's injury, illness, or damage to the home — a homeowner-type policy funded as part of the project. Orientation meetings, fall open-house meetings with the parents of the Newark children, rainwear, and other extra clothing supply, was also discussed. It was stressed that requests for photos, interviews, and other information needed to be channeled through the office of the Superintendent.

Based on this meeting, principals organized their various schools. The principal of the F. N. Brown School invited all hosts or potential hosts to a meeting on September 18. In turn, the host parents of that school invited the parents of the Newark children for a Sunday afternoon get-together.

Meanwhile, the Verona Citizens for a Fair Decision continued to press its case in court, despite losing the preliminary decision, still claiming that the Board had acted in contradiction to a New Jersey statute by refusing to hold a referendum, and that it acted outside the scope of its statutory powers. An attempt by Anthony Ditri, counsel for the group, to argue that the "sharing plan is the first step in a state scheme to abandon the neighborhood school concept" was blocked by Judge Larner, who asked the attorney not to engage in "political speeches." Ditri quoted Commissioner Carl L. Marburger, and contended that the Sharing Plan may have even originated in his office. He argued that this could very well be the beginning of the end for neighborhood schools. Ditri thought that the court should have taken at least judicial notice, so that he could "attempt to show that my clients are not just taking issue with a harmless humanitarian gesture made by our borough."

Superintendent Mattis renewed his plea.

> We have been given legal clearance by the courts and I urge all citizens to cease badgering the board at this point, to permit the proper administration of the Plan. . . .

But the plea by the Superintendent was ignored. At Board meetings, the questions continued, even after the children had settled in. At the meeting of September 24, attended by 52 citizens and 3 representatives of the press, one resident asked how many white children had been bused in from Newark. When the Board responded that no whites were being bused, the man then wanted to know why there was not a single white child, because Father McDermott had told him there would be white children. It was explained that the students came from a predominantly black neighborhood.

Mrs. Richard Sandler, speaking for the Forest Avenue School PTA, expressed the concern that there were not sufficient children for the numerous volunteer parents, and that it was hoped that the children could rotate in their lunch visits. Marshall A. Butler (who would later run for the School Board) wanted to know what information was being sought by the evaluation of the program, what the results were going to mean, and who the tests were going to be compared with. It was answered that primarily achievement and attitude results were wanted, that the results would be compared with a control group in Newark that was then being set up, and that the results might be made available to other Boards of Education.

William B. Schmidt wanted to know whether future busing plans would be based on the test results. Mattis replied that the Board was not committed beyond one year. Schmidt then wanted to know if *no* improvement would be a factor in the decision whether to renew the program. The answer he was given was that many factors had to be considered. Frank Lytle asked whether the program would be put for a vote by the people after the test results were available. The Board responded that that was a matter of litigation right now.

The *Newark Evening News* of September 25 described the Sharing Plan's success after one month:

The Verona educational sharing plan, which enters its fourth week today, has proven a delight to teachers, parents and the 38 [*sic*] children being bused from Newark's hard-core poverty area, according to a report presented last night by Superintendent of Schools John Mattis of Verona.

The children had "adjusted quickly," "were accepted by their Verona classmates," and "settled into regular classroom routines." The home-away-from-home lunch program, it was reported, also worked smoothly.

According to the *Verona-Cedar Grove Times* of September 26, Governor Richard J. Hughes praised the borough for "embarking upon the 'Sharing Educational Opportunities Plan'."

The first public report by John E. Mattis was also part of the local paper's story. "Surprisingly the young urban children adjusted quickly to their new surroundings," and were well accepted by their Verona classmates. The implementation of the Plan was "unbelievably smooth."

On October 6, the *Newark Evening News* reported, "Verona Scores with Bus Plan for 38 Newark Kids." After a recap of events leading up to the admission of the Newark children, the newspaper reported on the initial success of the project and the objection of the group who had fought the idea. Three photos illustrated the acceptance of the children. Joan Hughes, spokesperson for the host mothers, was shown waving goodbye to her two children and their guest, Eula Jackson, as they left for the afternoon classes. A mixed group of children was shown in a reading class with Regina Klein. And, smiling proudly, Joseph Rock was pictured holding his schoolbooks, ready for his new school.

The *Newark Evening News* of October 17 quoted Board president Hilda Jaffe:

> Now that all of the intensive preparation has been justified, the easy atmosphere prevailing in the classrooms and homes is proof that Verona has really accepted the need for sharing our educational opportunities with others who aren't so fortunate. It's been well worth it.

The story was a recap of the idea of the Sharing Plan, and it recounted the "six months of planning by the Board of Education to get the plan underway in the face of considerable opposition from some residents," the resistance by the Verona Citizens for a Fair Decision, the status of their court case against the Board of Education, and the way the Newark youngsters had been accepted — "enjoying every minute of it."

> Encompassed in the experiment are two first-graders, two third-graders and two fifth-graders at the Brookdale Avenue School; eight first-graders at the F. N. Brown School; six first-graders, four second-graders and four fourth-graders at Forest Avenue School, and six second-graders and four third-graders at the Laning Avenue School. . . . [*The plan's major purpose was*] to provide an educational program and environment which would help correct some of the serious educational deficiencies experienced by some Newark children. . . .

Joan Hughes, who spoke for the host mothers, felt the program was progressing well and "the Negro and white children were having no problems getting along, and were sharing an important social contact."

Throughout all the Board meetings, questions had been raised concerning the rights of citizens to inspect, copy, and have made available to them the minutes and other Board records. During the meeting of October 29, which was attended by over 100 citizens, a letter signed by Board attorney George Buermann addressed these questions in great detail, citing various statutes and court cases. The attorney's opinion was that the public was guaranteed the right to be admitted to all Board meetings at which official action was to be taken, but that the Board was not prohibited from conducting a meeting in advance or a closed conference, where no official action was taken. Further, he stated that all minutes and all Board records were public. In general, he said, the public was entitled to know, inspect, and copy public records. However, this right had never been an unlimited one, and was subject to the requirement of a lawful, proper, and legitimate purpose, and the inspection could not interfere with the performance of official duties. It was incumbent upon any Board not to release information that could seriously damage an individual's right to privacy, and where more harm than good might result to the public interest. The right of citizens to inspect, copy, and purchase copies of Board records was defined by statute and provided that: the right should be exercised during regular business hours; the right to copy by hand should be under the supervision of a representative of the custodian; and the custodian should make and supply copies. Even the costs of making these copies were stipulated in the law. Buermann's letter ended with:

> Conclusion: In general, the public is entitled to know, to inspect and to copy the public records of the board but the board has the right and in fact, the obligation to consider the nature of the public records, motives behind their use, and the effect on public interest in determining the extent of right.

All members of the Board except Tomecek voted in the affirmative for a motion that the Verona Board of Education would make copies of the minutes of regular and special public meetings available for public inspection at the Verona Public Library and, further, that copies of minutes and all other public records required by law would be maintained or kept on file and be made available to the public, in accordance with the opinion rendered by the attorney.

Tomecek was in favor of the motion, but he suggested changes. He then moved that the agenda of each meeting be published in newspapers five days in advance, that the Board members would receive copies prior to the publication, and that individual members could introduce other matters not included in the agenda. Gustavson seconded his motion, but when the vote was called, Gustavson voted against it. Wizda and Jaffe abstained, and Tomecek's motion lost with only one vote in favor. Most members of the Board were not really against his resolution, but complained that they did not have sufficient time to study and evaluate the motion.

During the open discussion period, Tomecek summarized his thinking:

> . . . the state establishment, having failed in its earlier proposals on two-way busing, is now proposing to bus city children into the suburbs where the suburban educational establishment doesn't know even what the city problems are. Diluting the problems by busing will not help the thousands of city children who need the help so desperately.

Tomecek complained that he was learning more about Verona's busing plan from newspapers than from Board meetings. He cited a report that the New Jersey Commissioner of Education, Dr. Marburger, and fellow Board member Hilda Jaffe had spoken in Morristown on October 17, hailing the success of the Verona busing plan and urging other communities to follow Verona's example. This occurred, he pointed out, when the Verona program was only about six weeks old, and without the benefit of a testing agency.

> He [*Dr. Marburger*] is talking like a politician, not an educator, when he makes such premature judgments. I say to the politicians, "Stop exploiting these thirty-eight children. Let the Newark children reap the benefits of this charitable gesture without interference from the politicians."

Tomeck charged that

> politicians disguised as educators are busy laying the groundwork for changing the educational system of the whole State of New Jersey.

Tomecek then quoted Dr. Harold J. Ashby, president of the Newark Board of Education, as saying that while he appreciated Verona's program, the system must be solved in Newark without exporting their children. Tomecek further quoted Frank Overlan — formerly a consultant in Dr. Marburger's division and the man who had advised the Verona Board on the proposal — in a statement to members of the New Jersey Boards of Education at their annual meeting in which he advocated "closing all ghetto schools and shifting the students to the suburbs." Tomecek added that in a closed meeting on May 12, he welcomed the Newark proposal as a charitable gesture, but thought the whole business seemed to be integration. He reported that Overlan, who had attended that meeting, had replied, "That's what this is all about."

Tomecek continued:

> Let's unmask all the talk by the educational politicians about busing ghetto children into the suburbs. They're really talking about busing non-whites out of the cities and into the subsuburbs. . . .

Tomecek worried about a possible takeover of the Newark schools by

> . . . a State Department of Education whose personnel feel that the schools of Newark should become bus terminals for Newark school children traveling to and from the suburbs. . . . In many ways, I believe that when these busing proposals are peddled as general solutions to the educational problems of the cities' non-white children, the busing proposals are nothing more than political attempts to fool poor city parents by diluting the problems rather than solving them.

Comparing the similarities of educational problems of many children in Verona with the children from Newark, Tomecek discussed his own special interest in helping the underachievers.

> I am extremely interested in providing the poor young black children, young white children, young Puerto Rican and other Newark children, with an education that will enable them as adults to get the kind of a job that will make it possible for them to live in a suburb such as Verona if they so choose, but they must have a real choice. Let's not be hypocritical. Let's not say that you can come, but we don't want you next door. We must help these children get the basic education in Newark without separating these children from their families, friends, and loved ones. Let's not forget that the parents of city children have the same feelings toward their children we have towards ours. The city parents want to keep in close touch with their children in school; this close contact is only possible in a neighborhood school. I would like to reiterate that I had accepted Verona's Proposal for Sharing Educational Opportunities as a charitable gesture whereby, while steps are being taken to solve Newark's educational problems in Newark [*underlined in original minutes*]. . . . However, I could not accept a proposal which failed to get broad community acceptance because of the manner in which it was jammed down the collective throats of the community.

Tomecek suggested that the people of New Jersey tell the Governor that

Marburger's primary job was to promote education, and that he should concentrate his efforts on working with the many dedicated teachers and administrators, especially on the education of the poor of the cities. He asked for more local participation, for questioning candidates how they felt about neighborhood schools, for asking whether schools with many non-whites have to be bad, and for asking what the candidates would do to promote proper education of the poor. He urged the public not to believe in promises, but to look at voting records.

In the ensuing general discussion, many topics were brought up. Jaffe first explained her participation at the earlier mentioned meeting with Commissioner Marburger in Morristown. She said that all kinds of legislation generally thought to be of benefit to New Jersey schools is passed in Trenton and Washington, without consideration of the effect on the local School Boards.

Richard Marashlian said the basis for the success of the busing plan seemed to be social, not educational, and Andy Downie felt the success or failure of the busing proposal should be based on the experience of a year's time, rather than six weeks. Mrs. Harry Dee felt that Tomecek was trying to undermine the public's faith in the Verona Board of Education, to which he replied that he was elected to help the students at the bottom of the ladder, and found the only way to get results was to bring things into the public meeting.

The Mancuso Report, which focused on the possible consolidation of school districts, was questioned by D. E. Jordan, and Jaffe pointed out that the Committee's recommendations were not the law as yet. Richard Meehan commented that people should not sit back or they will not have any input regarding the implementation of the Mancuso Report's findings.

Questions to Tomecek included whether he had seen Superintendent Mattis's report on teachers working with students; whether he had ever spoken with the Superintendent about the people on the Committee for Study of the Underachievers; and why he concentrated on underachievers. Tomecek felt that the cost per student in the top classes was excessive, compared with cost per student in average classes, and he said that this needed correction. He also felt that cities were in trouble because the educational establishment aimed teaching at what they thought the student should know and the teaching had not been relevant to underachieving children. "The education of some Verona children is irrelevant, the same way it is irrelevant to the city children." He wanted to alert the public that much of what goes on in the local community is determined by people in the political structure.

Because Tomecek had made a political statement in a public school building at a public school meeting, Mr. Downie questioned, would he allow a teacher to have the same right in the classroom using his lectern. Tomecek replied that he had respect for the judgment of those who were teaching.

Robert Dickinson wanted to know why the citizens' liaison committee had been consulted on the acquisition of property for administrative offices, but not on the busing plan. It was explained that the Board was required to go to the residents on issues dealing with money, but that school policy was decided by the Board.

Before adjournment, a few minutes before midnight, Jaffe expressed her great surprise that there was not a single comment on the notable success of the Verona football team and its able coaches.

Following the October 29 Board meeting, an October 31 editorial in the *Verona-Cedar Grove Times* conceded that the pilot program had a significant meaning and importance, and should serve as an impetus to other suburban school districts to follow, but it should not be viewed as solving the massive problems of urban school systems. Plans like Verona's were emergency measures, and what was needed was a realistic fiscal reorientation by the Legislature in dealing specifically with urban communities to help them improve their school systems.

A letter to the editor of *The Star-Ledger*, signed by Emil F. Tomecek, was printed on November 5, 1968. Tomecek again charged that politicians were trying to alter the state's educational system, and concluded with the same point he had made at the October 29 Board meeting — that the Sharing Plan had been "jammed down the collective throats of the Verona community."

Barbara Mackey's column in the *West Essex Record* discussed the Coalition of Concern, a Livingston group that had started to study the Verona plan. Lamenting the lack of national publicity, she said,

> We checked with Mattis on a rumor that the Walter Cronkite, CBS-TV, news program had asked to do a report on the Verona

Plan. He told me that a representative from the program had made the request but it had been turned down.

Mackey hoped that in the future Mr. Cronkite and others would ask again and would get cooperation. "Previous experience," she said, "has shown that the children will not suffer from the publicity, despite the fears of many educators and board members," and a coast-to-coast television report would broadcast the idea to millions of people.

On November 21, the Verona paper reported that the Concerned Citizens planned to hold a group of meetings in private homes to study local attitudes and problems. "A lot of people have stated that they would welcome a chance to meet other Verona residents who are interested in the future of our town," James M. Hughes, president of the CCV, stated. "The evening of December 8 is designed to give us all the opportunity."

Seventy-five citizens attended the November Board of Education meeting, a much higher number than usual. Tomecek requested that Superintendent Mattis include reports on patriotic observances held in the schools. Robert Dickinson asked how the projected enrollment figures had been arrived at, and Mattis agreed that the Board's forecast was very similar to one done by a citizen's group. Other than Hrant Yousoufian's question on how the Board decides which books to adopt and Marshall Butler's question on the role of evaluation of the Sharing Plan, no other pointed questions were asked.

In a letter to the editor printed in the December 5 issue of the *Verona-Cedar Grove Times*, Hrant Yousoufian lauded the Board of Education for taking a stand at the November 26 meeting on publicity involving the presence of the Newark children. Not everyone agreed with the Board's position, as evidenced by an earlier letter to the editor by Barbara Mackey (Bakst), which Yousoufian took issue with. The previous publicity, especially the *Newark Evening News* article of October 6, Yousoufian found objectionable, "in view of the apparent campaign to promote busing statewide by Education Commissioner Carl Marburger — in which Jaffe was again involved." He complained that there had been a direct quotation by Board president Hilda Jaffe, as well as photographs of the Newark children, which obviously were taken with the permission and help of the Verona school administration — something that had not been mentioned at the Board meeting.

In the December 27 issue of the local paper, a reflective article stated that "1968 was a time of conscience for many Verona residents, . . . a year in which they found peripheral questions in juxtaposition to moral responsibility." The article noted that issues raised exhibited racial overtones, and "wide polarization" was evident. After a recap of the events of the school year, the newspaper concluded that the Sharing Plan certainly had caused "alarm" in the community over the possibility that State educators wished to "integrate city and suburban school districts."

> One member of the local board who voted against the plan charged politicians with assuming the role of educators . . . [*and that the*] Verona experiment was to be the basis of a similar statewide program. . . . Board sessions often were marked by argument and harassment. Attendance, which usually had been small, now materialized into groups of 60 and 100. School officials termed the working of the plan a success, promising that there would be a report by the Princeton Evaluating Service at the end of the year.

A letter signed by Amy Bostwick, Chairwoman of the Verona Citizens for a Fair Decision, was read at the December 30 meeting of the Verona School Board. She offered that her group, in lieu of a suggested committee of local citizens, "do an in-depth study of the plans for the high school athletic facilities." Board president Jaffe welcomed any input by citizens, but only after the improvement plans were much more developed, and after the liaison committee had had a chance to study the proposals. Another question was the need for office space when a property being used by the school district on Bloomfield Avenue was returned to the town in 1970. Marshall Butler suggested that the public should be notified much earlier in regard to such items. A timetable was discussed on both issues, and Tomecek also agreed that the public should be made aware of issues now, in order to know how to question candidates at election time.

Thus ended the last meeting of the year.

*The initial planning between Verona and Newark had been be-
tween the two School Boards, with some help from the state. But
when it came to the actual nuts and bolts, the work had to be done
by the Superintendents and their staffs.*

Chapter 14

Parents and Teachers of Newark's Hawthorne School, Past and Present

NEWARK'S HAWTHORNE Avenue School
opened on September 13, 1897, with two permanent classrooms and a total seating capacity of
100, though the Newark Board of Education cautioned that there
were only 80 proper seats. The school was erected by the Clinton
Township, which was annexed by Newark on March 29, 1897.
The primary school district borders were at "the beginning of the
western city line, Avon avenue, South 10th street, Madison
avenue, Chadwick avenue, Clinton township line, thence following the course of said line to the Western city line." The report that
year by the Newark Board of Education indicated that it operated

55 schools, of which 44 were owned by the city and 11 were rented by the city.

The average enrollment at Hawthorne during the 1897 school year was 104; salaries for the teaching staff came to $752.70; expenses for school books, stationery, and printing were $651.68; and the total expenditure was $1,084.72. The average cost of books for pupils was $63, the average cost per pupil was $10.28. The size of the school building did not change the following year; the same two classrooms were used in 1898, which by then held 95, but the proper seating still was only 80.

There was a difference, however, in payments to the staff members — male employees were paid more than females. The job descriptions were for principal, vice principal, head assistant, and assistant. The last two positions were reserved for females, while the most important principal-ship, the one for many classrooms, was definitely a male bastion. The in-between positions, principals with fewer classrooms, and vice principals, could be of either sex, yet pay for a man was $1,800 per year, whereas the women received $600 less. The first year an assistant received $475; the salary increased to $600 the second year. An added maximum pay was available, but this was not easy to receive. It had to be certified by the principal and then endorsed by the Superintendent of Schools.

During 1898, the Hawthorne Avenue School staff consisted of Georgia B. Crater, the vice principal; Clara L. Danforth, an assistant; and Ada T. Moffet, also an assistant, who had already been employed at Hawthorne the previous year. The total salaries for the school year was $1,408.87; the total expenses were $2,083, which included the costs of school books for $130.15.

Until the middle 1950s, the Newark Board of Education printed a book-length report either yearly or biennially. In the 1910 report, the Hawthorne Avenue School was described in this way:

> Location Hawthorne ave, near Clinton pl; erected by Clinton Township, (Annexed March 29th 1897); opened September 13th 1897, enlarged, 1900, 1908; classrooms twenty-one; Janitor, F. W. Shortman. . . .

Over the years, the Hawthorne Avenue School populations seesawed between overcrowded and below capacity. In the short time span between 1898 and 1910, not only did the school increase from 2 to 21 classrooms, but 2 of the classrooms were deemed unsatisfactory, with classes being held either in the courts or hallways.

The total enrollment in Newark had increased from 40,619 in 1902 to 57,742 in 1910. At Hawthorne, the total enrollment at primary and grammar had increased from 104 pupils in 1898 to 1,004 by 1910, to which a kindergarten class of 96 needed to be added. The school report complained about the many half-day classes in Newark during the year of 1910; and the increase in enrollment was nearly 3,000, "an increase not surpassed by more than half a dozen cities in the whole United States." The recommendation was for at least three new schools, each seating 1,000 pupils, or an increase of 75 classrooms just for this increase — an average of 40 students to each classroom.

The combined report of 1916-1918 indicated that Hawthorne School, thanks to its 1914 addition, now contained 32 classrooms. The enrollment decreased slightly, from 1,108 in 1916 to 1,094 in 1918. The estimated value of the land was $22,000, the building was worth $199,000, and the furniture was appraised at $9,500, for a total value of $230,500.

The combined 70th and 71st report by the Newark Board of Education for the years 1925 through 1927 indicated that the Hawthorne School had, as would be the case some 40 years later, an enrollment well beyond the capacity of the school. During the school year of 1926-1927, 903 students were enrolled, or an average of 41 children per classroom.

> The condition of the Hawthorne Avenue School and the Maple Avenue School require immediate relief. The Hawthorne Avenue School is a "platoon" school and has, in addition, 3 portable buildings in the yard. There are 6 classrooms in these buildings. The school has 24 classes on part time.

The report does not specify what happened to the 32 classrooms that had been indicated ten years earlier.

The Superintendent recommended that, when possible, the old section of the Hawthorne Avenue School should be razed and an addition erected with eight modern classrooms and a teacher's room.

Obviously, overall school conditions in Newark had worsened, and in 1942 a 571-page report of a survey of the public schools was published, made by the field division of the Institute of Educational Research in the Teachers College of Columbia University in New York. It indicated a lack of space in old and overcrowded schools. A total of 68 school buildings were reported, with no replacement of outdated buildings. Two of the schools had been built between 1840 and 1849, two in the 1850s, and four in the 1860s. No fewer than 70 schools had been built between 1890 and 1909. The buildings were rated, with very few given a superior grade.

Hawthorne was judged to be in the middle, with a fair rating. A few of the complaints listed included substandard lighting, overheated class-rooms with poor ventilation, no modern toilets, and a drab interior with poorly lighted and damp basements. According to the report, the Haw-thorne School and the district it served housed kindergarten through fifth grade, plus ninth grade. While the building was rated fair, the playground was rated poor. Enrollment on November 1, 1941, was 959, with a build-ing capacity of 1,050. Three additions had been made to the school, the last one in 1914; one room was vacant. The percentage of classrooms in the basement or on the ground floor was 6.7. The school served a total community population of 8,696, with almost no increase having occurred in the population during the years between 1930 and 1940. It was esti-mated that 63.3 percent of the citizens of the community were native white, 31.1 percent foreign-born white, and 0.6 percent were black. No other races lived in the district. The population of the 5- to 14-year-old age group was 12.9 percent.

Today, Hawthorne School, a massive three-story building, towers over the neighboring structures. Huge for the neighborhood, built of brick and heavy masonry with many windows seemingly permitting bright light, and airy, high-ceilinged rooms, it looks its age unmistakably. The school seems to anchor the area, holding all the various smaller pieces together. It is located on a fairly busy street corner, with a few small stores located nearby. The side streets are filled with homes, some with boarded-up win-dows at basement and first-floor levels. Across the street from the school is a small neighborhood supermarket. On the other two corners are a very small church and a day care center, which is now run by Marguarita Bush, who had been head of Hawthorne's PTA in the 1968-1969 school year. Parking spaces are limited; cars are parked all around the school where they can. No parking is permitted on Monday mornings on one side of the surrounding streets, and Tuesday morning no parking is permitted on the opposite side.

Esther Elliott, who taught at Hawthorne in 1968, is the current prin-cipal. She graciously permitted me to visit the school several times.

According to Elliott, the school now has a capacity of 500 students but only 450 attend. The student population is nearly all black, including its principal and most of the teachers. This is not an appreciable change since 1968.

Elliott said that there had been several physical changes since the last report. The gym-auditorium had moved, and now occupies the center of the building, up one flight of stairs from the entrance to the main floor. An existing space in the basement was changed to a cafeteria in 1992; paint is peeling from its walls. Near the cafeteria I saw a computer room, and another filled with stoves for home economics.

When I asked why Hawthorne School had been selected for the Verona Sharing Plan, no one seemed to have an answer. But as I continued to ask questions, I came to see that the selection of this particular school made sense.

Hawthorne School was overcrowded in 1968. According to the minutes of the Newark Board of Education, it had the third largest enrollment in Newark, with a total of 1,417 students. First and second graders were on split sessions. Mobile classrooms had been brought in, as they had been more than 40 years earlier. The infrastructure certainly was not optimum. Teachers remembered that during the winter months, part of the school was hot, and part very cold — everyone brought extra sweaters. A bid to replace the boilers that year had been turned down by the Newark School Board because of cost.

An outside agency, Educational Testing Service in Princeton, New Jersey, was retained to study the Sharing Plan. Dr. Stanley Zdep, the ETS scientist who had tested the Newark children before they were accepted for the Plan and again after the school year was over, commented on the condition of Hawthorne School in a later meeting with the Verona School Board:

> the heating plant wasn't functioning properly. Children in first grade were sitting around in their coats, kind of shivering, and paying very little attention to any kind of academic program. So this is the kind of contrast [*you have*] between a ghetto school and schools which you have here in Verona.

Another part of the selection equation had to be the kind of parents whose children attended this school. Vying for the 40 open spots in Verona were 176 families. Parents made sure the children who were selected were ready, properly dressed, and prepared for the bus trip at seven in the morning. The attendance record of these children was outstanding — another tribute to the parents. Even with all the extra work involved, 91 percent of the parents wanted the Sharing Plan to continue.

Although most of the people interviewed said that Hawthorne Avenue School offered a good education in 1968 as well as now, one source indicated that when the Verona program was discontinued, some Newark parents said that they wanted to move in order for their children to obtain better schooling.

These days, everyone has to sign in to the school. A security guard watches carefully during the children's movements from one area to another. But except for the added security measures, not much has changed. The school was built to educate, and while children in higher income neighborhoods may have a better and friendlier atmosphere, Hawthorne Avenue School still tries its best to fulfill its function.

The home of former Acting Assistant Superintendent of Schools Simeon Moss in South Orange is located in a quiet, tree-lined neighborhood, close to some of the elegant residential areas. The walls of his study are covered with plaques and photos, proud moments of a busy and illustrious career. Simeon Moss was born and raised in Princeton, and graduated from Princeton High School. He did undergraduate work at Columbia University, and graduated from Rutgers University in 1941. He then served in the Armed Forces, and after World War II earned his Ph.D. in history at Princeton on the G.I. Bill. He is a well-educated man; his interest, as evidenced by the books throughout his study, is still history.

While Moss was living in Princeton, the Assistant Superintendent of Schools of Newark, Paul Van Ness, broke his leg and asked for a leave of absence. Moss was asked to take over for that year. When Van Ness didn't return, Moss was asked to continue in the position, which he did for the next two and a half years.

Simeon Moss was involved in the early stages of the Verona Sharing Plan. The initial planning between Verona and Newark had been between the two School Boards, with some help from the state. But when it came to the actual nuts and bolts, the work had to be done by the

Superintendents and their staffs. Moss, who was in charge of the Newark public schools, did his best to overcome the negativity of some of the older principals. Subsequently, he recommended several young and enthusiastic educators, including Woodrow Davis, the new principal of the mostly black Hawthorne Avenue School.

Indeed, the total cooperation of Davis may have been the reason Hawthorne School was chosen. Another explanation could be the strong interest of the many Hawthorne parents who were eager to get their children into the Verona program.

Simeon Moss, with Ruby Dixon — the teacher retained by Newark to accompany the children and to help while they were in Verona — selected and timed the bus routes. Moss kept in touch with the parents of the selected children; he regretted that more families could not have been chosen.

During the year of the program, Moss visited Verona four times, monitoring progress and speaking with all concerned, including some of the host parents. His impressions were not all positive. While Verona Superintendent Mattis was all for the program, Moss felt that the principals of the schools were courteous, but not enthusiastic, and that they were only paying lip service to what they had been forced to do. At best, he felt tolerated. But these visits were part of his job and he accepted the slights.

During their trips to Verona, Moss and Ruby Dixon visited all the Verona schools, talked to the principals, and visited the classrooms. Dixon was highly enthusiastic, and together they tried to straighten out any incidents or concerns. It was Dixon's job to keep the children happy, to talk with them, and hear their problems; she also substituted when a Verona teacher was absent. She liked the program and everyone seemed to like her.

After his stint as Acting Assistant Superintendent, Simeon Moss was appointed County Superintendent of Schools, a job he held for seven years. His interest in the Verona Plan never faded.

Moss remembers Robert Fleischer of Nutley, New Jersey, and Julius Bernstein of Livingston — who was the former principal of Weequahic High School — both expressing an interest in pursuing similar sharing programs. But probably due to local opposition, nothing ever came of it. There also was the worry whether the necessary funding was in place. Yet, as the first and only participant in such sharing, Verona was amply paid. It is Moss's impression that Verona actually made money.

Simeon Moss was sorry that the Sharing Plan stopped after one year. He felt the program's duration was not sufficiently long to prove anything. While Moss had been skeptical of its ultimate acceptance, he certainly expected the project to last longer than one year. The failure of the Verona Sharing Plan, as well as ongoing deterioration of the Newark school system, prompted him to accept an offer in a different school system.

From 1964 to 1982, Elizabeth A. Quinlan was the vice principal at Hawthorne Avenue School. She was born and raised in Newark, and lived there until she retired in 1988, when she moved to South Jersey, still keeping in touch with her old friends. A graduate of New Jersey State Teacher's College (now Kean University) with a Bachelor of Science degree, she obtained her Master of Arts degree at New York University, and did additional graduate work for certification in administration/supervision with courses at Columbia University and Seton Hall. Quinlan started her career at McKinley School as a kindergarten teacher. Her next three positions were as vice principal, all in Newark schools, until she retired from the Wilson Avenue School in 1987, after 36 years of service.

Quinlan remembers attending at least two meetings during the summer of 1968 concerning the proposed Verona Plan. She worked at least two days compiling the names and addresses of children and parents to be involved. Most of those who were to participate, she recalled, seemed pleased and looked forward to their school year.

She spent part of one day at the Newark Board of Education, at the office of Mr. N. Potts, who she believes was in charge of community relations. It was during that same summer that Woodrow Davis was assigned as principal of Hawthorne School.

Enrollment was increasing. Quinlan is not sure of the dates when the six portable classrooms were placed in the Hawthorne playground and when the two annexes — one at the South Ward Boys Club and one on Clinton Avenue — had to be used. But only after all these additional facilities were in place was it possible to eliminate the part-time four-hour session classes in grades 1 and 2. The two annexes were closed a few years later, but the portable units remained in use for many years to come.

Quinlan also remembers the Verona High School students who came to the Hawthorne School one afternoon a week, driven by adult volunteers,

for an "after-school study program" for the third and fourth graders, as well as the summer camp in Verona Park for Newark children. To quote Quinlan, "I believe the Plan had many positive aspects for the Newark pupils and for the Verona children."

Marguarita Bush, the soft-spoken but strong-willed chairwoman of the Hawthorne Avenue School PTA in 1968, had no idea why the Newark Board of Education chose Hawthorne as the school to participate in the Verona Sharing Plan.

After the turmoil of 1967, the South Ward — in which Hawthorne School is located — was undergoing rapid changes, as many of its primarily Jewish residents began to move out and blacks began to move in. At the time of the Verona invitation, Bush recalls, the school still had a mixed population, as well as white teachers — some of them Jewish. More importantly, neither Bush nor many of the other parents felt that Hawthorne's educational standards were bad. And the split sessions were considered tolerable.

After they were informed about the project by the Board of Education, the Hawthorne PTA held several meetings to discuss its ramifications. While many thought there was no need for their children to go to Verona to obtain a better education, they nevertheless felt it was a good idea to send them in order to continue the pattern of integration that was diminishing in their school. At the same time, the children would gain new experiences. The parents did not consider that sending the children to Verona was an experiment. Rather, they felt it to be more in the nature of a comparison, with a broadening of their children's horizons. One of Bush's daughters had been placed in a test group, and she felt that comparison testing was probably one of the least desirable aspects of the whole Sharing Plan.

Marguarita Bush, as well as some of the other parents, was an advocate of high standards in education. But she feels that even more important is the help that parents offer to their children. At that time, nearly all of the families at Hawthorne School were two-parent families, many strongly interested in their children's education.

Bush, a former teacher, is now in charge of the Clinton Hill Day Care Center, directly across the street from Hawthorne School. She is evidence that the combination of a good school and strong parental advice works. All five of her children have good jobs, all went to college, and three have college degrees. Continuing with the next generation, one of her three grandchildren is already in college.

Since 1970, Ethel Melvin has worked in the office of Hawthorne School. She remembers that when she started working there, the school was already predominantly black, and it was terribly overcrowded, with more than 1,400 students. Today there are only about 500 children in the school. At the time the school was filled, there were four classrooms in the Boys Club nearby, more in the annex on Clinton Avenue, and even mobile units in the playground. First grade had only half a day at school.

But the teachers, she says, both white and black, struggled valiantly. It was still a good school, with many of the parents active in the PTA and very interested in their children's education — much as they are today.

Her own two children attended Science High School. Her daughter took Business Administration at Essex County College, and Fashion Design at Centenary College, and today she is manager of a retail store. Her son attended William Paterson College and now works for the U.S. Postal Service.

Since 1967, Benny Graham has toiled at Hawthorne School as a custodian worker. He, too, has seen many changes, from a racially mixed school to a predominantly black school. Much of the building has had to be restored or replaced — he remembers that the heating units were replaced around 1972 and the system was switched to oil. Most of the school today is in pretty good shape, except that there is not sufficient money to modernize the playground or straighten out the fencing. For a while there was hardly any money for repairs, though recently, he says, there seems to be an influx of some funding.

It is Graham's contention that the kids really do not have any place to play, nor is there sufficient recreation. But then, he says, the kids of today need more discipline; they are much less polite, have much less respect, and often run wild. This seems to be true not only at the Hawthorne School in Newark, but across the nation, what with both parents working or with single parenting.

Four former Hawthorne teachers — Rosalind Denes, Rosalyn Bernstein-Harnes, Daphne Swaggerty, and Louise Morrison — each taught during the school year of 1968-1969. It was somewhat difficult for them to pinpoint exact events of 30 years ago. However, they do remember that in 1968 the first and second grades were on split sessions. Two teachers would work overlapping hours. One year, Denes taught from 11:00 a.m. to 3:30 p.m.

They remember when the portable classrooms arrived; each truck brought one half, and then workers put them together. None of these temporary classrooms had toilets. During the winter, the kids had to put on overcoats or sweaters to go to the main building. The radiators were difficult to control — they were so hot that the crayons melted. In hot weather, the temporary rooms were sweltering; there was no fresh air.

The main building had its own quirks; one part was always too hot, and the other could not be warmed up. A sweater was a must, depending on which part of the school they had to be in.

The playground was busy; after-school activities were offered, and many of the kids were kept occupied and off the street. They also had summer school.

The four teachers remembered sad and amusing events, and reminisced about some of the other teachers, four of whom had died; one now lives in Florida, one in Israel, one in South Carolina, and one had simply disappeared.

The four teachers did not especially like the white principal who had been at Hawthorne when they started. There were all kinds of problems, and the parents finally formed a review board. After that principal left, Woodrow Davis arrived, and suddenly it was a different school. Everybody seemed to like him.

They remembered Barry Gimelstob — father of the tennis player Justin Gimelstob — who was Hawthorne's physical education teacher at one time. Allen Paul Vishinsky, a member of Manhattan Transfer, and Illio Morino, of *Star Search*, are both alumni of Hawthorne.

The four teachers, all good friends, continue to meet from time to time.

They represent the old neighborhood — two black, two white and Jewish. They remember when the Hawthorne School was mostly Jewish and when it became predominantly black.

Hawthorne Avenue separates Weequahic from Clinton Hill — one side of the street has a different zip code from the other. And one side was more Jewish than the other. The Drs. Alma and Thomas Flagg, future school Superintendents, were among the first black people to move into the neighborhood. Everyone agreed that they were nice people. And all four teachers said that most of the black people moving into the area were intent on seeing to it that their children would make good. They valued a good education, worked hard, and were very active in the PTA.

Rosalind Denes and her brothers graduated from Hawthorne Avenue School, and her older children started out at Hawthorne. Her father had owned a six-family apartment house nearby, and when she got married, she and her new husband moved into the building. The school was within walking distance, but instead of being a student, she now was a teacher. About ten years later she and her family moved, but she continued to teach at Hawthorne, mostly first and second grades, for a total of 45 years. She remembers that when she first started, classes of 40 kids were the norm, but somehow it seemed easier to control such large classes in the early days, easier even than the much smaller classes of many years later.

Recently, a young man who appeared to be in his forties approached Denes in a shopping mall. He asked her whether or not she was Mrs. Denes, his favorite teacher. When she confirmed that she had taught at Hawthorne, he was delighted to have recognized her. He said that he could hardly wait to get home to his wife and family and tell them all about her.

Rosalyn Bernstein-Harnes, who had been born in Brooklyn, also lived within walking distance of the school. With degrees from Jersey City State University and Newark State, she taught at Hawthorne School for 31 years. She met her former husband, Lee Bernstein, at a dance at the Essex House. Mr. Bernstein was an elected Council person who objected to the realtors' "block-busting" — a practice in which realtors visited adjoining property owners each time a house was sold to a black family, warning whites to sell before they got caught by falling real estate values. Because of his opposition to this, a movement to recall Mr. Bernstein was initiated, and it succeeded.

In 1963, the neighborhood was still racially mixed, with more and more blacks moving in. A few years later Bernstein-Harnes' classes were at least three-quarters black.

Bernstein-Harnes taught third and fourth grade. When the classes were large, up to 38 children, she, too, had less problems than in later years when there were fewer children in each class. After 1989, the problems really became serious.

During the 1967 riot, threats were made to burn down the homes of all the elected officials. The family fled to relatives, but nothing happened to their home.

Daphne Swaggerty was born on the Eastern Shore of Maryland. After she completed her schooling in Bowie, Maryland, she moved to New Jersey, and for over ten years lived with her sister's family on Nassau Street in Verona. At that time, her niece and nephew were among the very few black children in the Verona school system. She applied for a teaching job in Newark, first commuting from Verona and later from Montclair, where she still lives. Before she even started teaching she was told that Hawthorne was to be her school. And there she stayed from 1950 to 1988. Swaggerty remembers that her first salary was $2,000 a year. She also remembers that she was the first black teacher, and that had created all kind of pressures and problems. But she made friends with everyone.

When she started teaching in 1950, Hawthorne was an all-white, mostly Jewish school. It didn't start to change until the Sixties. At the time of the riot, Hawthorne was an excellent school. All the black families who had moved in were interested in higher education for their children. The parents were active in the PTA, and insisted that the children go to school and behave. Swaggerty is especially proud that her room became a hangout for the kids. She is sure that children appreciate discipline, and she thinks that this is the reason her room was always full.

I showed her the list of children from Hawthorne who were bused to Verona and she remembered Kenneth Durdin, one of her students. She also recalls a visit to the F. N. Brown School in Verona during the time the Hawthorne children were being bused.

Though now retired, Daphne Swaggerty still works, supervising student teachers all over New Jersey.

Louise Morrison was born in Virginia and moved to the Newark area in 1946. She worked for many years as a long distance operator for the telephone company, and then decided that she would rather teach. After taking courses at Seton Hall and Newark State, she started to teach at Hawthorne in 1967, and stayed there until she retired in 1995.

Reverend Lillie Minnigan is a concerned mother and grandmother. During 1968 she was active in the Hawthorne PTA; about ten years later she became a part-time helper at the school, and she is still working there. Call her at her home, which is the same address she had in 1968, and the phone will be answered with "Praise the Lord." Her church is the First Zion Hope Missionary Baptist Church. A gospel singer, she and her choir, "Wings of Faith," also performed once at Hawthorne School.

Reverend Minnigan, like so many others I met, is positive that Hawthorne School offered its children a good education. She feels that it has always been one of the best of the Newark schools. She points with pride to her four children, who all graduated from the school and then went on to obtain additional education. All four children are married and still live in New Jersey, although not all in Newark, and several have built their own homes. There are nine grandchildren altogether, the Reverend Minnigan proudly told me, and the educational process continues with the next generation. Every Sunday is family day, with many of her offspring joining their parents and grandparents for dinner.

But today's generation is different, Reverend Minnigan laments. Many of the parents of the Hawthorne children are not much older than their kids. It's not the same anymore. But life goes on, and so does Hawthorne School, offering the best it can.

Lillie Asarnow was born in Brooklyn. She grew up in Newark after the family moved there when she was 12 years old. She stayed in Newark until she retired as a teacher.

Her three sons are all graduates of Hawthorne School. There was a span of nine years between the oldest and the youngest son. When her oldest child started school, it was predominantly white. By the time her youngest started, it was mostly black. But children, she said, really do not see skin color. When she finally decided to leave Newark, her youngest son wanted to complete his schooling at Newark's Art High School, a prestigious and very selective school.

Lillie Asarnow had been active in the PTA, at one time its president. During 1968, Asarnow worked part time in the office of Hawthorne School, while at night she continued her education at Newark State. While she was working at the office, she heard and saw what was going on, and heard all the rumors and scuttlebutt. She remembers writing a term paper about the Verona busing plan, but did not keep it.

Asarnow knew there had been considerable talk about the parents of the children who were bused to Verona. It must have been a tremendous effort to get the children up, scrub and dress them, feed them, and get them to the bus before seven in the morning, regardless of the weather. And no doubt the children were tired at the end of the day, arriving home late, with little daytime left to play or prepare homework. Despite that, the parents still wished their children to participate.

Even more than the children's own parents, Asarnow believed that the host parents in Verona were greatly admired. Everyone was amazed at the love, devotion, and care showered on these children by the host families. This made a deep impression.

There was great dismay when the Sharing program was discontinued after only one year. It was Asarnow's impression that the bused children were like lost sheep. For a whole school year, they had lost a great deal of contact with their previous schoolmates and friends. They arrived too late and often too tired in the evenings to go out and play, especially during the short days of winter. The children felt disoriented and threatened in their own neighborhoods; it was very hard on them. There was talk that many of the parents had started to look for other towns to move to. Their children had had a taste of better schools, and a better life — and parents wanted the best for their own.

Lillie Asarnow taught at Hawthorne School until the 1980s.

Every week the local newspaper was filled with letters to the editor, each making points in support of either Butler or Hartke in the forthcoming School Board election. Those who took the time to write represented a cross section of the population, but neither ethnic nor economic considerations seemed to play a part.

Chapter 15

Butler *vs.* Hartke — The Election

EBRUARY 11, 1969, was the date set for the annual Verona School Board election. More specifically, as the *Verona-Cedar Grove Times* headlined as early as January 16, "SHARE PLAN SEEN AS PRIME ISSUE."

On January 9, the local paper made it clear that two of the three candidates had "indicated their support of the Sharing Educational Opportunities Plan." As his first statement, Bill Hartke, one of the new candidates, submitted a transcript of the remarks he had made at the May 13 meeting. Aaron Kriegel, another candidate, termed the Plan "morally necessary and a politically forthright experiment."

Originally three candidates had declared themselves, but Kriegel soon withdrew, not wanting to split the pro-vote. This gave the electorate a clear choice. Marshall A. Butler, associate director of the evening division at Montclair State University, declared that as an elected official he "would find it impossible to deny a mandate by the people — as was the petition for a referendum — to put such a proposal with such far reaching implications, unclear goals, unstated objectives and undefined methods, up for referendum."

In his prepared statement, Butler suggested that those who accepted the Sharing Plan had done so emotionally, with inadequate information regarding the students involved or the educational objectives. He did not feel that the program would solve any of the problems of the urban schools — over-crowding, the need for teachers and administrators with abilities to stimulate and motivate, funds for facilities, socio-economic conditions, housing and linguistic barriers. Butler, who claimed to have attended every meeting of the Board of Education since the previous February (the Sharing Plan had not been announced until April 30 that year) stated that he was "appalled at the unavailability of information relative to this 'Plan'," and attacked the opposing candidate for advocating its "continuance . . . in complete disregard for the conditions under which it was implemented, two of which conditions could have a major effect on the education of Verona children." He questioned whether the Plan would be continued if federal funds dried up, and wondered whether there would be sufficient open space during the next school year.

> The board, by its refusal to submit this proposal to referendum, has in effect implied they are our elected officials and in this particular instance . . . [*the citizens of Verona*] are not intelligent or rational enough to weigh the facts and draw a fair, just, honest conclusion regarding the fate of the proposal.

In contrast, the previous week, Bill Hartke had stated that he was heartened by the many who had called with questions to the special phone he had installed:

> . . . it's time for us to go on record as a community of people who care enough to help those in unfortunate circumstances to

better themselves through education, to relieve the congested, mean educational facilities of Newark so that these children may have an opportunity to join the main stream of American life and not to follow their parents into further economic despair or onto the relief rolls.

A meeting on December 8, which had been organized by the Concerned Citizens of Verona, was not reported by the local paper until January 16. However, more than 250 people had attended the opening session at the Presbyterian Church, where Reverend D. C. Rice spoke on "Human Relations in the Suburbs." After the talk, pre-assigned groups went to different homes to discuss town attitudes and problems. The findings, as reported on January 16, were based on the summaries of the various meetings. Concern had been raised regarding the developing problem of housing segregation in Verona, as well as the difficulty a black citizen might have in buying a home outside the Martin Road-Cliff Street area.

On January 19, the *Newark Evening News* agreed that the forthcoming election for the Verona Board of Education centered around the "Bus Plan Vote Issue." The newspaper pointed out that this might set the stage for a referendum-like election. Butler, the anti-Plan candidate, continued to criticize the Board for its failure to list the goals.

Other than [*providing*] lunch for these youngsters, Verona residents play no other part in helping to solve the inner city problems.

Most of the 200-plus residents who attended the Concerned Citizens meeting, according to the paper, supported the Plan, but were concerned about the divisiveness in the community and "the effects" of this division for the future.

At the formal public hearing on the school budget on January 27, Ed Wizda, in a lengthy statement, explained the philosophy of the proposed budget. Because the New Jersey statutes demand a thorough and efficient system of public education, Wizda said, the Board felt the prepared budget would meet the educational needs of the children of Verona, carefully balancing short- and long-range plans for strengthening the instructional program and improving the physical structures. Each member of the Board then discussed specific parts of the budget and the meeting was opened for discussion. The questions ranged from the need for another principal, to the hiring of another groundskeeper, to the money spent on textbooks and salaries for teachers.

Following the discussion, the vote to introduce the budget passed by three to one. Although Elmer Gustavson was absent, he had endorsed the budget by sending a letter. Emil Tomecek, who had voted for the budget's introduction on January 7 (with no citizens attending that special meeting), voted against the budget on January 27. After the vote, Tomecek explained that he opposed some of the raises, particularly because Verona did not have a merit system. He also reminded the Board that throughout the year he had requested additional information on the educational plan for the coming year, tried to stimulate written reports on various matters, requested written reports from the Superintendent from the High School Underachiever Committee that had been formed, and reiterated his opposition to hiring a principal at Brookdale School. During discussion, when Tomecek was asked why he opposed a principal at Brookdale but voted for an additional groundskeeper, he replied that he was certain what a groundskeeper does, but not certain about the duties of a principal. He had also voted against hiring the architect for the high school athletic field project, because Verona did not have a five- to ten-year capital improvement plan.

The regular meeting of the Board was held the next day, on January 28. Superintendent John Mattis reported that the Sharing Plan was showing encouraging results. Verona had the advantage, he said, of knowing the educational design and experiences of similar programs, and had fashioned Verona's after Hartford's Project Concern, then in its third year, with 13 suburban public schools and one private day school accepting approximately 980 students from Hartford. Mattis reported that the overall attendance record of the 37 bused children was 91.17 percent, that the large majority were working to capacity, with some exceeding expectations, and that there was no adverse effect on Verona teachers' classroom attention and time. In addition, he reported that the children had adjusted socially very well, that it was the consensus of Verona teachers that the Newark children had broadened the Verona students' view of the world, and that previously many Verona children had not been aware that everyone did not live as they did.

In the ensuing discussion, Hilda Jaffe said that there were no plans for an extension of the program, and John McDonald pointed out that any decision must await the pending court action. Tomecek said that plans for the future would be based on the evaluation.

Peter Zales, who had also spoken at the May 13 meeting the year before, asked about the announcement on the public address system in the high school calling attention to a civil rights rally to be held in Newark. Superintendent Mattis explained that the statement had not been scanned beforehand and that an apology had been offered to the local Catholic parish, because several dissident priests from other communities were involved in the controversy. Zales polled the Board and all opposed such announcements to the students. Zales also questioned whether some poems regarding Vietnam were read over the public address system and wanted to know what that student had said about the flag. Mattis explained that it is customary for students to have readings first thing in the morning, and that the student showed proper respect toward the flag.

Every week the local newspaper was filled with letters to the editor, each making points in support of either Butler or Hartke in the forthcoming School Board election. Those who took the time to write represented a cross section of the population, but neither ethnic nor economic considerations seemed to play a part. Many of the letter writers made unusual and different points. And even though there was enmity in the campaign, with rare exceptions the tone of the letters was upbeat and friendly.

In the January 23 edition of the paper, Robert McInerney lauded Marshall Butler "for having the courage to oppose the methods by which the Educational Sharing Plan was implemented in Verona."

James M. Hughes, however, pointed out that Butler's statement "devotes a thousand negative words to deriding the Sharing Proposal and then sums it up as an 'inconsequential program'."

Mrs. Robert Rubin, even though she had never met Hartke, was impressed by his support for quality education, and by the Sharing Educational Opportunities plan. Doris and Carl Erickson were pleased that Bill Hartke was a candidate, and were sure he would "do the kind of job that needs to be done."

The following week, Mrs. Frank McCoy wrote that she intended to vote for Hartke because he "never attempts to straddle an issue; we always know exactly where he stands." Mr. and Mrs. Joseph R. Thomas pointed out that both candidates agreed on the need for better communication between the Board and citizens at large, but that only Hartke addressed current educational issues. The writers feared the alignment of Butler and

Tomecek, "because it was not too long ago that Tomecek was in high dudgeon because other board members had the audacity to discuss public matters without clearing their comments with him!"

In that same issue, Richard Marashlian, backing Marshall Butler, was "impressed by his refusal to let the busing question become the end-all of the current discussions," as well as his "promise to be more responsive to the will of the voters." Mr. and Mrs. V. Maglione objected to a previous letter, which they felt had been "a diatribe against a candidate, a letter strongly reproaching negativism which is itself couched in such negative terms that it offers no positive thoughts." They ended the letter with, "May the best man win, and Marshall Butler, good luck!"

Edward F. and Barbara A. Newkirk wanted their candidate to be a man of integrity, sensitive to the opinions of the people who elected him, willing to try innovative educational ideas after evaluations, well versed in the problems of education, keenly aware of the financial burden education imposes on the citizens, and someone whose own young children were in the school system. They felt these criteria described Marshall Butler.

Lawrence Hill wrote that he had gone to the office of the Board of Education to obtain details on the budget to be voted on, and was told that the information they had was the same as printed in the local newspaper. This reply, and his observation of several Board meetings, gave Hill the impression that the present Board disclosed as little information as possible. He therefore endorsed Butler, who "is not a picked man and who will not become a rubber stamp." Marie Kraeutler supported Butler because he was "the kind of man who would give the people credit for being mature enough to give support when fully informed, and can fully believe those to whom they have given authority." Sharon Leedham was sure that once Marshall Butler was elected "our community will have taken a giant step forward to achieve a better school system for all our children." At a Board meeting, she had queried his opposition to the Sharing experiment, and Butler replied that this was not an experiment, because there was no control group for comparing academic progress, and there had been no pretesting of attitudes or aptitudes before the children came to Verona. Further, he had told her, testing after two months would be meaningless, because by that time the children might have undergone significant changes. That was why he had thought the Plan was poorly conceived and poorly managed, and he claimed that if it had been done properly, it could have provided data to aid all 100,000 children in Newark.

The Board's proposed budget was under discussion as well, and Mrs. Robert Linde, former PTA president of one school, supported the budget, while Susan B. Sandler took the Citizens and Taxpayers League to task for "using irrelevant comparisons and half-truths." According to Sandler, Verona's school costs were rising at a lower rate than all of the neighboring communities; she, too, had examined the administrative costs of Montclair versus Verona, and had come to a different conclusion than the Taxpayers League. Also of importance, she compared the 40-point increase in the tax rate in Montclair to the 24 points in Verona, and concluded that "an atmosphere of hostility to educators and school boards benefits no one. . . ." Renee Olinger also questioned the veracity of the statement by the Taxpayers League.

One of the longest letters was written by Richard J. Meehan, who compared communication problems perceived by the governing body of the borough with those of the Board of Education. In two instances cited, he claimed that the Mayor and Council had offered concerned citizens an opportunity to question them on specific matters, and therefore seemed to have "recognized the communications gap in Verona, and have moved rapidly and constructively to build bridges to the citizens of Verona." Meehan compared these small gatherings with the 2,300 residents who had signed a request for a petition, which was ignored by the Board of Education, and said that the Board "in fact told the citizens 'we will dictate what is right for the people'."

Constantine Kallas quoted from Richard Nixon's inaugural address, that America was suffering from a "fever of words; from inflated rhetoric that promises more than it can deliver; from angry rhetoric that fans discontents into hatreds. . . . We cannot learn from one another until we stop shouting to one another . . . ." These words helped Kallas decide to vote for Bill Hartke.

The letters continued to pour in, and many more were printed in the *Verona-Cedar Grove Times* issue of February 6. Mr. and Mrs. J. A. Daar were "appalled at the prospect of further property tax increases mainly due to the highly extravagant administrative practices of all but one member of the present school board." They felt that Verona had been a highly desirable community prior to the advent of the present Board. On the other hand, Bernice Belverio supported the budget "so that the high goals we have for education can be accomplished." Norman H. Butt applauded the directors of the Citizens and Taxpayers League for its fine statement on the school budget, and also reminded the taxpayers that "our Board of Education has already lit the fuse on a time bomb expected to go off sometime in May. I refer to the proposed expansion of athletic facilities at the high school, the cost of which is fast approaching the million dollar mark." The Brookdale Avenue PTA Executive Board, however, in support of the budget, noted that the 11 percent increase was one of the smallest of the neighboring communities.

Donald "Zeke" Zukosky believed that "Marshall Butler is just the man we need to bring harmony to the present Board of Education." He assured everyone that he was not a racist, and he supported sending underprivileged children from ghettos in New York into the suburbs each summer.

> During the past two years our family has been privileged to have a Negro child share our home for an overall period of two months. This has been a meaningful experience because it was one of choice, not force.

Irene Szkryybalo pointed out that there was not a single businessman on the Board who would be careful with expenses, purchases, and profits, and that was why she supported Bill Hartke. Ruth and William Springer were mostly concerned with the quality of education in Verona and therefore supported Bill Hartke. Hank Mulas originally felt he would vote for Butler, but changed his mind because he did not want to have two educators on the Board. Mr. and Mrs. Michael Zichelli, Jr., pointed out that they had been interested in the educational process of Verona for a long time, had been actively involved, and therefore were not "Johnny-come-lately" in their concern. They asked other like-minded citizens to join them in voting for Bill Hartke.

Mary Hill endorsed Marshall Butler because, she wrote, he always wanted to know additional facts, such as the plans for the athletic field, and also because he thought that the busing program was poorly planned and executed.

Richard J. Heaslip, the campaign manager for Bill Hartke, spoke of the many people he met who wanted to continue the high standards of education in Verona and therefore would vote for his candidate. A. G. Calvanese did not want another carbon copy of the current majority of Board members, and therefore found Butler to be his choice. W. Henry Bowman thought that the complaint about "communications" was just a smoke screen for those who did not want to hear another point of view. He supported Hartke.

Peter Petrucelli wrote:

> The professional liberals employing the old Double Standard are again trying to cloud the real issue in the school election. Thirty eight children are the tip of the iceberg, while hidden below lies the destruction of neighborhood as well as city districts. The remarks of Mrs. Jaffe at the last candidate forum was an indication of methods these people will use to gather passengers for a ride on another Titanic.

His candidate was Butler.

Florence Jacobson liked the idea of a businessman on the Board, and also noted Bill Hartke's support of the Sharing Plan. Barbara Mackey Bakst echoed similar sentiments, but also noted that there already was one educator on the Board.

Mrs. B. J. Ferguson opted for change and voiced her support for Butler.

Another lengthy letter, signed by Joseph R. Thomas, questioned the fact that a news release by the board of governors of the Verona Citizens for a Fair Decision indicated unanimous support for Butler, without indicating who the board of governors were, how they were chosen, or how many people they represented. In the same issue of the newspaper, Thomas said, letters in support of Butler were signed by Edward Newkirk as well as Richard Meehan. Both men were members of the board of governors, but this fact was not mentioned. According to Thomas, these men, along with six others, were nominated for the board of governors, though he does not know who nominated them. In addition it seems that the group failed to hold an election, even though it had been advertised for May 23.

> Although the organizers of the meeting had been highly vocal in their criticism of the board of education for not permitting sufficient discussion of the Sharing Plan, they ended their own meeting in one hour, even though no election had been held and their supporters were still clamoring for an opportunity to air their views.

The question, according to Thomas, was who nominated these governors, why was there no election, and if there had been one, why had nobody been told? Furthermore, he claimed, this was a group that wanted "public officials to be more responsive to the electorate," yet did not give its members a chance to elect their own officers, nor did it issue a second newsletter after the August 1968, Volume 1, Number 1 issue. Thomas stressed that none of the groups he was affiliated with were planning to endorse any candidate, and that he and his wife, as individuals, would support Bill Hartke.

Both candidates had long releases in the local paper of January 30, under competing headlines — "Hartke Lists Prime Need," versus "Butler Urges Evaluation." Hartke felt the main issue was "communication through understanding for improved relations" between the Board and the public. He also explained his views on capital expenditures, published agendas, monthly Board reports, and other suggestions for a better dialogue. Butler pressed for "a unified plan of direction through a new evaluation of the school system," as well as equalized classes, integrated departmental goals, and guidelines for teachers to achieve maximum education for all children.

A recap of the issues and status of the upcoming School Board election was printed in the *Verona-Cedar Grove Times* on February 6. It was felt that the outcome of the election would determine the fate of the Sharing Plan. A single vacancy had to be filled, and both candidates had discussed the Plan through newspaper releases. According to the paper, supporters of both candidates had indicated that opposition to the project over-shadowed all other issues.

Indeed, it was be a one-issue election. Of those who went to the polls, approximately 500 failed to vote on the budget expense items, and 400 did not opt either way on budget capital outlay. It was not school matters that interested them, it was the Sharing Plan. The man who opposed it, Marshall A. Butler, garnered 2,003 votes, while his opponent, William Hartke, received 1,070 votes. The proposed budget also lost.

Though only a fraction of all registered voters came to the polls, as School Board elections go, the turnout was huge. A snowy day could have had something to do with low numbers, but the issue seemed too important to deter most residents. The vote that favored the Sharing Plan, in the person of Bill Hartke, was dismal. But even though he lost by a two-to-one margin, Hartke still garnered more votes than any previous candidate for a School Board seat.

Oddly enough, while 2,300 signed the petition for a referendum, only 2,000 voted for Butler. These results clearly leave room for interpretation.

Even more significant was the large number of voters who did not turn out at all. Three months earlier, at the presidential election of November 1968, 3,995 Veronans voted for Richard Nixon and 3,027 voted for Hubert Humphrey — over 7,000 votes cast for the national race. Also, during that election, more Verona residents voted for the local candidates than for their respective presidential contender. Running well ahead of the presidential candidates, the top Democrat received 3,625 votes and the top Republican 3,610 votes. When absentee ballots were added to those totals, 7,394 votes were tallied, out of a list of 8,687 citizens who had registered. Thus, a stunning 87 percent of the population voted. Yet in the school election, which centered on an important issue that ultimately turned neighbor against neighbor, only about 35 percent of the registered voters bothered to go to the polls. Why were more people not interested?

Surely it cannot be blamed entirely on the weather. Did those who refrained from voting have no interest? Did they not care one way or the other? Approximately 2,700 children were enrolled in Verona's schools; many families certainly had two or more children in the system. A sizable percentage of Verona's children attended private schools, and would not have been affected by the School Board vote — but the budget affected everyone's taxes.

One letter to the editor in the February 20 issue of the *Verona-Cedar Grove Times* by J. Malcolm Simon went to the point.

> "Congratulations" are due to two groups of Verona residents. First, to the 20 percent of God-fearing citizens who voted, not for Marshall Butler or against Bill Hartke, but against the terrible sin committed last year by the Board of Education; the sin of showing compassion for their fellow man. Second, to the 70 percent of Verona residents who were so concerned with the moral and educational issue involved that they failed to register their opinions by voting. While I hold no sympathy with the first group, I am more disturbed that the majority of Verona residents are so unconcerned as to allow a minority to attempt to control Verona's moral and educational destiny.

The results of 13 School Board elections in West Essex were listed in the *Newark Evening News* of February 12 under the large headline "School Busing Foe Wins Easy Contest in Verona." According to their count, out of 8,687 registered voters, 3,124 — or approximately 36 percent — went to the polls.

Board president Hilda Jaffe called a conference meeting to re-examine the school budget measure, stating that "Verona citizens still want quality education." The votes on the budget were closer than those for the Board seat. An outlay for expenses totaling $2,467,518 lost by a vote of 1,449 to 1,192, while a request for a capital outlay amounting to $25,180 lost 1,514 to 1,206. The budget was opposed by the directors of the Fair Decision group, as well as the Taxpayers League. It seems that not all their members agreed with them on the budget.

The Verona Board of Education had the opportunity to ask the citizens to vote a second time on their revised budget. During a special meeting of the board on February 13, to which member-elect Marshall Butler was invited, Jaffe pointed out that while the proposed budget did not lose overwhelmingly, its rejection made it mandatory for the Board to come back to the voters with a leaner, reduced budget. The assumption was that the voters had requested a slowdown in the expansion of the school system. The Board managed to trim the proposed outlay by $37,400 and called for a second vote on Monday, February 24.

The accusations raised by Joseph Thomas in regard to the Verona Citizens for a Fair Decision were answered in the *Verona-Cedar Grove Times* of February 13, in a letter signed by Edward P. Newkirk. He explained that a group of people had met the weekend of May 12 to draw up a document petitioning the Board for a referendum. They then held a public meeting on May 23, which was well attended, but had to adjourn after two hours, because they had rented the school facility for only that length of time. On May 27, the group incorporated and named three co-chairmen. The corporate officers named a nominating committee who selected two people from each school district. The nominations were as follows: George W. Burnett, Robert A. Dickinson, Lois G. Leffler, Fred R.

Mahn, Robert I. McInerney, Richard Meehan, Edward F. Newkirk, and Calvin Touw. The three co-chairmen were among the incorporating officers: Mrs. Kenneth Bostwick, Anthony Calvanese, and David Ford. A second public meeting, the letter went on to say, was held on June 19, and the nominees were unanimously elected.

The forces of change are as evident in Verona as in the entire country. Public education is at a major crossroad. The direction we take in Verona will affect our own children immediately. Our neighbors and our country will also be affected by our local decisions. — *Hilda Jaffe*

Chapter 16

The New-Old Board Takes Over

*T*HE REORGANIZATION meeting of the new Board was held on February 18, with only 30 citizens attending. Hilda Jaffe thanked the Board for reelecting her as president for the last four years, but declined to stand for the office again. She addressed the gathering with the following statement:

> The forces of change are as evident in Verona as in the entire country. Public education is at a major crossroad. The direction we take in Verona will affect our own children immediately. Our neighbors and our

country will also be affected by our local decisions. I pray that we do not move backwards or go off on a side road. We must continue to go forward here in Verona. I intend to support the forward-looking actions of the Board and the Administration as vigorously in the future as I have in the past. Let us all work together to reunite the community. The well-being of our children must be our common goal.

John McDonald was nominated as president by Ed Wizda and received all but Emil Tomecek's vote. Wizda nominated Jaffe for vice president, and Tomecek's motion to nominate Marshall Butler was not seconded. Jaffe won with three votes, Tomecek and Butler opposed.

After voting on a few housekeeping items, McDonald, in a short speech, proposed better communications with the public, improved relations with the municipal government, and a curriculum that would meet the needs of all children. Tomecek added that Board members could agree and disagree, but should make an effort to maintain personal respect for one another. He said that although he had disagreed with Jaffe many times, he could appreciate everything she had to go through as president.

Once again, the proposed budget elicited pro and con letters to the editor of the *Verona-Cedar Grove Times*. One, printed in the February 20 edition and signed by Edward I. Barz, pointedly quoted a group he had overheard — who thought themselves enlightened but did not know anything about the school budget — as saying, "as long as it involves more money I am voting against it." Hrant Yousoufian urged a "No" vote, which would subsequently take the decision on spending away from the Board and place it the hands of the Mayor and Borough Council, who might then come up with a reduced budget.

Two letters from opposing camps were printed in the same issue. Thelma Zukosky said she had been shocked at the apathy shown in school elections until two years before and was now elated that the "discontented" had finally awoken "and wanted representation." She continued,

The "establishment" retaliated with their familiar "anti-education" . . . followed by a verbal barrage of new words such as "troublemakers," "disruptive forces," "uneducated loudmouths," "bigots," and "racists."

Zukosky said she had visited the administration building after the vote and "saw the stunned look on the faces of the establishment . . . heard derogatory remarks. . . ."

Benjamin Veal, who had been an unsuccessful candidate during the previous School Board election, complained in his letter that the Brotherhood Week proclamation by Mayor Walter D. McKinley meant very little in Verona.

> Our small borough is divided as surely as the days of the Civil War, and proclaiming "Brotherhood Week" is about as effective as a sand shovel in the recent snow storm. . . .

Veal pointed out that most of the 300 blacks in Verona lived in a very concentrated area, and that

> Pompton Avenue serves the same purpose as the railroad tracks. Get the point local real-estate brokers; some of you can be quoted as saying that no other area will accept us, at least that's what you've said to some of us at the Pomptonian [*a local restaurant*] last year.

If the town wanted to truly proclaim "Brotherhood Week," Veal added, some of the homes should be sold on the open market, maybe even on the other side of Pompton Avenue,

> . . . and just maybe some black folks would like to buy and pay taxes and send their kids to schools in this town, then the kids from Newark could stay away, [*and*]. . . we might begin to have a more "perfect union" as the mayor says.

Veal was sorry that his candidate and the budget had lost.

> To further clarify for any mislead reader, I'm not on welfare. I work each day, pay my taxes gladly, have worked with Verona citizens to improve our community, support the police, schools and my church. . . . Your problem, if you haven't sensed it by now, is how to keep Verona "WHITE."

John McDonald, as the newly elected president of the Verona School Board, outlined three proposals with hopes that they might remedy the "negative approach the Board has had in recent years with regard to new ideas":

- that an agenda of the board's monthly meetings be made available prior to each meeting;
- that reports of the school system's progress be issued on a weekly or semi-weekly basis;
- that a closer relationship between the Board and the Borough Council be established through regular conferences.

"Verona Busing Going Smoothly, but School Election Threatens It," was the headline in *The New York Times* of Sunday, February 23. Written by Walter Waggoner, this special report for *The Times* gave a thumbs-up account of the six-month experiment in this "virtually all white suburban community" as "encouraging," but noted that the recent School Board election had reduced the supporting members from a four-to-one to a three-to-two majority. The plan originally "split residents into hostile camps," though "the animosities stirred up by the original proposal . . . appear to be easing, according to the views of some." But Hilda Jaffe was quoted as saying that there were "still tensions in the community" and that she expected them to continue.

The Sharing Plan opposition leaders, after their victory at the polls, emphasized in *The New York Times* article that the voters had merely expressed their disapproval of "high handed" School Board tactics. Emil Tomecek, who had cast the single vote against the project, indicated that he was not opposed to the busing proposal itself, but rather to how the plan had been "jammed down the . . . throat of the community, mine included." Hrant Yousoufian — who was first a supporter, then an opponent of the busing plan and president of the newly formed Citizens and Taxpayers League — also complained of the Board's poor response to the wishes of the people. The final decision on the legality of the Sharing Plan by Superior Court Judge Larner was expected the following Friday. The article quoted Jaffe as saying that it was too early to judge the educational results, "but the social smoothness of the operation is a key factor in its success and the children are obviously contented and at ease."

Waggoner also interviewed a number of parents who hosted the Newark

children every school day for lunch. Seven-year-old Gail, who had a poor attendance record at her Newark school, had not missed more than four days in Verona, and was "very upset when they called off school because of bad weather," according to her host, Judith Zichelli. Six-year-old Kenneth Durdin was very insistent that Lois Grebe came to all his school plays and programs. Nancy Blakney's youngsters always brushed their teeth after lunch, and after watching this for four days, ten-year-old Joseph Rock, their lunchtime visitor, arrived from Newark with his own tooth-brush.

Superintendent Mattis noted in the article that the Newark children had no adverse effect on the teachers' classroom control and management.

School Board Notes, the bimonthly newsletter of the New Jersey School Board Association, also described Verona's experiment as apparently working, and quoted Superintendent Mattis at length. Aside from the educational progress, it was his impression that the young Newarkers had broadened the Verona children's view of the world, creating an awareness of "the times" that was especially beneficial to the host families. Verona students, Mattis said, realized that children of different skin colors thought and acted alike, and had much in common. He stressed that color had little bearing on childhood experiences, and indicated that the visitors had brought out good qualities such as thoughtfulness and kindness, and made the multi-ethnic reading books in Grade 1 come to life.

Even the election of the new School Board member did not diminish citizen interest in the Board proceedings. Eighty residents attended the regular session of February 25. During the discussion and subsequent votes, mostly on their annual housekeeping chores, all members seemed in harmony, voting together and approving all motions. McDonald announced that the Board would soon present the proposed budget for the Borough Council to either approve, reduce, or take no action, in which case, within ten days it would be forwarded to the Commissioner of Education in Trenton. Other than the proposed athletic field changes, no controversial questions were asked.

The court hearing on the complaint by the Verona residents opposed to the Sharing Plan was scheduled for the 28th, according to a short notice in the *Newark Evening News* of February 27.

On February 28, Superior Court Judge Samuel Larner upheld the constitutionality of the New Jersey statutes under which the Board of Education of Verona had acted. His written ruling, which was actually rendered on March 12, read, "It is, on this 12th day of March, 1969, ADJUDGED that judgment be entered in favor of the defendant and against the plaintiffs on all issues between the parties and further that costs be taxed against the plaintiffs and in favor of the defendant."

The *Newark Evening News* reported Judge Larner's decision in the March 1 edition of the paper. When Anthony Ditri argued that the state did not sufficiently spell out standards that local Boards of Education should follow when admitting students without tuition, Judge Larner reasoned that statutes can only be effective when they are written in broad and general terms. He cited numerous court decisions that confirmed his opinion. The Judge stated that the statute simply gives the Board a specific power and is only limited by the reasonableness with which such power is used. The decision by the Verona Board was reasonable, he said, because no Verona child was denied a better education by adding the children whose tuition was financed by federal and Newark funding. On the question of the referendum, Judge Larner placed the emphasis on the word "may," which, according to the statutes, gives the discretion to the School Board. Otherwise, education policy would be governed by referendums. Judge Larner said if the citizens were dissatisfied with the Board's action, their recourse should come at the time of the School Board elections. The judge also denied that the Board exceeded its local authority, noting that the statute does authorize the Board to receive children from other districts if accommodations are available.

Meanwhile, the second time around the budget lost again, and P. F. Zales, in the February 27 issue of the local paper, exhorted the Mayor and Council to encourage a "constructive dialogue" with the community at large. It was his contention that the budget lost mainly due to the Board's neglect in taking the public into its confidence. Pat D'Entremont, in another letter, decried the failure of New Jersey Legislature to address aid to the cities, and instead handed to each school district, affluent and poor alike, $25 per pupil. She warned readers that soon suburban New Jersey would have to foot the bill to make improvements to the cities.

A letter dated March 4 signed by Mary Hill was mailed to the Mayor and Council members, with a copy to Board president John McDonald. Hill wrote that the recent election and the defeats of the school budget were indications of general dissatisfaction that Verona citizens felt toward the educational system. The letter complained about soaring costs and the myth of quality education in Verona.

> We must evaluate the innovations, eliminate those which have not been advantageous, cut down on experimentation, and concentrate on the task of education.

In Hill's opinion, the basic problems were over-specialization of professional functions, which reduced communication and cooperation; over-acceleration, which put undue pressure on students; curriculum gaps in basic subjects; and questionable judgment in hiring. Attached to her letter were two pages of questions relating to the budget.

Because the budget had twice been defeated, it was up to the Mayor and Council to decide on school expenses. On February 26, copies of the proposed budget were certified and delivered to the governing body of Verona. On March 7, a $58,500 reduction was ordered by the Borough Council. According to the *Verona-Cedar Grove Times* of March 13, this decision could have been appealed by the Board. As part of the Council's review, the budget resolution read:

> Reviewing the budget the Borough Council finds no provision in it for the tuition paid and to be paid by the City of Newark in connection with the Sharing Educational Opportunities Program. The Borough Council believes it should be considered in structuring the budget.

According to the *Newark Evening News*, it was the vote of Mayor McKinley that decided the cut in the school budget. The six-man Council had been split three votes to three. One member of the Council was sure that additional money could be slashed from the budget, while two members were afraid that the reductions would impair the education of Verona's school children. In addition to the Council's budget cut, Verona would also receive less money in state aid, due to a change in the funding formula. Board president McDonald said he was surprised by the decision of the Mayor and Council.

> The split vote is indicative of the fact that the council could not agree on all of the cuts involved. . . . It seems to me that the advice of the board was ignored in that the reduction of state aid was to be permanent and not to be restored by the State Department of Education.

About 100 residents had attended the Council meeting and voiced their opinions. Hrant Yousoufian, of the Verona Citizens and Taxpayers League, and others asked for a larger cut in the budget. The Verona PTAs, and about 900 who signed a petition, opposed a smaller school budget.

All members of the School Board were present at the March 25 meeting, with the Council's budget changes dominating the evening's discussion. John McDonald stated that the friction generated by opponents to certain programs had made the Board a symbol — to be for or against. The reduction in state aid for "atypical children" — those students with special needs — necessitated a cut in that program. The action by the Mayor and Council, he said, "have caused a situation wherein a reserve for emergencies cannot be estimated in the 1969-1970 budget," which meant that the Board would be without sufficient reserves for any contingencies. Tomecek questioned how the cut could be appealed, when during the previous year newspapers had been informed that the Board would buy a $76,000 property for office use. He opposed such an appeal, however. Wizda was for the appeal, because "the first duty of the town is to provide a good sound education for the Verona children."

Marshall Butler opposed an appeal. While he had not been involved in the budget process, he did feel that the cuts would not adversely affect the quality of education. Hilda Jaffe, while deploring the loss of money, thought the appeal too time consuming and that it would be better to face up to the fact that the belt-tightening was necessary. Thomas Sellitto announced that in order to show a net amount in the black, the Board had decided to reduce the budget an additional $6,000. The approval of this revised budget, plus a copy of the itemized breakdown, was moved by

Emil Tomecek, and seconded by Ed Wizda. Oddly, it was approved by all except Tomecek, who was the only vote against his own motion.

By explanation, Tomecek pointed out that the budget they had just approved, except for some cuts, was essentially the same one that was defeated twice at the polls. And he still questioned the acquisition of the previously mentioned property. John McDonald stated that the purchase of the property had been discussed when a $35,000 surplus was anticipated, but, as Tomecek reminded the Board later in the meeting, the greater part of the surplus had now been incorporated into the next year's budget. The balance of the meeting, which lasted until well after 11:00 p.m., was devoted to questions and answers on the budget.

"Share Plan Appeal Seen," was the *Verona-Cedar Grove Times* headline announcing the forthcoming meeting of the Citizens for a Fair Decision. The news release invited their members and the public to a gathering on April 16 at the F. N. Brown School. The following speakers were announced: Anthony F. Ditri, on the recent decision by Superior Court Judge Larner; Calvin Touw, one of the governors of the group, on proposed new legislation dealing with School Board budgetary procedures; Richard Marashlian on the future role of the citizens group; and an open discussion of the borough's recreation program. Pending legislation in Trenton and the future of the local group were also on the agenda. The group also set a $2 membership fee per family and asked for election of officers. It was not stated who would pay for the group's legal fees, which could surely not have been covered by the membership fee.

Several newspaper ads invited the general public to attend the meeting. Other guests were to include Esther Chernofsky from the Verona Recreation Department, Councilman William Venner, and Emil Tomecek.

The *Verona-Cedar Grove Times* of April 17 reported that the Verona Citizens for a Fair Decision, Inc., had authorized their counsel to appeal the Judge Larner's ruling. Anthony Ditri's prepared statement read,

> At stake is the fundamental question whether government can continue to ignore the will of the people and substitute instead their judgment for matters which they were not elected to serve.

In reviewing the history of the court case, Ditri reminded the audience that on August 30, an injunction had been denied. For numerous reasons, that decision had not been appealed. Final arguments had been presented on February 28, and on March 12, 1969, a judgment was entered in favor of the Verona Board of Education. No further reasons had been needed to appeal, Ditri said, and the plaintiffs felt a moral obligation to the 2,300 citizens who had supported their request for a referendum. What the association wanted from the Appellate Court was a decision relating to the duties and responsibilities of a local Board of Education. Title 18 of the New Jersey Statutes had become effective on the first of January, 1968, lodging tremendous power in the county and state Boards of Education. Ditri added:

> At stake are neighborhood schools and district lines. No longer can you as a parent choose a neighborhood or a community based on the location of a particular school, or the quantity of money spent for education in that community, as you can no longer be assured that your child will be able to attend that school.

Ditri concluded his presentation by explaining the appeals process. The Appellate Division of the Superior Court consisted of three judges, who, after reading the briefs, would hear oral arguments. In order to proceed beyond the Appellate Division, however, one of the three judges would have to dissent, or constitutional questions had to be involved in the appeal.

On April 9, one week before the Fair Decision group's meeting, a short article had appeared in the *Newark Evening News* concerning the continuation of *de facto* segregation in Newark. The story noted:

> Despite the fact that the school system as a whole is now 80.8 percent Negro-Puerto Rican, there are six elementary schools and one high school in Newark whose enrollments are almost completely white. Two of the elementary schools whose enrollment are almost entirely white — Alexander Street and First Avenue — share common boundaries with schools which are predominantly black.

This practice had continued even though school segregation as a result of segregated housing practices had been outlawed by the New Jersey Supreme Court. The article went on,

> A member of the Newark Board, who asked not to be identified because of the sensitivity of the question, said that the only practical solution in Newark would be to effect cross-busing, which, he said "would tear this city apart."

There was, however, some busing to former white schools as the population "in the ghetto areas" expanded. The article noted that Newark neighborhoods had changed dramatically in the past seven years: Maple Avenue School, 96 percent white in 1961, was now 95 percent black; Chancellor Avenue School, 98 percent white in 1961, was now 91 percent black.

The Verona Citizens for a Fair Decision appeal was filed by Anthony Ditri on April 17, 1969:

> Notice is hereby given that Amy Bostwick, *et als.*, plaintiff-appellants, appeal to the superior court, appellate division, from the whole of the final judgment entered by the superior court, law division, Essex County, in the above entitled matter in favor of Board of Education of Verona, defendant-respondent, on the 12th day of March, 1969.

After the elections, School Board meetings continued to be well attended and contentious. During the April 29 meeting, Emil Tomecek again moved to authorize Superintendent John Mattis to furnish written reports to any Board member who requested them. The motion lost by a two-to-two vote, with Marshall Butler and Tomecek voting in favor, but Ed Wizda abstaining. He was worried that the Superintendent would be too busy supplying reports to the schools. Another resolution, to have public meetings taped, was tabled in order to investigate what "machinery was needed, what effect it would have on a meeting, how beneficial it would be, and how widely used it is in other towns."

The Sharing Plan had not been publicly discussed for some time. But it came up during the April meeting when the contract with the Educational Testing Service was questioned. Although the testing procedure had been worked out earlier, both Newark and Verona had insisted on safeguards, and that took additional time. Newark, the prime signer, was paying for this service, but Verona entered into the contract "to protect the Verona Board's rights, to insure that the testing would be done properly and the result used properly." Hilda Jaffe explained the contract, stated that the final draft was dated December 19, and that it had been formally signed on January 20, 1969.

Not satisfied with that explanation, Tomecek asked when the public was informed of the signing of the final contract, when the Board was informed, and when the authorization was given to the president to sign this contract.

When the question was opened for discussion, Patricia Meehan asked if there had been any testing of the Newark children prior to their arrival in Verona. Superintendent Mattis explained that testing had been done two weeks after the school opening. In answer to another question, Mary Hill was told that the control group had been selected at random, and that it was doubtful that, as she had heard, $60,000 had been spent on the bused Newark children. Hill then asked if "the same thing could not have been done" in Newark with this amount of money. John McDonald replied that this would be up to the Newark Board. Richard Meehan asked whether the Verona Board had started discussing the renewal of the Sharing Educational Opportunities plan and McDonald told him that the Board had asked for reports. Meehan also wanted clarification on how the Mancuso Report would affect Verona, and Jaffe explained that the State Department of Education needed to consider this report first and then hold hearings.

During the spring of 1969, Hilda Jaffe made headlines again by winning an award from the Essex County Teachers Association at their 31st annual legislative dinner. She was cited for making the "outstanding contribution to education by a layman." The organization chose Jaffe for the honor because of her outstanding contribution to education in Verona and outside her own community, through her committee work with the Essex County Associated Boards of Education and the State Federation of School Boards of Education.

She also was praised for her leadership role in the Sharing Educational Opportunities program of Verona.

A newspaper story listed her accomplishments:

- first elected to Verona Board of Education, 1962;
- reelected to two additional three-year terms, 1965 and 1968;
- president of the Verona Board on four separate occasions from 1965 to 1968;
- vice president of the Board, 1964 and 1968;
- president of Brookdale PTA;
- vice-president of H. B. Whitehorne PTA;
- co-chairman of the "Know Your School" study, Verona League of Women Voters;
- member of the 1960 School Expansion Project Committee;
- founder of the first elementary school library in Verona — Brookdale School;
- Girl Scout leader;
- nurse's aide for more than 20 years at Community Hospital;
- Essex County delegate to the executive committee of the State Federation of School Boards; member of the executive committee of the Essex County Associated Boards of Education;
- Verona's delegate to the State Federation of School Boards and Chairman of the State Federation Annual Workshop;
- elected attendee to the conference on the National Assessment Program of the Public Schools.

In a letter to the editor of the *Verona-Cedar Grove Times* printed May 8, Barbara Mackey Bakst complained that the Board was not working together. She pointed out that Board president John McDonald had not received an answer to his suggestion for holding informational town meetings on controversial issues, such as a merit system for teachers and administrators. A request to newly elected member Marshall Butler to outline the proposals he had made during his campaign to open better communication with the public had also gone unanswered.

Hilda Jaffe, in John McDonald's absence, announced that the May 27 meeting was being taped for the first time, and that a microphone would be moved down on the floor for the public's portion of the meeting. Jaffe also read a prepared statement in which she expressed personal dissatisfaction with the tone of recent public Board meetings, and she expressed her belief that School Board members must assume responsibility for working together amicably for the benefit of the schools and the community.

> We must recognize that our responsibility as board members is not to run the schools, but to see that they are well run. Therefore, we must confine board action to policy making, planning and appraisal. We must refuse to represent special interests or partisan politics, or to use the schools for personal gain, or for the gain of friends or supporters. To that end, we must arrive at conclusions only after having discussed matters fully with members of the professional staff and board members at a meeting. Once a decision has been reached by the majority of the board we must support it graciously. . . . The members of this board of education must begin to work together. It is our only hope for bringing the community together again.

What cannot be read in the Board minutes, but was gleaned from the 1969 end-of-the-year report of the *Verona-Cedar Grove Times*, was the contentiousness under which the new Board labored.

> Questioning of previously recognized authority in matters of school administration brought heated exchanges at board sessions, encouraged critics to speak up at confused meetings attended by unusually large audiences. Almost immediately, the new board, which organized in February, became split, with John McDonald, Mrs. Hilda Jaffe and Edward Wizda generally constituting a majority and Marshall Butler joining with Emil Tomecek to form a minority.

Also at this time, a new group, the Verona sector of the Education Task Force, under the chairmanship of Mrs. Howard Kastner, held a series of meetings which culminated in the announcement of the six-week summer recreational program of games, sports, dramatics, arts and crafts, and other activities to be organized for the Newark children who had participated in the Sharing program. Most of these activities were held in Verona Park; Father Francis Carey offered Our Lady of the Lake Church across the street from the park for indoor activities and rainy days. More than 30 Verona mothers volunteered for every Tuesday and Thursday starting July 1.

The children, selected by the principal of the Hawthorne Avenue School from among the second- through fifth-grade students, arrived at 9:30 a.m. and returned to Newark at 2:30 p.m. The coordinator of Volunteer Services for the Newark Board of Education made all arrangements for the bus. Many of the children of the Verona volunteer mothers were to be included in the program, while older Verona students would act as aides to adult leaders. Lunch sandwiches would be provided by a special committee of volunteers headed by Mrs. Robert Kiernan.

. . . We signed up at the first opportunity to become a host family. We were proud that our little town of Verona cared about the problems of inner city education and we were proud to be able to be a part of the "Sharing Program." — Ann Buckley

Chapter 17

Memories: Teachers, Parents, and Volunteers

*S*OME OF THE stories of those directly involved in the Verona Sharing Plan are touching. More important, these "slice of life" anecdotes prove that children are children. Some were aloof and others were friendly; some were lonesome and some were not. Credit must be given to Verona residents. No one, not even those who opposed the Plan, had harsh words with the guest children. They may have stopped talking to the host families, they may have frowned upon their own children becoming too friendly with the children from Newark, but nobody ever bothered one of the visitors.

Nancy Edelhausser, one of the Verona teachers, stated,

From my vague recollection, the two Newark children in my first grade adjusted nicely to a daily routine and enjoyed and were enjoyed by their classmates. Due to the early hour and long trip from Newark, the two, at times, fell asleep during the day.

Doreen Weiler, another Verona teacher, did not have any of the Newark children in her class. She remembers the principal telling the teachers that they would not have to spend any additional time in school due to the Sharing program. That held true, except for several times when the driver called that the bus had broken down, and one of the teachers would volunteer to stay with the children.

Ann Buckley, a Verona mother, wrote:

> At the time the program began, we were a family of six. . . . Jim, the Dad; Mike, 7, second grade, F. N. Brown School; Ann, the Mom; Kathy, 6, first grade, F. N. Brown School; Stephen, almost 4, at home; Maureen, 9 months, at home.
>
> Our church affiliation was Our Lady of the Lake. We participated in the Walk for Understanding and were active in many living room dialogues with good peoples of all faiths from the various churches in the Verona area.
>
> On Thursdays, the children and I participated in the "Summer Program," helping out with lunch and games. All I can remember about that program was the laughter and happy noise from all the children playing together. Children doing what they do best — being children, having fun together, regardless of the difference in color.
>
> Jim and I were immediately in favor of the proposal of the Board of Education to bring a small group of children from Newark to Verona and we signed up at the first opportunity to become a host family. We were proud that our little town of

Verona cared about the problems of inner city education and we were proud to be able to be a part of the "Sharing Program."

THE FIRST DAY: I walked to F. N. Brown school with Stephen and little Maureen in a stroller to meet our new child, April Nunnally. April was in the first grade with our daughter, Kathy. As I approached the school, there were two groups of women (parents), those waiting to meet their new child and to bring him or her home for lunch, and a group milling about to watch and also to make some unkind comments. As I recall, these comments were directed at the Verona moms and the Verona children, NOT the children from Newark.

When we got to [*our street*] there were a few neighbors gathered to watch us walk . . . home for lunch. These neighbors talked among themselves and did not yell anything at my family as we walked on. I escorted the children to and from lunch for about two weeks and then stopped, as there were no longer little groups of people that were staring.

Our first grader, April, was a darling girl. She was always impeccably dressed with matching ribbons on her pig tails. She loved chocolate milk and had it every day. She fit into our family easily and was never a bit of trouble at any time. We had the pleasure of her visits weekends until the program was canceled. April was lots of fun, friendly and had a great laugh.

April appeared to love the atmosphere of being in Verona: the playground and the library at the Brown school; Verona Park; our back yard [*swing set*] playhouse, grass.

And I can remember that April was totally awed by the Verona pool. She just couldn't get over the size or its beauty.

April fit in perfectly with . . . Kathy's friends. I feel that because Kathy was only six she was still at home most of the time and we knew her friends and their parents. These parents were supportive of the Sharing Program. April was just as quick intellectually as any of these little girls and I never noticed any difference whatsoever.

Now our son Mike, who was in second grade and very athletic, was just beginning to play with friends away from the neighborhood and at Brown after school. He was directly affected by [*our*] family having April at our house. He had two friends who he was very close to, and after April came to our home, he was never invited to their houses to play again. And they were not able to come to our house . . . again. However, I am happy to say that at school they were the best of buddies.

Steve, at almost four, was not affected at all, and I feel that the credit for this must go to my neighbors, the Fords, the Grassos, the DeGeronimos, who may have thought that Jim and I were too liberal, but they always treated Steve like the little child he was. I can remember one altercation that Steve got into. I got [*a*] phone call. . . . I dashed up the street and the four adults there acted in a loving way, and the situation was resolved. . . . I had to discipline Steve because he did something stupid, but there were no repercussions. After lunch, it was play as usual.

Maureen, as a baby, was not at all involved.

Now about Jim and myself. . . . I was never a part of the coffee group again. Jim and I were never invited to the "get-togethers." Even though [*ours*] was a very small dead-end street, the cohesiveness was gone.

But on the positive side, our neighbors were never vocally antagonistic to Jim or to our dear children, or to April, our dear guest. A hello or a wave was always responded to.

. . . My close neighbors were and are very good people and honestly felt threatened by the Sharing Program, and they also felt that it was being jammed down their throats by a liberal upper middle class Board of Education that had no clue what it was like to be able to live in a suburban town like Verona, the sacrifices, etc. They truly . . . felt that they had no voice whatsoever. It was a done deal, so to speak. I often wonder if more time should have been spent in discussion and explanation [*of*] the issue of monies [*and*] the Newark children, the exact nature of what was going to happen, etc. It was only four months after the initial proposal that the program was implemented. I really think that the rapidity of the implementation of the "Sharing Program" increased and heightened the fears and the anxieties of many of the good people of Verona.

Now, today, whenever I see my old neighbors, we hug and

kiss and exchange very warm greetings and wishes for good health, etc.

. . . This experience made me really think about what I wanted the children to know and to experience about people who were "different." I did not find the decision to attend the March for Understanding an easy thing to do. After all, I had a four-month-old in a carriage. I joined in the belief that it was time for people of good faith to stand and hope for awareness that the blacks of America had suffered enough.

The experience also made me so very thankful for the green grass in Verona, the schools, the pool, etc. I must say that the experience also increased my understanding [*and*] empathy for my dear neighbors . . . as to why they were so . . . afraid of the "Sharing Program." I also learned . . . that in taking a stand there was a potential for growth as human being.

THE CHILDREN: A childhood experience is at best fuzzy. But from [*their*] Mom's point of view [*they learned*]. . . . Stand up for an ideal; real friends; learning about a different culture; tolerance and respect of neighbors; being polite and respectful of others; saying hello; always being polite; [*and*] family togetherness.

I . . . have no negative thoughts or feelings about the experience. I view this time as a very special . . . period in my life and that of my family, and I only wish that the program could have continued because the children, [*who are*] our future, and the children in the Inner Cities (Newark) are being short changed. Children are children.

ADDENDUM: April lived in a well-kept home on the Newark-Irvington border. The neighborhood was NOT run down. It appeared that a grandmother was in charge of the home, as she was the one that I had telephone contact with whenever this was necessary. April had three brothers. When we arrived at her house to pick her up or to drop her off, these young men quickly left the front porch or the living room. It was very obvious that our presence was upsetting to them. After the program ended, our contact with April ended too.

April Nunnally still remembers her short year in Verona, and was happy to have contact again with the Buckley family. On her daily bus ride to Verona she met Elvira Miller, and to this day they are still friends. Elvira went to F. N. Brown School, but does not remember the name of her hosts.

I spent considerable time trying to find some of the children and their parents, but failed, even though the Hawthorne School had provided some names and addresses. After a short article in Newark's *Star-Ledger* on my quest, Jeremiah Kelly called. He still is friendly with Joseph Rock, another of the bused children, and both remember their year in Verona. Laurette Hamilton was a student at Brookdale, which had the smallest number of Newark children. She only vaguely remembers her host, but does recall a birthday party and going ice skating. Despite efforts to find out what happened to the rest of the children, the above were the only ones found.

Jack and Lois Grebe remember Kenneth Durden as a very vivacious, very active, always-on-the-go first grader, who just enjoyed life. His older sister, Connie, also was one of the students bused into Verona.

In the beginning the boy always wore brand-new clothing, but after a while, he began to dress just like his classmates. Since the Grebe's children were older, they did not really make friends with Kenneth, except that their son Darren, who was two years older, on several occasions came to Kenny's defense when he was being harassed by other students. But he was outgoing, and soon other children were inviting him for lunch.

Because his own mother could not come, Kenneth insisted that Mrs. Grebe attend all his school plays and programs.

After reading an article in the *Star-Ledger* in March of 2000 that referenced a "Kenneth Durden," the Grebes were able to contact Kenny by phone and reminisced for over an hour. Even after 30 years, Kenny vividly recalled his lunchtime and school experience, during his stay in Verona — some pleasant and some not as pleasant. Ken now owns his own home in Newark and is an architect in New York, married to an African American from Ethiopia. Ken's sister Daphne, who is an attorney, works for the city of Newark in the Cultural Affairs Department.

During their recent conversation, Kenny told Mrs. Grebe that one day he was watching as she was sewing several Scout patches on Darren's uniform. He greatly admired the patches. This made him later join the Boy

Scouts, staying in for years, and working his way up to become an Eagle Scout.

Stephen and Mim Connolly sometimes had as many as three guests for lunch. But it was the youngest, Stephan Johnson, who stole Mim's heart. He used to sit on her lap, cuddle up, and read to her. Sometimes he used to tease her, suggesting that she would not believe that he knew a specific word.

The older two boys were much more quiet, aloof, and difficult to get close to. One of them seemed to get into trouble with his classmates and was taunted by them on the way home. So Mim Connolly began to walk down to the corner to meet the boys. Soon the older boys began to receive invitations to other homes for lunch. Mrs. Connolly treated all of them as if they were her own, including correcting them when necessary.

It had been suggested that the hosts not make telephone calls to the children's parents, but little Stephan called his mother occasionally, and then the two mothers started talking to each other. They finally met when Hawthorne School hosted a reception. There were flags outside the school, a large group of black people were in attendance, and they all applauded as the Verona contingent came in. A sit-down luncheon was held and everybody socialized. The principal's opinion was that money was not really the problem in Newark, but rather that he needed better teachers; he blamed the tenure system. It was a day Mrs. Connolly would not forget.

But she would rather forget the problems in Verona caused by many of her friends, acquaintances, and neighbors, who were quite upset that the Connollys hosted black children. She lost a good friend who berated her in the kitchen of the Episcopalian Church. But Mim Connolly was never sorry for the experience, and she still thinks of little Stephan.

Reggie Klein was already a school teacher before she moved into the Verona school system. From 1967 to 1977 she taught at Forest Avenue School, and after that she was the principal for an additional 14 years. Mrs. Klein wrote:

I had two of the children in my first grade class, and I must say that they arrived exhausted each day from their very early getting up and the long trip to Verona. The girls, one of them I remember was called Tracy, were generally accepted by the children [*in my classroom*] except for one youngster whose father's store had burned down during the riots. He refused for a long time to sit near either one of the children, and blamed them for his family's troubles.

Sally B. Foster, for 15 years the secretary of the Verona Recreation Department, volunteered to help out when the Hawthorne children were in summer camp at Verona Lake. Her pleasure and expertise is story-telling. Near the end of the first summer, she remembers, she brought a large suit-case full of clothing, and all the kids participated; the girls dressed up, imagining themselves to be princesses.

In Verona Park there is a pine grove between the two paths leading to the small footbridge near the dam. This was Sally's favorite place; there she gathered the children, sitting on the pine carpet, surrounded by the aroma of pine needles. There, in the hush and quiet, she told her stories.

She also recalls a lack of money, the scrounging of materials for arts and crafts, and the devotion of all the volunteers.

Foster's daughter, Meg Slotkin, who still lives in Verona, was also a volunteer at the park. She has a vague recollection of playing finger games with the younger children, and she remembers helping to prepare a the-atrical stage skit.

Years later, Natalie Lipton recalled that summer when she was a volun-teer at the Verona Park program. The one memory that always flashes through her mind is of her on her knees, scrubbing the floor of the cafe-teria at Our Lady of the Lake Church.

Boris Weller was the elected chairman of the VEA — the Verona

Education Association — a forerunner of the union. Originally only teachers and administrators could be members; later custodians were also able to join. Bargaining in 1968 was a courtesy, not a right.

> It was really more important . . . to further the goals of education than to bargain for additional benefits. . . . There was a very close relationship between the Board and the VEA — since it was the goal of the Board of Education to retain all good teachers.

Each Verona school elected representatives to the VEA. The smallest school — Brookdale — only had one member, while others, depending on their size, had two or more. The representatives elected an executive board, which met at regular intervals, usually monthly, moving their meetings from school to school.

Boris remembers well when the Sharing Plan was introduced and its "enthusiastic" reception by the executive board of the VEA. To his best recollection, all members of the executive board supported the Plan, and he does not recall a single teacher in any school objecting to the decision of the executive board to support the Plan. When the Board of Education called the initial public meeting at the high school, Boris Weller prepared a statement indicating the support of the VEA. This statement was important; without the teachers' support, the program would surely fail. But to his chagrin, he was not allowed to address the Board during this crucial meeting, because he was not a resident of Verona. To this day, Boris feels that this was the wrong decision. It did not matter where he lived; he was the elected head of the VEA that year, an employee of Verona's school system, and he had been elected to represent an important faction of the educational system. It was, in his opinion, an illegal ruling, because it was his prerogative to address the Board on any matter. So John Burguillos, the vice president, had to read the speech instead. Some time later, one of the Board members, speaking privately to Boris, admitted that the Board had been wrong.

The days of the Vietnam discussions were the "glory days" of Verona High School, according to Boris Weller. Both sides spoke up, freely and openly, and discussions were encouraged. He doubts that this is what is happening today in either Verona or other school systems. It is Boris's impression that most of the students opposed the war in Vietnam and were in favor of busing in the black children. It is quite probable that the kids were a shade more liberal — or at least more open-minded — than their parents.

No repercussions came from the VEA support of the Plan. The opposition only targeted Board members. Even after the Board membership changed, no teacher suffered because of his or her support for the Sharing Plan.

Bob Neff also was an active member of the VEA, one of the more than 100 member teachers in the school system. The association received a copy of the yearly contract, which they certified after meeting with the membership.

Bob and his wife were active members of the Democratic Party. He told me that as many as ten years later, when district leaders met to select candidates for Mayor or Borough Council, candidates were asked whether or not they had supported the Sharing Plan. Feelings ran deep on that subject for years.

Mrs. Neff, who was active in the PTA, remembers that the Laning Avenue PTA was quite opposed to the move to serve lunch at the schools. Both parents working was not as common as today. Many of the mothers felt that the kids were better off eating at home than staying at school, although not all the PTAs felt the same way. Those who wanted their kids to come home for lunch sometimes hinted that other mothers might just want extra time to play tennis or other "frivolous" activities. So the children had to go home for lunch, and because of that, parents could participate in the Sharing Plan.

For a while, the Neffs hosted one of the older black children, Craig Boone. After the first days, like most of the other visiting children, he decided to dress like the Verona kids. The Neffs both agree that this was a good experience for their family and for Verona, and told me that they would support it again today. According to Bob Neff, "It was an excellent idea, but what we did to the Newark children was terrible."

The family of Herb Babb, principal of the Forest Avenue School, was not so compatible with their guest. The Newark girl who came into their home for a brief time was highly competitive and constantly argued with Babb's daughter. Even at school, the two disagreed vehemently. "They were like two sisters, constantly trying to gain recognition. They acted like jealous siblings," Babb said. They competed even at lunch, over where to sit, what to eat, and who said what. The parents felt that this pressure was not good for either child and another home was found for the girl.

Janet Boeck's Newark guest, Regina, joined her daughter in walking to and from school, but the two did not develop a close relationship. They shared no common interests, played different kinds of games — a friendship just didn't materialize. There was no animosity, nor any mention of skin color as a factor.

Janet remembers the luncheon in Newark, where for the first time she met the grandmother who took care of Regina. It was a nice experience, she says, and she felt some regret at not having met the black mothers any earlier. She also felt sorry for the kids, getting up so early in the morning and having to endure the long bus ride and the strange environment. "It must have been quite upsetting for those little ones," she reflected. But she felt the children had adjusted. "The program should not have been stopped once it had been started. It was a shame!"

Jean Campbell moved out of Verona in 1968, but not because of the Sharing Plan, nor because of the dozen or so anonymous nasty phone calls she received. It was the impending move that prevented her family from hosting a child, but as the president of the Forest Avenue PTA at that time, she not only fully supported the Sharing Plan, but spoke out in favor of it, and she helped the principal in finding host parents.

Still living in the Essex County area, Campbell keeps in touch with former acquaintances, but she says she lost at least one whom she had thought was a good friend. When Campbell came out in support of the Sharing Plan, she received a phone call from that friend who berated her in no uncertain terms and then never spoke to her again.

Russ Nugent has been with the Verona school system for over 30 years. During his first 16 years in Verona he taught fourth grade at Forest Avenue School. Then he was enticed to join the Laning Avenue faculty, where he stayed another 12 years, again instructing fourth graders. When the fifth grade moved, Russ, deciding on a change of scenery, moved with the fifth graders to the Whitehorne Middle School.

Nugent was born and raised in Cedar Grove, just north of Verona, and he still lives there. He studied at William Paterson College, which is now a university, and as a student teacher was assigned to F. N. Brown School in Verona. He was hired and never left the Verona system.

An outspoken Liberal, Nugent well remembers the time when black children were bused into Verona, putting the whole town into an uproar. He remembers when Reverend Walter M. Moore preached tolerance, and a good part of his congregation walked out.

Russ Nugent also remembers Ruby Dixon, the black teacher who each day accompanied the children from Newark. She was, as he put it, a disciplinarian, a practitioner of the tough-love school. She was outgoing, vivacious, attractive, and well dressed — he guesses she was in her forties — and she was a true friend to the children. He feels she was well chosen for that particular job. Nugent also remembers a student aide, but does not recall her name.

Russ Nugent appears to love his job, because he recalls so many of his pupils — even those from 30 years ago. Remarkably, he has kept all the class pictures and can lay his hands on any of them when he wishes. The names of two black children from Newark who attended his fourth grade class at Forest Avenue School came immediately to his mind. One was a boy, Jeremiah Kelly, about ten years old, whose parents came to school to meet the teachers. And the other was a girl, Monica Evans, also about ten, whose mother seemed to be a single parent.

One of Nugent's major complaints was that all the children were rushed at the end of school to get on their bus. The time to make real friends, he says, was not during the short lunch period, but after school was over. The Newark kids never had adequate time to play with their Verona counterparts, to get acquainted. Some kids seemed upset that they always had to leave right after class ended. It appeared to Russ that an opportunity for real friendship had been lost.

Doris Erickson was a substitute host mother. When a volunteer parent was unable to meet his or her obligation, the Erickson family jumped into the breach. They did not have a chance to get well acquainted with most of their guests, but they enjoyed the company. All were nice children, Mrs. Erickson said. They had the run of the house and always behaved.

Doris Erikson was hard put to recall the names of her more frequent luncheon guests. But she did remember a little girl who visited her home. With a laugh, she recalled feeling that the child was very street-wise — a survivor. Mrs. Erickson still chuckles about the many "birthdays" the girl seemed to have. She just liked parties, Doris said, and at least twice during that school year she had a birthday.

This might also have been the girl whom Doris Erickson shared with Gert Janett, another one of the host mothers. This girl, obviously lonely and looking for more than just food, was apt to call late in the evening, sometimes as late as 11:00 or close to midnight to tell Gert she was lonely — her mother was out and she was left home alone. Gert felt that this was a nice child, but perhaps left too much to her own devices. She was, however, always well dressed, and Doris Erickson tried to see to it that she felt herself a part of the Erickson family.

The Ericksons also asked a couple of times if the girl could stay after school with them to play with their daughter Pamela, rather than going home by bus. On these occasions they drove her home. The two girls played together and stayed on friendly terms, especially when the girl stayed over on weekends.

Doris Erickson also remembers one little girl who complained of her mother being drunk most of the time. She had been a guest at the Erickson home early on. At that time the youngster was not able to read. Months later, when she had her lunch with the Ericksons again, she proudly and quite fluently read to them.

Doris Erickson sometimes wondered if her daughter, Pamela, felt left out, especially at lunch, and whether she had some vague feeling of jealousy. This was an impression not uncommon to other mothers, and some wondered whether they paid too much attention to the guests at the expense of their own children.

Not all the Ericksons' friends and acquaintances agreed with their actions in hosting these students, and a few people told them that they had gone too far. Doris Erickson especially remembers one lady who scolded her in no uncertain terms when the two met in a department store. But Doris was as open-minded with her Verona friends as she was with her new friends from Newark.

Doris Erickson met many of the black mothers during the luncheon at Hawthorne School. After the program was canceled, the Ericksons' little guest continued to call, at least for a while. Like many of the hosts, Doris wonders what happened to the child and whether one year was sufficient to achieve the goals of the Sharing Plan.

Marion Peer now lives in South Jersey. But Saundra Robinson, her Newark guest, loved the Peers' Verona home and their large family of seven children. Saundra just seemed to belong; she was the same age as the Peers' twin daughters. A close relationship developed between Saundra and the Peer family, with numerous phone calls, in which Saundra's mother sometimes participated. Mrs. Robinson was impressed by the way her daughter talked about the Verona family and their life. Mrs. Robinson was invited to their home, and she came to visit — a very gracious lady, Peer said.

Saundra was a quiet young lady, and a good student who was eager to learn. When Mrs. Peer prepared colonial-style dresses for the twins to go trick-or-treating on Halloween, she also made one for Saundra. When the program ended, the families remained in touch for a time. Then Saundra called to tell the Peers that she and her mother were moving away.

Judith Zichelli's guest was never shy; she had somewhat of a chip on her shoulder, and was proud of her father — a lieutenant in the Black Panthers — who was in jail. She also mentioned a baby brother, but no matter how hard Judy or her daughter Lisa tried to draw her out, no other information was forthcoming. The Zichellis felt they were never able to get close to the youngster.

Judy Zichelli tried to make the noon meals special, but the child simply came, ate, and left, with hardly a goodbye — expressing no interest in relationships.

The Zichellis had been looking forward to having this luncheon guest, but they felt that neither they nor their guest was enriched by the encounter. Even so, Judy was aware that the girl, who had had a poor attendance record at the Newark school, had not missed more than four days in Verona and was "very upset when they called off school because of bad weather."

Judy Zichelli had given birth to another child about six months before the Plan started, so she had little children at home and her time was limited. Nevertheless, she volunteered again when the summer program began.

Eugene and Debbie Waldstein's son Mark described his newly found friend Donald Boyer as "looking white." Mark still remembers Donald well; he was very happy with the arrangement that his parents provided — an instant friend delivered to his doorstep. The two became good pals; after lunch they played together until it was time to return to school. Donald was always happy and cheerful, and to Mark he was no different from any other kid.

The Waldstein kids were surprised when, after lunch, Donald carried his dishes from the table to the sink. A couple of times their new friend even slept over. "It was a lovely year," Debbie Waldstein said.

The first time the two boys played outside, one of the neighbors, surprised at seeing the white and black child together, drove into a tree. He didn't speak to the Waldsteins for a couple of years.

During the summer following the Sharing Plan year, once everyone knew the Newark children would not be returning, the Waldsteins invited Donald to come and stay with them. Mr. and Mrs. Boyer drove their son to Verona, and the visit was cordial. When the Waldstein family took Donald back home, Mark was surprised to see where his friend lived. There were no backyards in the inner city, not many green spaces, and the houses were very close together. Mark realized that his good friend led an entirely different life from his own.

Numerous children were always present at the home of Mr. and Mrs.

Milton Klabanesh. Ruby Klabanesh was associated with a foster care program, as well as with a private adoption agency, and children of all ages seemed to be guests at one time or another. All her life Ruby has taken care of children. She still has a newspaper clipping of an interview she gave when Pamela Daniels, of Hawthorne School, was her luncheon guest.

Eight-year-old Stephanie Klabanesh had refused an invitation to a birthday party because Pamela, her Newark friend, had not been invited. When the parents of the birthday child were told, they immediately agreed that Pamela could come too, but because Pamela did not have a suitable gift, neither child went. The two children were good friends and Pamela slept over a few times. She was one of the few Newark children at the Brookdale School.

Stephanie remembers that her family gave Pamela a Christmas present. In return, Pamela brought the Klabaneshes a set of glasses decorated with blue flowers, which they used for years after.

Jack and Elaine Dennis volunteered to host a child, but had to forgo when their two-year-old daughter Sandy needed to be hospitalized. Elaine became a substitute host when Sandy recovered. Whenever anyone had an emergency, the Dennis family was ready to provide lunch to one of the Newark children. Elaine's mother, Unadine Sanger, a teacher at Forest Avenue School, was especially taken with little Barry, from Hawthorne School. On days when he did not attend, Sanger called his home to see that he was okay. Often Barry himself answered; when he did not attend school it was usually because he was babysitting his younger brother and sister. At a very young age, Barry was extremely self-reliant, very bright, and always came to school well dressed.

There is only one story Richard and Kathleen Citrano remember about their little guest. The boy was sitting at the piano trying to play a tune, with Richard beside him trying to teach him. The young man turned to Richard and said, "You really must like me. You touched my hand with yours!"

For one school year after the Sharing Plan had been terminated, Clara Levinson and three companions drove to Newark twice a week to work as volunteer teachers' aides at Hawthorne School. They were used wherever and whenever the need arose, but when it was possible, the Verona volunteers were put in classrooms with former Verona students. The same group of ladies continued their help during the summer camp at Verona Park.

Eileen Hartke, the wife of Bill Hartke — who lost to Marshall Butler in the School Board election — had nothing but praise for Debora Alexander, who with her daughter Karen attended first grade. The two girls played together, especially "dress-up," and behaved like other kids, usually getting along and sometimes arguing. Debora was respectful, bright, and did well in school.

Debora's mother, Barbara Alexander, always went to PTA meetings and made sure that Debora did her studies. Mrs. Alexander always packed a very balanced lunch for Debora to bring. Only after the Hartkes suggested that she could share with them did Debora stop bringing her own lunch. Sometimes Debora was invited to stay over the weekend, and on occasion her mother, who worked in a hospital, joined them all for lunch.

The story they all remember vividly is the time when Eileen Hartke bought dresses in the latest style for her daughters. The new clothes were much admired by Debora. For Christmas, as a surprise, the Hartkes bought another dress, the same style but a different color — brown with pink decorations. When Debora opened the gift, she broke out in tears and cried that she hated the dress. "I am brown all over and now you bought me a brown dress," she sobbed. Bill Hartke remembers sitting with her, his arm around her, consoling the little girl, and apologizing. And then their daughter Karen found a way to heal the hurt; she took the brown dress and gave Debora her own.

Fifteen years later, Debora called Karen and the two girls had a long chat, reminiscing and updating family news. Debora was still living in Newark. She had two children, and was soon to get married. She told Karen that she remembered her school year in Verona very well.

Carolyn Cheatle supported the Sharing Plan and spoke up at one of the meetings. A woman sitting next to her remarked, "You people talk a good game but you didn't even volunteer to be a host." That concerned Cheatle, and the next morning she called the school, and signed up to be a host parent.

She and her husband Walter, a captain in the Verona Police Department, had just adopted a three-year-old son. Their other son, Jim, was seven years old, and when the Newark children came, their guest was to be a boy. Carolyn Cheatle did not remember his name, but thought he was probably a fourth grader at Forest Avenue School.

The boy was very tall and large for his age. In the beginning, everybody at school wanted him to be on their team, but he was not very well coordinated. He tended to drop the ball, and was slow in running. Even so, he had great strength. One afternoon, during play in the backyard, he accidentally pushed Jim, who fell.

The Cheatles decided that with a little child in the house they did not want to take chances on any further accidents. However, Carolyn now feels she could have handled the situation better if she had thought it out. The boy was nice, neat and clean. She felt sorry for him; even more so when later, at Hawthorne Avenue School, she met the boy's mother. He would have liked to continue his relationship with the Cheatle family. And the two mothers had a long chat.

There was only one other comment by Carolyn: some of the children from Newark used unbelievable language!

On October 6, 1968, a photo of Joseph Rock appeared in the *Newark Evening News*. Joe, a fifth grader, was showing off his school books. He was a good kid, polite, whose parents — according to his host mother — were very strict. Girls were the majority in Joe's host family, and the son of the house wanted another boy to even things up. As it turned out, the two became good friends. In the kitchen, where they all had their lunch, the boys always sat on one side of the room, and the girls on the other. Even the two sets of parents got along; once, the Verona parents were invited to join the black family at a Newark restaurant for dinner. There they were introduced almost as celebrities. Another time, both families enjoyed a picnic in a Newark park. Among the games they played that day was softball. It did not bother the host family to realize that most of the people in the park were black.

Once, on his way home from school, Joe had a scuffle with other kids. His host mother pointed out to Joe that he was in the spotlight, that everybody was watching him, and that he represented the children of Newark. There was never another problem.

It was a good experience for all, the host mother told me. She remembered that after the Sharing Plan was discontinued, there were a few more phone conversations with the Newark family. But then the contacts stopped.

Joan Hughes maintains that those days in Verona changed her and her family's entire outlook on life. Politics aside, she says, she is happy that everyone in her family roots for the underdog. Both Joan and her husband, Jim, were in the forefront of the pro-Sharing group. Jim Hughes was the chairman of the Concerned Citizens of Verona, which held a number of public meetings, and Joan Hughes acted as spokesperson for the host mothers.

Both of them remember the night a bomb threat was received at their home. Linda Caulfield, the 14-year-old daughter of their neighbor, was babysitting that evening. Linda called her parents, and Jim Caulfield, her father, came over and sent his daughter home, then calmly waited for Jim and Joan Hughes to return. Jim and Joan Hughes remember his act with gratitude and admiration.

Jim Hughes also served as a juror during those days and, by coincidence, one of the opponents of the Sharing Plan was also on the same jury. While they disagreed on Verona politics, in this trial the two men were the only hold-outs who thought the accused was not guilty. Jim also remembers long discussions with Ed Newkirk, an opponent of the Plan, describing him as one of the nicest people he knew.

During one meeting, Jim was assailed as a "pinko." After a PTA meeting, while Jim was standing beside some friends and neighbors, one gentleman admired his daughter Janice's blond hair and good looks, and then asked Jim how he would feel if Janice were to marry a black man. Jim replied that his primary concern was that his daughter meet a good man who loved her, took good care of her, and was a good husband.

The Hughes family was host to a sweet girl from Newark, who presented no problems. Their son Courtney, who was eight years old at the time, still remembers Daphne as tall and thin and poorly dressed, with holes in her stockings. If there was a problem with the arrangement, it was Courtney. While he was the same age and in the same class, he was also at a stage where girls were ignored. Furthermore, the parents of Courtney's best friend, Michael, were strongly against the Plan. So there was no bonding between Courtney and Daphne when the two children shared their lunch period at home. Yet Courtney and Michael, regardless of the views of their parents, made sure that Daphne was always protected. And the parents of the boys, unlike others whose friendship collapsed, have maintained their relationship.

Courtney's sister Janice, who was nine years old, also remembers Daphne as somewhat shy, stiff, and hesitant to engage in conversation. Neither Courtney nor Janice remember being hassled for their parents' beliefs, although Janice recalls a Halloween incident when the lady of the house where she was trick-or-treating with other kids asked her to go to the end of the line. Janice remembers that she and a couple of others were picked for a special photo session with some of the black students. She is sure that only children whose parents were in favor of the Sharing Plan were picked for the photograph.

Both Courtney and Janice were proud of their parents. When questioned by his father on what he might have remembered, Courtney added that he felt every child should be exposed, as he had been, to children of different beliefs, color, or circumstances.

Joan Hughes was particularly proud of the strong stand her husband took during a strategy meeting with Hilda Jaffe, Barbara Mackey Bakst, Father McDermott, and others. Much later, she learned that Father McDermott thought that while Jim Hughes' statements were politically correct, he should have considered the feelings of the other side in the situation and chosen his words more carefully.

Mr. and Mrs. Hughes, like a few other families who fought for the Plan, all belonged to the Catholic Christian Family Movement. It is Jim's belief that the seeds for the Sharing Plan were sown during one of their discussions, which were always led by different members each time. He remembers that John McDonald and his wife were members, and that the

McDonalds were concerned about the education problem in Newark. Because John was a member of the Board of Education, the discussions of the group may have given John the impetus to bring the problem up at one of the Board meetings.

Joan noted that even though Verona was divided by the Plan, it was a different mix from what had existed before the controversy. Previously there had been little contact between the various religious leaders, civic leaders, and local organizations. During and after the Sharing Plan, all that mattered was whether one had Liberal or Conservative leanings.

The Sharing Plan, however, was the high point of Jim Hughes's life. While he still has the same sentiments, he never got so involved again. He is perfectly happy with what he is doing now, retired and pursuing his own interests, but there are times when he regrets that he has not continued to use his talents to participate in movements that help other people.

When the Sharing Plan was first proposed, the clergy were among those who spoke loudest in favor. But it seemed that although they marched ahead, not all of their flock followed. This is not an uncommon feeling among many Veronans. Whether or not this sentiment was more pronounced in the Verona Catholic Church, some of those who led the opposition seemed to feel it was so. Two of the most active priests expressed their regrets, not for the support and leadership they offered at the time, but for the way they categorized their opposition.

Father John McDermott made a speech during the town-wide meeting at the Verona High School in which he used the word "ashamed" when he referred to the efforts of the opposition. Now, when Father McDermott reflects on the speech, he tempers his sentiment, saying, "I am embarrassed by the word 'ashamed' on my part. That is too judging. But I did say it. I was out of order."

Father Jack Martin had come to Verona just out of the seminary in 1965, and as the youngest priest, was mostly working with children. He remembers that one Sunday a statement was read at all the masses that as part of the baptismal call, support should be given to efforts to grant the Newark children an educational opportunity. And he, too, remembers that the word "ashamed" was used. He also said that, in retrospect, he and his colleagues were right in supporting the effort, but were wrong in the way they spoke to parishioners who opposed the Plan.

Later, Father Martin volunteered to drive Verona High School students to Hawthorne School for their tutoring sessions. And many remember Father Martin leading the summer camp children in song with his guitar.

To this day, Father Martin can quote the May 13, 1968, speech given by the Reverend Donald Webb of the Methodist Church at the Verona School Board meeting where the Sharing Plan was first discussed:

> . . . because you believe in little children you will do it. Because you believe in America you will do it, and because you really believe in God, you will do it.

Father Martin sent a letter to Reverend Webb after that meeting, calling him a "remarkable Christian."

Father Martin still works actively to promote social issues. He is a leader in the Interfaith Community Organization, and the president of the Haitian Solidarity Network.

Joseph Thomas, who at that time led the Verona Council for Inter-Religious Activity, also felt that the tone in 1968 was too controversial and confrontational. He said that in the Catholic Church of Verona, social conscience is still very much alive, that the work still proceeds in soup kitchens, helping the homeless, and assistance to the Appalachian area. But the work is done much more quietly these days — peacefully!

Adele Sunshine spoke at the May 13, 1968, meeting about being a teacher of neurologically impaired black children in Newark. She had stayed there for 17 years!

Sunshine started teaching just prior to the 1967 Newark riots. Among her notes was the following:

> A couple of months after the riots in Newark I started teaching educable children in Newton Street School. The children were poor. My sons had outgrown their winter clothing over the

summer so I brought things to school for my class. Before
Halloween there were rumors of another riot and we were told
to park our cars in the playground that day. The week before,
neighborhood teenagers were beginning to mark up cars either
with chalk or paint. I left my class and walked to my car with
another teacher who came in with me. There were a couple of
boys near my car looking at an angry black woman holding a
broom. She was screaming at them to get "aways" from that
car. "It belongs to a teacher!" They went off. I thanked her pro-
fusely. She replied "I see you bring clothes. I see you go back
with no clothes. I watch your car." Relieved, I thanked her
again. It struck me that we whites were being watched and evaluated.

Sunshine maintained a notebook, and some entries were dated years
later:

Dean came in and hugged me. He had given me a great deal of
trouble the day before. . . . It was a bad day in class all around.
The children were all getting edgy and quarrelsome. Horace
became angry and grabbed the pen from my hand and threw it
across the room. . . . We went through one Gym teacher who
lasted three days and two Music teachers. The first lasted two
days, the second, forty minutes — and he did not have my class.
Now we have two young fellows who will last. I wonder
whether I will. The children fight, curse, throw things —
crayons, desks, chairs, food, etc., spit, run from the room,
refuse to work, assure me that their mothers will kill me, etc.
But they all do their math, they all read, they all write and do
craft work. And I am exhausted — the ride home through traffic revives me, however, and I live to go back another day. And
to enjoy the earth around me.

Even though we live in a democracy and we have the right to differ, it
was disheartening to hear so many years later that some former friends and
neighbors still do not talk to each other.

It is also disappointing that not a single host family tried to keep up with its host child, at least to the point of finding out how the child fared after one year in Verona. Now, so many years later, some of them expressed to me the same regret.

Statistically, the number of children bused from Newark is too small to draw any conclusions about the Sharing Plan. Each of the individuals interviewed was employed; most had graduated from high school, and college courses were mentioned by some. And those parents to whom I had spoken about their children indicated that these students also had graduated at least from high school.

The board . . . has agreed that continuation of a reduced Sharing program would not be wise. The benefits to be gained by those few Newark students selected to stay with the program and by the smaller number of participating Verona children, teachers, and families would be far outweighed, first by the high cost, and secondly by the continuation of board and community tension.

Chapter 18

Rationalizations and Excuses

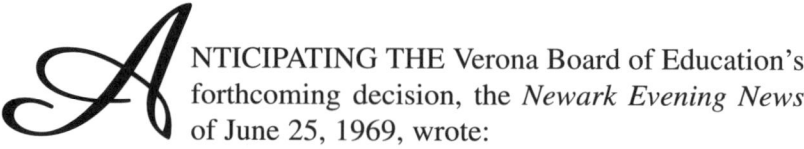

NTICIPATING THE Verona Board of Education's forthcoming decision, the *Newark Evening News* of June 25, 1969, wrote:

The controversial Newark-Verona racial busing plan reportedly will not be resumed in the fall. . . . The reason for the Verona Board of Education's expected termination of the program is believed to be the deep division it has caused in the community and among members of the board.

The next day, June 26, a much larger headline — "Verona Says Space Dooms Busing Plans" — confirmed the reporter's previous assumption that the Plan would be terminated. If the educational Sharing Plan were continued into the 1969-1970 school year, according to the three-page statement by the Board of Education, it could be offered to only "approximately 19 of the 37 Newark children" in order to maintain the Board's mandated 25-pupil class size.

> Since classroom space is at a premium and the spaces may be located in classes at schools other than the school now attended, continuation of the plan would not only eliminate some youngsters, but it would also require some Newark children to attend a class at a different Verona school next year. In weighing space limitations, and faced with the prospect of further curtailment in future years, along with the high costs of pupil transportation and the supplemental teacher, the Board felt it could not recommend the renewal of the contract for so few students.

According to the reporter, Verona officials refused to estimate enrollment in the school the coming September. Quoting unnamed sources "close" to the Board, the newspaper reported that it was not actually the space and cost that caused the termination of the program, but rather the dissension the project has caused within the borough and among Board members. Still, educators declared the project an "apparent success," and the Board statement noted that this decision should "not be interpreted to mean that the plan had been either sociologically or academically ineffective." The release by the Board noted the various tests that had been made and other evaluations that were in progress.

> The board, after considering all of the foregoing aspects, has agreed that continuation of a reduced Sharing program would not be wise. The benefits to be gained by those few Newark students selected to stay with the program and by the smaller number of participating Verona children, teachers, and families would be far outweighed, first by the high cost, and secondly by the continuation of board and community tension.

"Space Need Terminates Share Plan," was the headline in the *Verona-Cedar Grove Times* of June 26, 1969. The termination of the Sharing Plan had been announced after the schools were closed for the summer vacation. The newspaper reported that the Board had also discussed the hiring of the Educational Testing Service of Princeton, and the various tests that had been given in September and again in May to all first- and second-grade pupils in Verona schools and in the Newark control group. Other tests had been given to grades 3-5, and it was stated that results would probably be available by late summer. The Board statement asserted:

> The Newark children, after nine months of sharing classrooms and home lunches with suburban children, feel kindly toward their teachers, their classmates and their host families. The parents of the Newark children appear to appreciate the educational environment in Verona and indicate that it has been a worthwhile experience for their children. The host families have registered positive feeling about the plan and are pleased with the comfortable social relationships which have developed among the Newark children and their families.

The headline of Newark's *Star-Ledger*, also dated June 26, read "BUS STOP: Verona Drops Program for Newark School Kids." On the next day, June 27, a *Newark Evening News* staff writer reported that the Newark Board of Education had termed the decision by the Verona Board "unfortunate . . . especially when data presently available points to the effectiveness and success of the plan." The statement mentioned that parents, teachers, administrators, and pupils — those most closely involved — "agree that the sharing plan has been beneficial to both Newark and Verona participants." The Newark Board commended the Verona Board "for its courageous and pioneering efforts in initially developing and adopting the interchange program."

Even as far away as Long Island, New York, the news made headlines. *Newsday*, the Long Island daily paper of June 26, wrote about the termination of the Plan and quoted Hilda Jaffe as saying, "It was definitely a success. The children got a great deal from the program and they gave a great deal to their classmates, their teachers and their classmates' families." According to this account, the cost of the program was estimated at about $1,000 per child and was paid for entirely by state and federal funding. *Newsday* reported that Board member Emil Tomecek, the only member opposed to the Plan at the time it was adopted, had refused to comment until the Board made its official announcement.

The *Newsday* account went on to say that similar plans had been suggested and rejected in Great Neck, Long Island, and Newburgh, New York. In addition, it reported that Governor Nelson Rockefeller had signed a bill the previous month prohibiting the New York Department of Education from ordering busing of students to achieve racial balance.

According to the *Newark News* of June 27,

> The Newark Board of Education termed "unfortunate" the decision by the Verona Board of Education to discontinue the Sharing Educational Opportunities program.

On June 29, the *Newark Sunday News* questioned whether pupil busing was only occurring in one direction — toward the suburbs. Many of the Newark officials thought that the termination of the Verona agreement only confirmed that there is a one-way street, as far as Newark's relation with its suburbs is concerned. Although the Newark museum and library were widely used by surrounding communities, the article said, little was known about the existing use of educational facilities of Newark by its suburbs. It went on to note,

> While Newark students are not permitted any more to attend Verona public schools, even in token numbers, Newark permitted this year 133 pupils, including one from Verona, into the Newark school system.

Scores of pupils were bused daily from the suburbs into Newark, often for special educational services that only Newark offered. The *Sunday News* continued:

> In the past, and presently as far as is known, there have been no complaints to the Newark Board of Education by either black or white parents that such mixing might undesirably raise community tensions either in the city or in the suburbs from which the students come.

In all, 61 communities had had children in the Newark special education programs, most of them handicapped.

The *Star-Ledger*, also of June 29, pictured three little girls with the caption,

> Three first-graders in Verona talk about summer vacation plans. Because of the opposition to the town's busing plan, only one of the girls will be returning in September.

The caption under another photo taken in a classroom stated,

> Just children in a classroom — but the presence of Newark youngsters in Verona schools caused an uproar.

Two little girls, one black, one white, were photographed standing very close to each other.

> Oblivious to the controversy which has divided Verona, two first-graders — one from Verona, one from Newark — say goodbye on the last day of school.

"Town Split Over Busing Experiment," was the headline in the accompanying empathetic story that noted there were 37 fewer children in Verona now than the week before — the children from Newark, who would not come back.

> . . . The 37 children went to school for a year. They made friends, went to their friends' homes for lunch and they learned their lessons in class. And they learned them well. Three-quarters of the children, according to the Verona school superintendent, progressed academically better than they would have had they remained in the South Ward's overcrowded and understaffed Hawthorne Avenue School. They learned that white children were no different from themselves, they could be played with, that they could be trusted, that they could be fast friends.

The article went on to note that Mrs. Louise Rock of Newark was surprised at the change in her son's behavior and that he did his homework every night. Ten-year-old Johnny Blakney in Verona expressed his disappointment when he heard that his friend Joseph would not be coming back. Mrs. Robert Rubin in Verona thought that the little boy who came to their house had changed their son.

> We live in a ghetto, too, a white ghetto. Our children are growing up in a world that is unreal, colorless.

Dr. Virginia Bennet, an associate professor of child psychology at Rutgers University, was quoted as saying she thought the Verona Plan "is just one more bit of evidence for the black kids that 'whitey' is totally unreliable." Further, if the children were accepted by their peers and suddenly the program were discontinued, they would feel totally rejected by the white society.

> And they will be heartbroken. But many people in Verona feel that statements like that are sentimental, not businesslike, not at all like the Verona way of doing things.

Verona is not an all-white town, the *Star-Ledger* article went on to say.

> There are about 240 black people in a population of 15,000 who have lived in Verona on an average of 15 years, with a median income of $13,000 — compared to the white median income of $14,000. Most of them live in the area bordering Montclair and there is no problem in the relationship between the blacks and the white population.

The balance of this *Star-Ledger* report, written by Robert J. Braun, delved into the history of the Plan — how it was developed, how Verona first greeted it with applause while under the surface the opposition grew.

> . . . Board members now would rather shun new and often progressive programs — not only out of fear for their political lives and private peace, but also out of the genuine

concern that an outraged public will commit the self-defeating act of not providing enough money to operate the schools.

This had happened in Youngstown, Ohio, where the schools had to close because "its townsfolk were fed up with paying for them." There had been a bomb scare in Rahway, New Jersey, when the School Board complied with a controversial integration program. One Board member in Monmouth County explained that no one was willing to take a stand on a controversial issue — Board members now had unlisted phone numbers. The February 1969 *Birch Society Bulletin* was quoted in the article as saying that educational attempts to teach safeguards against narcotics and sex abuse were merely excuses to weaken the fabric of American life by letting young children learn how they could become sexual perverts and drug addicts. And a member of the New Jersey Board of Education was quoted as saying that fear had become a partner in education and leadership was needed — but then added, "Look, don't expect me to be your hero."

The *Long Island Press* reprinted the *Star-Ledger*'s story in its entirety on July 6. In its introduction, the paper reminded its readers of the discussion regarding busing children from Queens to Great Neck elementary schools. The New York City Board of Education had turned down the plan because the Great Neck School Board would not commit itself to a two-year project. "During this debate, frequent reference was made to the busing of Newark's ghetto children to suburban Verona," the article reported.

But Richard Meehan did not like the *Star-Ledger*'s article and wrote to the paper that it was an insult to the intelligence of its readers. Printed on August 9, his letter stated that Braun's article "was composed of half-truths, generalizations and gratuitous assumptions." Meehan took issue with the reporter's assumption that Verona had gained financially. He also wondered whether the addition of a Newark child to a class of 24 had forced Verona to divide the class and hire another teacher, at Verona's expense. "I also believe that this program was a direct attack on the concept of the neighborhood school in New Jersey," he wrote, and he blamed Education Commissioner Carl Marburger and the Mancuso Report.

Some 125 residents attended the regular Verona Board of Education meeting on June 30, 1969. By a unanimous vote, the Board agreed to lease the Leone property, which had previously been a contentious subject as well, for two years at a monthly rate of $400. Board correspondence included two letters from host mothers expressing their gratitude for the luncheon hosted by the Newark mothers.

Board member Ed Wizda could not be present, but he had prepared a statement, which was read at the meeting, with copies distributed to the press. He explained that at the Board conference meeting held on June 17, the Board had received an exceptionally favorable report on the Sharing Educational Opportunities project. Even so, he said, the majority of the Board had chosen to disregard the highly favorable aspects of the Plan, and was against continuing it. He went on, "Unable to find anything about the Project which would justify their actions, the majority then had to seek other reasons for the Project's end." Wizda complained that the lack of classroom space as the deciding factor was incorrect, and claimed that if all Board members had agreed, space could have been found easily for the 37 children, and possibly even 15 more. If a majority of the Board had voted to continue the project, he went on, 25 children could have been taken care of.

> If only fifteen students were to be accommodated, I believe that the program is educationally sound and worth continuing, even if we have to bear another year of harassment of board members and administration.

The Board had also mentioned as another reason to discontinue the Plan the high cost of pupil transportation, Wizda said, disregarding the fact that Newark had paid for these costs, and that the Newark School Board, which would have liked to see the project continued, felt that the excellent results justified the cost.

Ed Wizda went on:

> It is plain and simple, two members of the Board openly opposed the Project, and one member previously in favor now joins them. I do not intend to question their reasons for not continuing the Project, but I do question other organizations which throughout the year have remained silent and have not aided or

> supported the Verona Project. When West Hartford initiated its sharing plan, several other Hartford suburban communities joined in. What has been the response of other suburban Boards of Education in Essex County to Verona's Project? On the whole, negative. Have we received any aid or support from our legislature? No. From the State Department of Education? No. From such worthy civic organizations as Kiwanis, Lions, Rotary? No. Silence on all fronts. We are most thankful for the moral support of the Verona clergy and those citizens of Verona who truly practice the belief that all men are brothers. Without their support the past year would have been unbearable.

Wizda's statement called the abrupt halt of the Plan "tragic," and he hoped that the friendly relationships between the Hawthorne School families and those of Verona would continue.

Emil Tomecek responded, saying that it was his impression that there was less outright opposition to the Plan and less division than there had been the previous year. He felt that if a referendum had been held in the first place, the candid discussions would have promoted broad community acceptance.

> . . . Verona citizens are properly questioning other Board decisions, including mine, . . . and that's the way it ought to be. Isn't that what community control is supposed to be all about? The legitimate questions by Verona citizens on other school matters are all being misinterpreted as opposition to the busing proposal and evidence of community division. These Newark youngsters have made a most significant contribution to community control of education in Verona. The success of programs can no longer be guaranteed solely by the vote of the Board. Programs and proposals, because of increased interest, will be scrutinized more closely and will require that most important element — broad community support.

Tomecek explained that the dearth of quantitative information on the effectiveness of the program in meeting its goal made it difficult to make a decision for either continuing or canceling the program. And in light of these uncertainties, he concurred with the termination of the program. If it had been planned properly, he said, the Newark first-graders could have stayed in Verona until they reached the fifth grade.

The newly elected member of the Board, Marshall Butler — who had been opposed to the Plan — did not quite agree with either Wizda or with Tomecek. Butler stated that the previous Board had made it quite clear that it had been a one-year program with no further plans at that time. Therefore, the present Board had not discontinued the Plan,

> but rather it has not considered the renewal or initiation of a new program. This program might very well have been continued on a very limited scale, and probably serve very little purpose at a high administrative and per pupil cost.

He repeated his campaign opposition statement that the program was ill-conceived, poorly planned, and inadequate in experimental design, and he felt that this was the reason the Plan had not progressed.

> I firmly believe that one of the most unfortunate failings of this program has been the apparent inability to study both educational environments and to ascertain why the Newark children have succeeded, if indeed they have, and it seems to be so at the moment. We might have learned how to create a better learning environment for all children instead of just a few. I have struggled with the consequences of these children returning to the city, and have been advised that as a result of this experience they are better equipped to meet the problems besetting the urban schools. . . .

Hilda Jaffe accepted the decision to terminate the Plan "with deep sorrow." She had not agreed with the majority, and had voted against cancellation. "I will not carry my minority viewpoint to excess," she said. "This board cannot afford further permanent splintering over one issue." Jaffe explained that the Plan had been conceived to correct some of the serious educational deficiencies experienced by some Newark children. In addition, it was to have provided an opportunity for research and evaluation that might serve many other students. The program proved, she said, that sharing educational opportunities could work, and that disadvantaged children could benefit from a change in environment and goals. If there had been broad, enthusiastic community support, the Newark children could have been kept within the Verona school system. Publicity, she stated, might have increased public support for the program, but the Newark children and their parents were promised that the children would be treated as normally as possible. For that reason, TV, radio, and press coverage of the classes was refused. She continued,

> After all, the disadvantage we were trying to relieve is education. The city school is the problem — not the children. The children have never been termed by us "socially disadvantaged" or "economically disadvantaged." Those patronizing descriptions would reflect, and quite wrongly, on their families. It is an attempt to help a few innocent victims of a too large, too poor, overburdened school system.

Jaffe remembered her own upbringing in the city and spoke about the apparent success of the Plan, the interchange between the children, and the lunchtime program provided by the host parents. Despite her disappointment, she expressed her hope for the future.

> A year ago I was proud to live in Verona — tonight I am sad. The Board of Education has moved the community back into the mass. Someday perhaps we can step out again.

John McDonald then made his own statement.

> A preliminary report on the Project indicates that it was more successful in terms of goals achieved than had been dared to hope for, when Verona first sought to respond to the desperate situation facing the Newark children.

He went on to say that experiments by their nature are terminal, once sufficient data has been accumulated. Unfortunately, he felt that while some of the children could have been accommodated for the coming year, the following year an even smaller number could have been allowed. He also felt that the cost per pupil was quite high — in excess of $1,000 — and there had been no assurances that federal money would be available.

Verona alone cannot solve or even make a significant contribution towards solving what is obviously a regional problem
requiring regional cooperation. In this regard, the lack of initia-
tive on the state level, or expressions of interest by other local
boards has truly been disheartening.

McDonald regretted, but could not ignore, the opposition to the program,
and the distrust toward the Board, which had spilled over into other areas
of educational concern. "The need to restore harmony has become
urgent," McDonald stated, adding that he was impressed that 91 percent
of the Newark parents said they would send their children to Verona the
following year — a fact he felt was highly significant. The educational
growth of the children was similar to findings from other parts of the
country where such programs had also been attempted.

Surely the evidence strongly points to the direction which
should be taken if society is to correct the educational imbalances which are at the heart of many of the problems facing
society today. But just as surely, these imbalances cannot be
corrected by piecemeal action. One local school district alone
cannot do it. . . . At the moment all I can say here is that what
we in Verona would like to do we are unable to do — but what
we set out to do we did. It seems to me that little more could be
asked of any experimental program.

A few of the citizens in the audience commented on the decision. Herb
Rappaport recalled the meeting of the previous year and commented that
he had been proud to support the Board then. But that night he opposed
the Board's action.

Jim Fogarty congratulated the Board for its foresight during the past
year, but did not want to criticize the Board for canceling the Plan.

They are, after all, only reflecting the attitudes and desires of a
majority of Verona citizens who elected them to office. . . .
Rather, our society and specifically the townspeople of Verona
deserve the criticism. Verona has failed to realize that the problems of Newark and other urban areas of Essex County will
eventually be ours. . . . And with this program being morally

right, anyone who professes a belief in a divine Creator cannot
turn his back on this issue. This issue is not dead. . . .

Fogarty asked the elected officials, churches, and businessmen to join
forces for the future, and to follow the example of the Board in developing constructive, original programs for the state of New Jersey.

Bill Hartke also had been proud of the Board for daring to be different,
but tonight, he said, he was sad and ashamed. Eleanor Rubin chastened
Marshall Butler for claiming that the Sharing Plan was ill-conceived and
poorly planned, as it had been a smashing success. She went on to say,
"Your decision to terminate the plan has been made without regard to educational reports, without regard to the experience of the Verona parents
and children." Amy Bostwick said that she was surprised that some in the
audience had complained about not having been asked whether to discontinue the Plan, when she and her group had complained that they had not
been asked whether to start the Plan.

Don Ellicott, a teacher in Verona, suggested that the question of the
Sharing Plan should be on the ballot the coming year and for years to
come. That way, he said, the voters would always be reminded of what
they didn't have, and might have to rationalize for its lack. Otherwise the
issue would be forgotten, "consciences will be soothed and everybody will
be smiling and back to business as usual."

Peter Petrucelli was elated that this was the year of the quiet people, and
he objected to the inference that he was a racist. When John McDonald
interjected that such a word had not been mentioned, Petrucelli continued,

> . . . people call me a bigot when I get up — I'm going by what
> I've been told on my own. . . . I disagreed — I'm a racist. Mr.
> Tomecek disagreed — he's a bigot . . . the progressives have
> had a monopoly on education for years and . . . now the quiet
> people are speaking.

Petrucelli reminded everyone that the Plan had not been approved by the
people, but it had still been passed. He pointed out that there were many
poor whites in Newark, and he felt the Board should have brought in Italians, Polish, Irish, and Germans — not just blacks. If the Newark School
system were really that bad, he said, they should fire all the teachers there,
and some of the pupils and teachers of Verona should transfer to Newark.

Henry Fields claimed to be startled by the press release handed to those in the audience, which stated that the Newark children felt kindly towards their teachers, and appreciated their educational environment; the host families had registered positive feelings; and there had been a dramatic measurable academic growth. And then, "on page three, in the middle paragraph, first sentence [*says*] 'after considering all of the foregoing aspects, the board is agreed that the continuation of the school sharing program would not be wise'." Fields said he did not understand the conclusions the Board had drawn. According to the press release, the benefits would be outweighed by the high costs, as well as Board and community tensions. Statements like those, Fields contended, are exactly those that create tension. As for the lack of space and the desirable 25-pupil class,

> Well, I'd like to offer a very dramatic proposal — that is, increase this number of 25 to 26 — it seems to me this is a revolutionary proposal, but it would allow the other Newark children to participate in the program.

Andy Downie, who was a teacher, took issue with Emil Tomecek's desire for quantitative information and broad community support, and claimed that the need for that in educational matters would force all schools to close. These were just shallow rationalizations for discontinuing the program, he said, and added, "the Board of Education has snuffed out that candle of hope."

Peter Zales remembered the time when the supporters of the Plan were gloating, but he did not think that this evening was the moment to gloat over the dropping of it. He also was unhappy with the press for "heightening and sensitizing polarization. . . . I think they're to be criticized because they seem to do more, not just in Verona, but by and large, in agitating, stirring up these things." He concluded by saying that the press should report the news and state their opinions only on the editorial page.

Ann Buckley, who had been a host mother, expressed her disappointment in the citizens of Verona for not being more tolerant with each other and the Board of Education. Also, and she included herself, she felt citizens should have been more vocal in their approval, and she felt that the community of Verona would no longer be considered by other suburbs an example of concern for others.

Near the end of the meeting, Marshall Butler appealed to the people not to forsake the Board because this issue had been laid to rest. The meeting was adjourned about 10:15 p.m.

Both Newark papers reported on this meeting at length. "Charges Fly — Verona Ends Busing Plan" appeared in the *Newark Evening News*. "BOARD MEMBERS RECALL THE GAINS" and "Verona Reflects On Its Experiment" were the two top headlines in the *Star-Ledger*. On July 2, the *Verona-Cedar Grove Times* gave an overview of the June Board meeting, which they said was attended by over 150 citizens.

The following week, the League of Women Voters issued a special news release asking the Verona Board of Education to reconsider its decision to terminate the busing program. The League criticized the Verona Board, announced that a resolution had been sent in support of the Sharing Plan, and expressed regret that it had ended. In 1964 the League adopted its current national position to "Support equality of opportunity for education, employment and housing." This press release was in a number of newspapers, including the *West Essex Record* of July 23.

On July 10, Mrs. Howard Kastner thanked the more than 100 Verona volunteer fathers and mothers, as well as the Verona teenagers who had offered to contribute their services to the six-week summer recreation program to be held in Verona Park and at Our Lady of the Lake Church. The idea for the summer program had been suggested by Barbara Mackey Bakst. It was formalized by a planning committee of the Verona Task Force, headed by Sister Michael Maurice, and consisting of Bakst, Mrs. John Boyle, Mrs. Richard Heaslip, Mrs. Howard Kastner, Mrs. Marty Lipton, Mrs. Robert Peer, and Mrs. Michael Zichelli.

Mrs. Kastner stated in the local paper:

> We decided many months before the board canceled their program that we wanted to continue the ideas behind the Sharing Program — the opportunity for Verona and Newark children to work and play together and form solidly based friendships, the opportunity for Verona and Newark mothers

and fathers to plan and carry out the program, the idea of sharing our facilities with others, and the two-way concept of lending a helping hand — Verona to Newark and Newark to Verona.

Margaret Branch, one of the mothers of the participating Newark children, was the volunteer who supervised the children on their bus trip to Verona. The bus usually arrived around 9:30 a.m. Each child was then assigned to a group headed by a Verona mother, and assisted by a Verona teenager. The morning program was supervised by Mrs. Henry Marsh, a physical education teacher, Ann Hunt, who led the group in dancing and singing, and Sylvia Strauss, a French teacher, who led the children in a series of French rounds and songs. Father Jack Martin was scheduled to play his guitar, and Reverend Sargent Desmond would do magic tricks.

In the afternoon, the program for the children alternated between arts and crafts conducted by volunteer mothers headed by Mary Keenan, or creative dramatics and story-telling headed by Sally Foster. A committee of 32 mothers, headed by Mrs. Robert Kiernan, was to prepare sandwiches for lunch. Before the bus left at 2:30 p.m., the children were to gather for a cold drink and cookies or ice cream, which had been donated by Verona citizens.

Five photographs of Verona and Hawthorne school children enjoying various activities in Verona Park were run in the local paper in the July 17 edition. The program ended early in August with a picnic for all the Newark and Verona children who had participated. Invited also were representatives of the Hawthorne Avenue School, and the Fathers of the Queen of Angels Church in Newark, who had arranged the bus transportation, as well as the Fathers of the Verona Church, and the Verona officials and citizens who had helped. All in all, 35 youngsters had been guests of Verona's volunteers twice a week.

. . . The decision by the Verona Board of Education to "yield to the vocal segment of the community is regrettable."

Chapter 19

The New
School Year

ON SATURDAY, JULY 5, 1969, the *Passaic Herald News* ran an editorial titled "Oh, Pioneer . . . ?" The newspaper claimed that the decision by the Verona Board of Education to "yield to the vocal segment of the community is regrettable." Even stronger, it "indicted" the other communities in suburban Essex "for their complete detachment," and asserted that the silence of service clubs and other organizations had helped drive the nails into the Sharing Plan's coffin. In discussing the action of the majority of the Board members, the paper agreed with the youngsters of that day not to trust anyone over 30.

No one expected Verona's plan to solve the problem of the city, but it was a small light in a vale of darkness. And now the light is snuffed out.

No Board meetings were held in July, and only 48 citizens were present at the August 26 meeting. Although a considerable drop in attendance from the previous meetings, it was still above the norm. Bills had to be approved to replace broken glass and copper piping stolen from the schools by vandals. The Board also approved an expenditure for transporting 25 special education pupils.

Later in the evening, Emil Tomecek, in a prepared statement, notified the Board that he had filed a formal petition of appeal with the New Jersey Commissioner of Education, Dr. Carl L. Marburger, about two actions taken by the Board without proper authorization.

First, on December 19, 1968, a contract between the Boards of Education of Newark and Verona and the Educational Testing Service of Princeton, New Jersey, was signed. Second, a board advertisement costing $320 was placed in the February 6, 1969, issue of the *Verona-Cedar Grove Times*.

According to Tomecek, New Jersey statutes provide that a School Board cannot enter into a contract until the contract has been presented and passed at a public meeting and further, that the statutes forbid making decisions at conference meetings and then merely going through the motions of a vote at a public meeting. While there were exceptions, Tomecek did not think that these exceptions applied to those two cases.

John McDonald responded briefly to the charges, "which, in effect, are only allegations." He explained that the Commissioner of Education had asked the county Superintendent of Schools to determine if there were cause for such a complaint, but that Tomecek had refused to meet with the county Superintendent and the Board to discuss the complaints. Because Tomecek had filed what he called an appeal, it had now become a matter of litigation. "In effect, Mr. Tomecek has charged that this board has acted improperly on two occasions. . . ," McDonald said, and the Board's attorney had responded, and the matter was now before the State for a determination.

> The mere fact that Mr. Tomecek thinks that the board has acted improperly does not make it so. Now, Mr. Tomecek, in many instances comes to conclusions and then relates that, in effect, it is a fact that has happened. It is not.

Emil Tomecek asked that the record be corrected. He had addressed a letter to the Commissioner of Education. A Dr. Twitchell had called Tomecek and arranged to meet with him and the Board of Education, and the matter was to be settled in private without attorneys. But the president of the Board, without consulting anyone, had chosen to invite the Board's attorney. For that reason, Tomecek decided to make a formal appeal. McDonald replied that when the Board was challenged, he would always call an attorney to represent it. The two disagreed, Tomecek saying that it was his letter that was being acted upon, and McDonald insisting that he would not have the Board challenged improperly.

Tomecek asked when the results of the Educational Testing Service would be available, and whether he could propose a resolution that the results of those tests should be made part of the minutes. McDonald answered:

> Just a minute — I don't want the inference left that it is not a matter of public record. All of this is part of the procedure we went through one year ago, and I would . . . request the secretary to table that resolution since it's no formal resolution until you can put it in writing and present it before the board. In my opinion there is no need for such a resolution, but if you feel it's needed, bring it to the board at the next board meeting.

Emil Tomecek responded:

> . . . You don't decide whether my resolution can be voted on or not. I made a resolution — there is no policy of this board that says a resolution has to be made in writing. In fact, we just corrected a couple of resolutions here without having it done formally in writing. . . .

After a heated debate on procedural rules, the president asked whether

there was a second for Tomecek's motion. When there was none, Tomecek was satisfied that the proper procedures had been followed.

During the open discussion time, Mrs. John Kraeutler brought up the question of Verona's sex education curriculum. It was explained that Verona had a guide to health and safety education. She was told that the Board preferred to teach "health study" in its entirety. Within the program is education on personal health, care of the body, community health, mental health, and how boy/girl relationships would come into play at different levels. The program was to start in kindergarten and continue to grade 12. Mrs. Kraeutler explained that she had been in Trenton for 14 hours looking at this matter, was a little concerned with some of the materials that were to be used, and therefore wanted more information. She was assured that this would be supplied.

Early in September 1969, the Verona Task Force met to explore the possibility of continuing a series of volunteer programs with the children of Hawthorne Avenue School for the fall and winter. A preliminary meeting had been held with Woodrow Davis, Hawthorne's principal, and Bernice Smith and Marguarita Bush, president and vice president of the Hawthorne Avenue PTA. A special tutoring program was also under discussion. The group also asked the Board of Education to possibly reassess its position after the test results were announced.

At the beginning of the year tests showed that on average the Newark youngsters were lagging behind and were fearful of the future. This had changed by the last day of the one-year experimental plan — June 24, 1969. The transported first-graders had achieved significantly greater gains than their counterparts in Newark in the areas of reading, mathematics, and listening skills. Second-graders had also gained collectively. . . .

Chapter 20

The Test Results
Test Verona

ON SEPTEMBER 1, 1969, the Educational Testing Service in Princeton, New Jersey, released its long-awaited report entitled, "A Study of the Effectiveness of Education of Urban Children in a Suburban School District." The authors, Stanley M. Zdep and Diane Joyce, acknowledged the cooperation of the two Boards of Education, the administrators, teachers, teachers aides, and parents, as well as the host parents, "and last but not least, the children themselves." The statistical analyses were carried out by F. Reid Creech, of the Office of Computational Sciences of the Educational Testing Service. The evaluation focused on 26 of the children in first and second grades. They were referred to as "transported" children, and they were to be compared with a similar group, matched by sex and grade level, who had remained at Hawthorne Avenue School. These children were referred to as "counterparts." The transported children, the report said, had been dispersed to 12 of the 19 classes in Verona on the basis of existing vacancies. Those classes with transported children were referred to as the "experimental" classes, while the others were the "control" classes.

There were differences between the Verona and Hawthorne schools. In Verona, in first grade only, the schedule provided for reading instruction with a reduced pupil-to-teacher ratio of approximately 11 to 1. Traditional math was taught at Newark, versus contemporary mathematics in Verona. Hawthorne Avenue School was on split session, one in the morning and the second session starting at 11:30 a.m. Starting in February, Hawthorne School had employed a specialist in mathematics to work with the children and their teachers.

The methods of this study were fully explained in a released booklet. Pre-testing during September 1968 had been done in both schools by first-grade teachers, who had administered the Metropolitan Readiness Test, and by ETS personnel, who had administered the ETS Cooperative Primary Achievement Tests as well as an attitude questionnaire. In Verona, the Metropolitan Readiness Test was administered to small groups, while in Newark the entire class took the test at the same time.

Post-testing was done in both schools simultaneously during the third week of May. No more than one test was given a day on ETS's Cooperative Primary Tests in reading, mathematics, and listening. The attitude questionnaire was re-administered at that time.

All examinations, except the attitude questionnaire, were standardized tests developed for the particular grade level. The attitude inventory was specifically adapted to the Verona Plan, and consisted of 30 pages. Each page contained two pictures, identical except for the racial composition of the classroom scenes depicted. The children were asked which class they would prefer, which they thought would be smarter, and which would give the teacher more problems.

Other pertinent data included a specially adapted version of the Classroom Operational Problems Check List, which had been completed by teachers of both schools, before and after, and which listed various types of problems that could be encountered by teachers. Post-questionnaires were also sent to the host parents. Newark students and Newark parents were interviewed by the supplemental teacher. Attendance data for the transported children and their counterparts had been collected by school officials.

The first question in the second section of the report, subtitled "Results," asked whether or not the transported children had benefited in terms of achievement as a result of the Plan. The pre-test, according to the tables included, indicated the same level of ability between the transported children and their counterparts, while a substantial difference was measured in post-tests. Results on the Metropolitan Readiness Test indicated that first grade transported children "significantly outperformed their counterparts on all three of the post tests" (reading, math, listening). Even after researchers adjusted post-test scores to account for variables between the two school systems, the result indicated that "there was a significant net achievement effect in favor of the transported children." There seemed to be no difference between boys and girls. Similar results were reported on tests for second grade. In neither grade was it possible to single out what aspects of the Plan were responsible for the greater achievement of the bused students.

The second major question that this study hoped to answer was whether there were any detrimental effects on the achievement of the Verona students due to Verona educators having to gear their teaching to accommodate less-advanced Newark pupils. Post-test scores of the first grade revealed that classes with transported children and classes without showed "no significant differences in achievement gains." Similar results were seen in tests of second graders.

Student attitudes were assessed with a "method of paired comparisons." The children were shown two pictures at a time, each depicting a classroom scene containing six children with variations in their skin shading. In some, all six children were black; in others there were four, two, or no blacks. All possible combinations of pictures were shown in pairs in a counterbalanced order. The children were asked to show their preference in ten different pairs of pictures in response to each of the three questions asked. Some of the children failed to respond to skin shading, and some would consistently choose either the picture on the left or right hand side — the responses of these children were therefore removed prior to analysis. On the pre-test, 20 percent of responses had to be removed; this number decreased to ten percent in the post-test — probably reflecting both learning and maturation.

ETS's complete report contained many pages detailing the statistical methods used. It was asserted that this had been a first opportunity to find out about some important academic and social attitudes.

The first question the researchers analyzed dealt with Verona children and whether they had developed racial tolerance after being exposed to the Newark children. The results indicated that Verona children preferred racially mixed classes that were mostly white.

The next question asked whether the Verona children felt that they suffered academically due to the presence of Newark children. According to the evidence, the young Veronans felt that a mostly white class might even be a little smarter than an all-white class. The ratings were not as favorable for black and mostly black classes.

There was a difference of opinion between first- and second-graders as to whether the proportion of blacks related to class disruptiveness. The first graders did not think so, but the second graders felt that the number of blacks and class disruptiveness were positively correlated.

On the other hand, the children of Newark seemed to differentiate far less on the basis of class racial mixes, especially at the end of the school year. The authors wondered whether the children at the Hawthorne Avenue School were taught not to differentiate on the basis of race.

In the beginning of the school year, both the transported children and their counterparts in Newark considered white and mostly white classes to be smartest. By the end of the school year both groups saw little difference. Did the transported children influence the stay-at-homes? Did talk about the host parents play a part in this change of attitude? These questions are not answered by the report. Oddly, by the end of the year, the transported children rated a mostly black class as being far less disruptive than any other racial mix.

Race alone, the authors concluded, or a combination of races, had little relevance at first grade level. They hoped that similar studies could be made at higher grades — which, of course, could have been done had the Sharing Plan been continued. But the Hartford program results did come from tests of high school children.

Statistics compiled by the study showed that 68 percent of the transported children liked going to school in Verona more than in Newark, and that 45 percent of their siblings and 43 percent of their friends would have been interested in a similar arrangement and were not put off by their friends' good fortune. A full 97 percent of the transported children liked their Verona teacher very much, and almost four out of five felt they were treated like any other student by their classmates. Eighty-nine percent of the visitors would have liked to continue school in Verona, and nearly three-quarters thought it would be good for their siblings to attend in Verona also.

The responses gathered from the parents of the transported children revealed similar sentiments: 88 percent had positive feelings about the Plan; 85 percent heard their children mention Verona youngsters frequently; 86 percent indicated they would enroll another child; and nine out of ten said they would have continued their children in the Plan the following year. One of the few negative factors reported was transportation in winter.

Of the Verona host parents, four out of five expressed positive feelings toward the Plan, while 17 percent had mixed feelings. Although the Plan was something they could live with temporarily, they expressed concern that better ways to upgrade the education of Newark children might be found. One-third of the parents said their children mentioned the Newark youngsters frequently and 63 percent reported occasional remarks. More than half noted that their children played together with the visitors, but one-fourth of the parents did not know the answer to that question. Over two-thirds of the host parents felt the Newark guests enjoyed their lunches, with an additional 25 percent adding that the children "enjoy it very much." When the Verona parents were asked if the Plan should be continued, 87 percent said yes, only 3 percent responded no, and 10 percent were uncertain.

The results of the questionnaires indicated that both the Newark children and their parents, and the Verona host parents, deemed the Plan successful. Many Newark parents attached letters to the questionnaires expressing their personal thanks to the community of Verona and their hope that the program would continue, because it had benefited their children academically. Host parents lauded the benefits to their children, who they said had begun the process of accepting skin color as a superficial difference.

The researchers did not poll any residents of Verona other than those who volunteered to be host parents. In hindsight, it would have been interesting to find out whether the visiting children were discussed in other homes, had ever been invited to homes other than those volunteered for lunches, and whether attitudes in general had been changed.

Despite the 25- to 40-minute bus trip, which could have proved formidable to young children, the attendance figures for both the transported children and their counterparts who stayed in Newark were very similar.

Of operational problems that the authors of the study documented, only two out of the top five mentioned by the Verona and the Newark teachers were similar. In Verona, the teachers' concerns included: "concerned about study habits," "under-achievement of many students," "teaching those who do not want to learn," "frustrated by wanting all my kids to learn," and "being impatient with my students." The Newark teachers listed: "teaching those who do not want to learn," "under-achievement of many students," "student destructiveness of equipment," "certain students taking up too much of my time," and "needing materials to teach slow learners."

At the beginning and end of the year, the first-grade teachers of Verona "control" classes — those in which no Newark children were enrolled — reported on average a greater number of problems than did teachers of the "experimental" classes — those with Newark children. However, second-grade teachers in both categories reported more problems, which increased throughout the school year.

Earlier in the year Verona teachers had been very concerned with under-achievers, especially children in the experimental classes. This concern decreased as the year drew toward an end.

According to the authors of the study, at the beginning of the year tests showed that on average the Newark youngsters were lagging behind and were fearful of the future. This had changed by the last day of the one-year experimental Plan — June 24, 1969. The transported first-graders had achieved significantly greater gains than their counterparts in Newark in the areas of reading, mathematics, and listening skills. Second-graders had also gained collectively, but their strides were not as impressive. However, there were no adverse effects on achievement among the Verona children in the first- and second-grade classes containing transported children, and no differences were found between children in the experimental and control classes. Students in both grades expressed their preference for a racially integrated class and felt such classes, mostly white, were the smartest. At the end of the year, the transported students expressed a preference for being in white classes, even though they no longer considered white classes to be smarter than black classes.

Near the end of the report, authors Zdep and Joyce cited a survey carried out in some 6,000 schools by James Coleman. Entitled *Equality of Educational Opportunity* (GPO, 1966), it concluded that a child is more influenced by socio-economic status than racial background. "Thus, a poor black child would benefit more from attending school with white or black middle class children than he would be attending school with poor white or black children." It also found that black children were more sensitive to peer influence than white children, implying that black children would benefit in an integrated class, whereas the white child would suffer very little. Both these points were borne out by the Verona Plan.

"In summary," Zdep and Joyce concluded, "it appears that this one-year trial Plan in Sharing Educational Opportunity did have a positive impact on the effects of such an educational program on various groups of children, parents and teachers."

At the request of their teachers, students of the Verona social studies classes attended the September 30 Board of Education meeting. They were welcomed by the president of the Board, who expressed the hope "that you will learn something of the processes of democracy as it is shown here at our Verona Board of Education meetings." According to Board records, 160 citizens attended the meeting (the minutes do not indicate whether the students were included as "citizens").

Bruce Levin, one of the students, brought up a question on grievance procedures. At the request of Marshall Butler, Superintendent John Mattis explained to the students the Board's responsibility:

> Recent instances of disorder and disruption in a number of the New Jersey school systems, have compelled the attention of the state board of education and the commissioner, and have required the issuance of this statement. . . . Local school districts are required by fundamental law to provide school facilities and to maintain an appropriate program of education. All children of school age have a right to attend the public schools and to receive a suitable education. Any disruption of the school or interference of their normal operation offends this right, which is constitutional in origin, violates the law and cannot be condoned or tolerated. . . .

According to Mattis, the directive spelled out the means through which the concerns of students might be effectively expressed, considered, and fairly disposed of. In Verona, that meant a process of going up the ladder — *i.e.*, first by taking a dispute to the teacher, and then, if no resolution was forthcoming, by approaching in the following order: the vice principal, principal, Superintendent, Board of Education, the county Superintendent of Schools, and finally, as a last resort, the Commissioner of Education, "who is expressly empowered to hear and decide controversies and disputes relating to the conduct of the public schools." It was strongly felt that the initiation of formal procedures, by which students and parents could have their concerns heard, could do much to produce concord and to avoid outbreaks of lawless behavior "which sometimes result from lack of communication."

Emil Tomecek wanted to make it clear that while "grievance procedures" were part of a labor contract, suggestions from students did not carry as much weight as procedures established by equals in a formal grievance hearing. Marshall Butler added that his main interest was in assuring that the Board had met its responsibility.

It was announced that copies of the report on the Sharing Plan by the Educational Testing Service were available at 50 cents each. Dr. Zdep, the noted psychologist who participated in the study and co-authored the report, had been invited to the meeting, and he was introduced.

Dr. Zdep explained the report in great detail, and during the presentation he revealed facts not previously known to the public. He reported that during the summer of 1968, the Newark Board of Education had sent out a questionnaire to all the Hawthorne School parents asking whether any of them wanted their children to participate in an educational program in Verona. Approximately 176 parents of children in grades 1 through 5 expressed an interest. It was from this group of affirmative responses that the random selection was made. "The names were pulled from hats, so to speak," he said. Children whose parents had indicated a desire for their children to participate in the Verona Plan, but whose names were not drawn, were selected as their counterparts. "They were matched by sex," Dr. Zdep explained, "because . . . at this level girls have a tendency to outperform boys academically." In other words, an equal number of boys and girls as that of the group traveling to Verona was selected for testing as counterparts. Using these two similar groups, it was possible to compare pre-test and post-test results. To study any adverse affects on the children in Verona, Newark students were deliberately withheld from some classrooms.

Dr. Zdep explained some of the numbers shown in statistical charts, and pointed out the difference in how the children functioned and felt before and after their school year in Verona. "It turns out that in every single area at the Grade 1 level — reading, math and listening — the post-test mean scores were significantly different and it indicated a net achievement effect in favor of the transported group."

If considered separately, the mean differences in Grade 2 test results between the transported children and their counterparts were not statistically significant. "However," he went on, "if all three achievement areas were combined in a multi-variate analysis, the result was to indicate a net achievement in favor of the transported children."

In order to measure the students' attitudes, new techniques were utilized. According to Dr. Zdep, children at this level do have attitudes on a lot of things, but they are very difficult to measure because most children at these ages cannot rank order.

> If you ask them to rank order on a set of statements, a list of things they like to do or what have you, they have a lot of difficulty, and only some of them can do it successfully. Also, if you present them with two events — suppose we presented them with a Tootsie Roll and a Hershey bar and asked them which they like least, or which they liked less — they would have great difficulty indicating which. But as you all know, if you asked them which they prefer, which they like better, they can all do that, and for our purposes this was fine.

For that reason, Dr. Zdep explained, the children were shown the pictures of classes composed of different racial groups. He detailed the methods used in this test, then offered several conclusions of the data. Dr. Zdep also noted that alternative conclusions could have been reached that might or might not have been supported by the data.

> However, it seems apparent to a lot of people who viewed the report, that in no case can the conclusions presented here be invalidated by the evidence, although you may come up with other conclusions which you feel perhaps might be better —

and they may indeed be better or more justifiable — but these are the conclusions that we used. . . . And in fact, you all realize that this was the type of class that the Verona Plan was designed to create, a racially mixed class that was mostly white, and it turned out that the Verona students preferred this class as much or better than an all-white class in most instances.

When questioned about the reaction of parents in Newark, Dr. Zdep spoke about the pre-testing in Newark and said,

the contrast was just amazing. Many of the windows [*in the school*] were out, the noise was coming up from the street. The heating plant wasn't functioning properly. Children . . . were sitting around in their coats . . . shivering, and paying very little attention to any kind of academic program. . . .

The host parents from Verona, Dr. Zdep told the Board, "not only answered the questions, but they wrote in the margins, on the back, between questions, on the reverse side, and where they ran out of space, some of them included additional pages." Obviously not all of the comments could be entered, and therefore a representative sample was compiled for the report. Dr. Zdep cited some comments:

"The benefits accrued by this program [*have*] been to my children. I may be prejudiced, but I feel my children have learned to accept black and white as superficial differences. . . ."

"Newark boys and girls certainly showed many Forest Avenue students good manners and respect for others. This should be the beginning of the end of bigotry."

"[*Name omitted*] had a very noticeable accent at the beginning of the year, a real drawl. It has since vanished. He speaks much more clearly and his vocabulary is much improved. There are no more double negatives or 'ain'ts'."

"After a month my son commented to me that the Newark students seemed to be getting lighter."

". . . My son and the child I have from Newark get along famously. They have their fights, as all children do, but

underneath runs something deeper that has brought meaning
and hope to my husband and to me for the future."

Dr. Zdep then summarized his findings and compared the Verona
results with those of the similar program in Hartford. Marshall Butler
requested additional time for "a thorough inquisition or discussion." Dr.
Zdep promised to do his best to return at a future date, and Butler said that
he had hoped that there would be more time at the meeting to question Dr.
Zdep further. John McDonald pointed out that the date of the School
Board meeting had been chosen because it was the same evening that
Newark was making the report public. However, he indicated, that should
not prevent the Board from meeting again with Dr. Zdep for additional
questioning. But other business still had to be transacted, which did not
permit any more time to be allocated to the report.

Butler did not agree. "I think," he said, "the board has a responsibility
to know this report and to deal with it now." McDonald agreed, but
pointed out that the report was really the property of the Newark Board of
Education and they had released it the same day. In order for the Verona
Board to take a position, he said, "we would have to sit with Dr. Zdep and
review it, as you indicated. I don't think that this is the time, or this is the
place to do it."

Marshall Butler again indicated his unhappiness, saying "this morning,
the *Star-Ledger* quoted personnel, administrators, and people from the
Verona school system regarding this, and if these people are going to
comment on it, I want to understand it, and I want to know what it's all
about. . . ."

John McDonald was puzzled as to how the reporter had received his
information, or to whom he had talked. To McDonald's knowledge, no
one in any official position had talked to the newspaper.

Emil Tomecek stated that he did not want a private meeting with Dr.
Zdep, but rather wanted the report to be discussed openly. But, he said, "I
believe, prior to the public discussion here openly, we should have an
analysis of this report by someone in the Verona system — our professionals — so that they could tell us . . . what they think of this report
before we release it to the public, so that we, as board members, could be
guided . . . giving our own positions. . . ."

McDonald, listening to the apparently conflicting requests of Butler and
Tomecek, remembered previous conflicting statements and stated:

. . . may I remind you, when you say you want everything discussed openly, why was it that you were so adamant about
bringing this report to the public tonight? At our last conference
meeting you didn't want to bring it out, you wanted to hold it
back. Not only this report but every report that we have. . . .

Then, McDonald reiterated that this was not the Board's report, not the
administration's report, and not the staff's report — it was the report from
the Educational Testing Service to the public and to the Board. If the
Board had wished to have a conference meeting to discuss it further, he
said, they should have requested one.

Ed Wizda doubted that the Board members were competent authorities
on testing, and pointed out that the Educational Testing Service, while not
necessarily the highest authority, was still the professional organization
hired for that purpose. If Mr. Butler wanted a page-by-page analysis, he
said, it would almost require a dissertation or thesis.

Butler insisted the word should be "inquisition." He said, "The only
reason I said 'page by page' is that, as things arose on a particular page, I
would like to ask [*about*] them rather than be jumping . . . all over the
place." Butler admitted that he was not an authority, but he wanted the
Board to agree to assume the responsibility.

McDonald spoke again:

Well, you prefaced your questions on a "page-by-page dissertation and inquisition" with respect to the report. I was going
to permit questions . . . from the floor tonight, and from the
board members, but I am not going to submit to, as you call it,
an "inquisition" with respect to every word that's contained in
this report. This is a night when we have a lot of business to
take care of and we have to go forward. If you feel that we have
to have a page-by-page dissertation on this particular report
. . . that we have it at a meeting of the board members and Dr.
Zdep, who would make himself available, and at that night we
could have a special meeting for all of the public to come forward, if necessary, after they have had an opportunity to review
the report. But this report tonight is for the purposes of presenting it to the public. . . . They don't even know what's on
page two here.

Marshall Butler made a few additional requests, and then asked that the Board be polled on the question. Emil Tomecek repeated that he felt that the public should know about the report, but not before the Board learned what was in it. He offered an alternate motion:

> And the reason why I'm making the motion is that we have to understand that the president doesn't make all the decisions for this board, the board makes the decisions. Now I'd like to make the motion, and it's going to be this: RESOLVED that the Board shall discuss this report openly here tonight.

Tomecek's motion was seconded by Butler.

John McDonald questioned whether the motion meant what it said, and Tomecek said that he wanted to question the professionals present so that he could make a judgment on the report. McDonald counseled a delay for a conference meeting, but Ed Wizda, while sympathetic to the motion, felt it would be unfair to discuss the report in front of people who had not had a chance to see it. Tomecek did not think this problem was "insurmountable," as the public could purchase a copy of the report at the meeting.

Wizda said, "But they have not studied it, Mr. Tomecek. You've had the report for the past month in your hands now."

Hilda Jaffe, too, sympathized with the intent of the motion. She also felt that the Board had taken the right step in receiving the report in public. "I have read the report more than once," she said. "I have some questions which are not easy to formulate. I feel that this would be difficult — to have a questioning of Dr. Zdep at this time by board members in the form of a bombardment or inquisition." Jaffe added that no matter what was being discussed that night, the press would report it in its own fashion, and there would be widespread dissemination. She agreed with Ed Wizda that additional time would be needed for a proper public discussion.

When John McDonald suggested the date of October 8 for a public meeting, Emil Tomecek reminded him of the resolution on the floor. Ed Wizda asked for clarification of the proposed meeting — whether it would be open to the public and if it really would be a page-by-page "inquisition," saying he liked to get to bed before midnight. Tomecek wanted the public to participate, "even if they criticize me — clap to show that they don't like what I've said." The resolution was moved and Tomecek, Butler, and Wizda voted for it.

Charles Alario, a Verona resident, asked to speak and — although it was not yet time for the public discussion — he was given permission. Alario said,

> I understood the busing issue was a dead issue. I interpret Mr. Butler's remarks tonight [*to mean*] that if tonight's dissertation and examination of this report indicates that it is correct and valid, that perhaps he intends to introduce a motion to re-institute [*the Plan*]. If this is not the case tonight, I can't see any reason at all for sitting here, with the public being invited to this, where there is no set goal or purpose. In other words, Mr. Butler, if you find out tonight that this is valid, do you intend to re-institute the program?"

Butler said, "No, sir," and Alario asked, "Then what is the purpose?"

It was Butler's contention all along, he explained, that if this was something the community wanted, he would put it to a referendum and have it re-instituted. "And I will still do that," he said. "But I have no intention whatsoever as an individual to encourage or ask the board to make any resolution to re-institute this program this evening." He just wanted to find out what had been done, and while he did not like to stay until late either, he still wanted to know what was going on.

Tomecek first asked what the objectives and purposes of the tests were, and who in Verona had approved those objectives.

Dr. Zdep quoted again the research objectives:

> In the case of the present plan, it was proposed to use as precise a study design as real-life conditions would permit, in order to answer important questions regarding the effect of the program on student achievements, student attitudes and student behavior.

This answer bothered Emil Tomecek, who remembered the words of the original proposal, which, he said, were "correcting some of the educational deficiencies experienced by some Newark children and an opportunity for research and evaluation." McDonald and Tomecek sparred as to whether this was a question or a statement. Tomecek felt that between the original version of the contract and the one that was ultimately signed, there seemed to be four different versions of the objectives.

Several members of the audience interrupted the meeting to find out if it would be possible to purchase copies of the report. One man also spoke up and said that Tomecek had been discourteous to Dr. Zdep, whose sole function was to explain the report, not to merely read part of it to Tomecek. The meeting was recessed so that audience members could obtain their own copies.

After the break, Dr. Zdep told Marshall Butler that he had been primarily responsible for the design of the study, but that the tests themselves had been reviewed by the entire Division of Educational Studies, which included eight to ten other professionals with Doctorate degrees. Marshall Butler asked Dr. Zdep who had decided what should be studied in order to determine the effectiveness of suburban education over inner-city education.

Superintendent Mattis pointed out that Butler's question was similar to the one asked previously by Tomecek, and stated further that the original proposal had been developed by the entire Board of Education and agreed upon unanimously.

Newark's Board had not agreed originally, and had requested certain refinements. Mattis stated:

> The proposal of the Newark board was further developed and afterwards there was consultation with the Testing Service. I indicated that I was also interested in attitude changes as a result of the change in environment in addition to academic growth.

While the contract had been left up to the Superintendent of Schools, the copies of the test, as developed by Dr. Zdep and the other professionals, were given to each member of both Boards in order that everyone knew the testing plan. That included the dates for pre-testing and post-testing. "That's how it happened," Mattis concluded. "Now the testing design, if that's what you want to call it, the research design, would not exactly parallel the proposal itself." Then Mattis asked Dr. Zdep to comment.

Defining objectives is a difficult procedure, according to Dr. Zdep. Educators define objectives as making children comprehend, instilling reading skills, reading more rapidly, etc. These objectives somehow have to be translated into a contract, into legal language. The appropriate tests that address these objectives must be selected. The School Boards also wanted to know something about attitudes, when no such test existed. An experimental research instrument was used, and questionnaires were added to get information thought to be meaningful.

Butler asked Dr. Zdep to explain the meaning of "enriched educational program," which was stated on page one as follows: "The proposal was designed to provide Newark children with an enriched educational program and environment." He especially wanted to know whether the word "enriched" meant "better than something that exists." Dr. Zdep explained that these were educators' definitions, translated into the tasks of reading, listening skills, and mathematics, while "enriched" meant the children would be in smaller classes, with a supplementary teacher to help them, and would have the added advantage of being invited to lunch with host families. "We did not define that particular part," Dr. Zdep explained. "That was defined by the people in Verona."

Butler said, "I contend that it was not defined by me." Mattis asked Butler whether he did not agree that Verona had something better to offer by way of physical facilities, equipment, class size, an enriched environment both in school and perhaps in a home situation. Butler did agree, but said that he wanted verification, because "we only *assume* that the Verona situation is better than the situation that these youngsters came from, but the question is, is it?"

Butler's next question concerned the availability of spaces in the Verona system, and how that tied in with the random selection of the children. Tomecek added that the children were spread over five classes — the first five grades — and if the children had truly been picked at random, there could have been a situation wherein most of the children had been fifth graders — for which there were only two spaces.

McDonald suggested that Butler and Tomecek were trying to invalidate this report by coming up with conclusions that did not exist. Mr. Butler said he was simply asking questions, and he next wanted to know whether the matching of the transported and control students by sex and grade level was sufficient for valid conclusions. The reply from Dr. Zdep was brief and to the point, "For what we were attempting to do, yes, this was adequate."

Marshall Butler said, "The socio-economic, the intellectual level, the motivation, the age of the youngsters, the teaching that was taking place in the control group then could be ruled out as effects that might have affected the achievement?"

Dr. Zdep explained that the randomization procedure within the terms of sampling error is a method of correcting these differences:

> . . . They are all students in the Hawthorne Avenue School. Presumably they have similar socio-economic backgrounds. However, as you pointed out, there may be the exceptions. Now the important point here is . . . they are a select population. We actually termed this group of children as "children whose parents gave a damn." Hence, you can generalize the results only to parents in this bracket, defined as having given their permission for their children to come to the Verona system. As far as other children in the Newark system, it would be an improper generalization to carry these results to students such as those. Again, the randomization procedure, by selecting from a hat on the basis of grade level and sex, if you get a bright child in one group, chances are, based on sampling theory, you're going to get a bright child in the other group. . . . If you don't, this comes out as error, and in the final statistical analysis, that in which we determine the ratio which we test for significance, this becomes the denominator term or term we call error, and all experiments contain error.

Several residents in attendance requested that the Board discontinue the questioning and call another meeting later, to give the citizens a chance to digest the report. Tomecek was opposed to this and said, "I don't see why we have to haggle here over whether we should ask questions or shouldn't. We've wasted at least thirty to thirty-five minutes over that question — let's get on with it . . . we ought to act upon [*the suggestion from the floor*] later at the proper time."

Jaffe moved to discontinue the discussion and set another meeting date. Wizda seconded. Butler and Tomecek voted against the motion, the other three members voted for it. The meeting on the report was subsequently scheduled for October 15.

A number of resolutions necessary to transact the normal business of the Board were passed. One final resolution, however, still concerned the tests. It was moved by Tomecek and seconded by Butler that "the contract between the Boards of Education of Verona and Newark and the Educational Testing Service of Princeton be included in the minutes of this meeting."

A letter that had been prepared by the Board's legal council was then read, stating that the entire contract had been performed by all parties, that the proper authorization for the agreement had been satisfied at the time the Board approved the proposed contract with the Newark Board, and that further approval was unnecessary. Further, the letter said it would be inappropriate to seek further approval because of the petition by Tomecek against the Board, which seeks to "declare that this contract was contracted in an invalid manner and to declare this contract to be invalid." For those reasons, the legal counsel went on, the Board should refrain from any consideration of the proposed resolution until the Commissioner of Education rendered his decision. Over the objections of Tomecek, the resolution was tabled. Only Tomecek voted against it.

A number of letters were read expressing disappointment with the discontinuance of the Sharing Plan. Emil Tomecek then reminded the Board that at the previous month's meeting, the president had requested that Tomecek submit his resolutions in writing and in advance. Yet this very evening, he said, the resolution moved by Hilda Jaffe, which had not been submitted in writing, had been voted on (his own resolution to continue the discussion on the report — also not in writing — had been voted on first, and Jaffe's resolution to table took precedence).

Tomecek repeated his previous motion and asked everyone to listen carefully. "Resolved that the contract between the Boards of Education of Verona and Newark, and the Educational Testing Service of Princeton, be included in the minutes of this meeting." He claimed that the only purpose of this motion was to get the contract into the library so that it would become a part of the public record. It was Tomecek's contention that the attorney had been misled, and that the letter did not mean that there had been an approval of the agreement. Therefore, the letter from the attorney, he said, was really not germane to the issue. He now proposed a modified resolution, which read that the contract should be placed into the library together with the minutes of this meeting.

McDonald took issue with this resolution, remonstrating that the problem lay with the single word "contract," which means that something has been entered into, and that's where the difficulty lies. . . . There is no reason why we have to hammer this each week, and you try to browbeat the board, to discredit the board, and to try and push this thing each week. If the Commissioner decides it is necessary, I will be the one who will move the resolution and put it wherever it should go. . . .

Tomecek then proposed to alter the resolution and get rid of the offending word "contract." John McDonald again repeated that nothing further would be done until the Commissioner of Education made his decision — a move which Tomecek termed "ridiculous." Tomecek's motion failed for lack of a second.

Charles Alario asked Hilda Jaffe and Emil Tomecek to explain the duties and responsibilities of a Board member — both the duties designated by the Legislature and those as interpreted by the individual. Each Board member offered a lengthy explanation. Jaffe said that when she first joined the Board, she was under the impression that a question like that could be answered easily. But she had found that the longer she remained, the more difficult it became for her to give a correct answer. According to the statutes, the responsibility resting in the Board is not directly to the people who elected it, but to the state, since the Board members are agents of the state — and as such were responsible for providing a thorough and efficient system of education. While the duties of the Board members are listed in the statutes, the responsibilities change as education changes, and as the Legislature adds or takes certain duties out of their province

> . . . as board members, take full responsibility for the excellence and the improvement and the manner of public education in our own community by encouraging the administrators and the other employees to perform their own duties. . . .

It was hoped that the community would offer honest criticism and support.

Tomecek explained that the Board, in deciding policy, needed to respond to the wishes of the community — "the people out there in the community — they are the boss." In turn, the administrators should respond to the Board and the teachers to the administrators. Policies should be based on recommendations by professional staff; the Board, however, did not merely approve, but needed to make final decisions. For instance, based upon recommendations from the staff, the Board had to approve books, make sure that all statutes were being followed, find out how the money was being spent for specific programs, and set priorities.

According to Ed Wizda, the word "community" as used by both Board members should not be limited by geography or maps. "Where education is concerned," he said, "I'm concerned about the best education, or a good education for all children, regardless of where they live."

Tomecek agreed that he was interested what was going on in Newark, but that was a personal responsibility. It was his contention "that we don't have the abilities, the capabilities, the time or the talents to do both . . . the board has been side-tracked from its main responsibility of providing for the education of youngsters residing right here in our school district." Tomecek cited as examples 159 known cases of high school pupils not receiving needed after-school help; the lack of progress after a contract was signed for the development of the high school athletic field; the lack of action in regard to revising the policy book that had been voted on in February 1968; and the lack of interest in the 124 youngsters who participated in the summer school program and were in dire need of help.

Jaffe objected to these allegations, saying she was certain that the Board had continued to act to alleviate the many existing problems. Reports do take time, she said, and people must be given a chance to work at their own speed.

> I'm not always satisfied with what's going on around me, and I hope I never will be satisfied, but I hope I'm not generally dissatisfied with the work of the employees of the school district, and I would never want to constantly prod or poke or criticize people because I feel that you get less done that way than by waiting patiently and pleasantly.

John McDonald commented:

> You have heard the first campaign kick-off speech for the election in February 1979. I think Mr. Tomecek has outlined his reasons why he feels the board isn't doing its job, forgetting that he is a member of the board, and also forgetting the fact that in many instances when we have a meeting Mr. Tomecek,

when 11:00 p.m. arrives, takes up and leaves the meeting, so
that we can conduct no further business. . . .

Emil Tomecek asked McDonald to address the issues, such as the children who needed after-school help. He wanted to know what was going to
be done to offer them an effective program, rather than waiting for a
report.

I said that one of the serious problems facing this board this
year was going to be to determine the degree and extent to
which time and energies of both the board and administrators
shall be spent on problems outside the school district. . . .

Both McDonald and Tomecek were asked whether they were candidates for the next School Board election. Tomecek had not decided;
McDonald indicated he was planning to run again. The meeting adjourned
at 11:50 p.m.

Ed Fox, editor of the *Verona-Cedar Grove Times*, in his weekly column
"High on a Hilltop," in early October, mourned the fact that the philosophy of the Sharing Plan had been lost in the controversy about whether the
Board of Education had the right to institute it without a referendum. He
thought it much more important that the test results, compared with those
of similar plans, should provide some basis for those with expertise to
decide the advantages and disadvantages, if any, of the Sharing Educational Opportunities concept.

Educators in general, and especially those who are at the
state level in New Jersey, may be expected to devote considerable professional study to the ETS report. Undoubtedly even
more detailed attention will be shown by sociologists who are
concerned at the schism in society caused by a great many factors, of which race is one of the foremost. . . . It is too much,
perhaps, to imagine that the ETS findings will minimize all the
furor of the past but now that one year of sharing has been
evaluated, a rational re-approach to the program would be to

consider it solely in the light of its analysts and its possible contribution to long-range educational planning on both the state and federal level.

Barbara Mackey Bakst, in a letter to the editor, wrote,

As excited eager children gathered before the first bells opened school doors from Grove to Brookdale Avenues, the rain showered down upon them like a giant burst of tears of sadness for those who were missing — their former fellow students and playmates, the 37 boys and girls from the Hawthorne Avenue School.

She found it incredulous that no space could be found for 37 children when over 2,800 were in the local system, and wondered how the majority of the Board members, who voted against the children, felt that very morning.

According to the *Verona-Cedar Grove Times*, the report by Dr. Zdep at the Verona Board meeting "was greeted with a mixture of praise and skepticism." The article went on to say that Marshall Butler, elected to the Board to oppose the Plan, favored "a thorough review of the study so we can have a clear understanding of what the words meant and what the statistics meant." It reported other comments, including those made by Board president John McDonald, who said that the study "substantiates the position of the board members who voted for the project in the first place." Originally McDonald had supported the project, the article noted, but voted against the renewal, because in his opinion the project had sharply divided the residents of Verona. Hilda Jaffe, who had been the president when the Board approved the project, had said the results were "gratifying," and were similar to the findings of the projects in Boston and Hartford.

On October 1, the headline in the *Newark Evening News* had read: "Newark-Verona School Busing Results Lauded." A short synopsis of the Educational Testing Service report was included as part of the story, as well as the reactions of the two School Boards concerned, which were markedly different.

The Newark board last night said it was pleased with the results of the nine-month study and said it would have liked the program to continue. The Newark group praised the Verona board for its courageous and pioneering efforts in approving the plan and carrying it through.

The paper then reported the Verona Board's contentious meeting, detailing Tomecek's motion for an immediate discussion, Butler's call for an "inquisition," and several residents' request for a special meeting to be held after the public had had a chance to read the report.

On October 5, *The New York Times* headline read: "School Bus Plan Termed Success." The subhead stated, "Shift of Newark Negroes to Verona Ended, However." The newspaper condensed the Educational Testing Service's report to a few paragraphs, highlighting the progress of all students — especially those who attended first grade but noting that it was not possible

to single out any particular aspect of the suburban experience that was responsible for the differences in scores between the groups. . . . Given the total educational experience, the achievement for the transported group of children was significantly greater."

This was the last time that *The New York Times* mentioned Verona or the Sharing Plan.

On Sunday, October 11, 1969, *The Christian Science Monitor* reported on the Verona Plan.

An experimental program to bus ghetto children from Newark, New Jersey, to grade school in a middle-income white suburb has been stopped, even though an Educational Testing Service report praises the program.

Briefly retelling the history, including the resistance in "this almost all-white community," the article stated that the problem stemmed in part from the fact that many suburban parents felt that "each town is responsible for educating its own children." They had moved from urban areas to the suburbs for "better education," were paying high taxes to that end, and wondered, then, why Verona should "take on the educational responsibilities of Newark." At the same time, however, they did believe that "wealthier suburbs must help, as the children often become victims — rather than beneficiaries — of a Newark education."

The ETS report, the article said, also laid to rest any fear that the quality of the Verona schools would deteriorate if black children were enrolled, and provided frank answers about racial attitudes of grade-school children, noting that by the end of the school year the Newark children preferred the racially integrated classes.

In November 1969, the professional magazine *School Management*, under the heading "Abandoned busing plan judged a success," quoted the Educational Testing Service's conclusions that the bused children "significantly outperformed" their Newark classmates. However, the article noted, due to the last School Board election, it was unlikely that the Verona Board would reinstate the plan, despite the report of its success.

The Elementary Teachers Supplement of the *Scholastic Teacher* of December 1, 1969, gave good grades to the Verona experiment, even though it had been discontinued, stating, "There seems to be little doubt that integrated learning situations are one way of improving academic achievement and racial attitudes."

> Tests show that academic achievement of black youngsters in integrated classes is considerably better than of those children remaining in ghetto schools. Other tests indicate that white students with an original antipathy for blacks now have a healthy curiosity and awareness. And, despite the relatively small numbers of busing experiments, it seems that it makes little difference if the busing is within city limits or from city to suburban schools. Academic achievement improves and racial attitudes change regardless of the location of the integrated classroom.

Three years later, in 1971, the *Journal of Applied Social Psychology* printed an article titled "Educating Disadvantaged Urban Children in Suburban Schools: An Evaluation," by Dr. Stanley M. Zdep, who at that time was director of research of the Girl Scouts of America. In the brief introduction, Dr. Zdep presented an account of the one-year experimental program — without naming the city — "that transported 'volunteer' disadvantaged city children to schools in a nearby suburban community." He concluded with the assertion that "transported first graders displayed significantly higher average gains in reading, mathematics, and listening skills than did counterparts who remained in the city school."

This article, which is similar to the report Dr. Zdep gave to the Verona and Newark School Boards, was called to my attention when I requested additional information from Educational Testing Service in Princeton. A fire in their warehouse had destroyed many of their older records.

Dr. Zdep stated:

> Today our cities face many problems; one of the most pressing ones involves the schooling of ghetto children. The children in inner city schools usually come from low SES [*socioeconomic status*] families; a high proportion of them are black; and they have been termed "educationally disadvantaged" for a number of reasons.
>
> Some of the educational disadvantages have been documented most vividly in the recent Coleman report on *Equality of Educational Opportunity* (Coleman *et al.*, 1966). Coleman pointed out that, on standardized achievement tests, Negroes from the metropolitan Northeast show a grade level gap of 1.6 years in sixth grade, 2.4 years in ninth grade, and 3.3 years in twelfth grade. Much of this lack of achievement has been attributed to language difficulties of disadvantaged children. Although differences in cognitive skills in relation to SES are not yet well understood, . . . [*evidence suggests*] that lower class children have restricted language patterns that tend to confine thinking to a relatively low level of repetitiveness. Other . . . evidence [*indicates*] that some low SES children have problems in reasoning and abstract thinking that also depend on language development.
>
> Another difficulty for disadvantaged children lies in the area of motivation. . . . A number of investigators found that these children are less motivated and have lower aspirations for academic and social achievement than do their more advantaged peers. Furthermore, this depressed level of aspiration seems to

be related to the child's perceptions of the opportunities and rewards that are open to him in society.

Various attempts have been made to close the educational gap existing between disadvantaged children and their middle class counterparts. Perhaps the greatest impetus in this direction was provided by the Elementary and Secondary Education Act (ESEA) of 1965, which provided financial support for various forms of compensatory education. Some of the educational programs undertaken under the auspices of the Act focus on the establishment of remedial reading classes, improvement of library resources, and teacher training programs. In other cases, various innovative educational programs have been developed. One example of such a program deals with the busing of ghetto children to predominantly white, middle class schools in surrounding suburban communities.

. . . Collectively, evidence from these . . . [*other busing*] programs seems to indicate that city-to-suburb busing can work, that it benefits city children, and that it does not harm suburban children.

Based on this initial promising evidence, a large eastern city (Center City) and one of its suburban satellites (Suburbia) entered into an agreement that called for the "sharing of educational opportunity". . . .

Without naming the "Center City" school, Zdep writes,

. . . the school suffers from a physical deterioration typical of many inner city schools. Makeshift classrooms have been added and classes are overcrowded. First grade children were on split-sessions. The first session met between 8:30 to 12:30, and the second session met between 11:30 to 3:30. Children from the first session had to move to other classrooms at 11:30 in order to provide space for incoming children from the second session.

In Suburbia, for grade one only, the schedule provided for reading instruction with a reduced pupil to teacher ratio of 11:1. But in Center City, teachers had two or three times as many pupils for reading. Contemporary mathematics was presented in Suburbia, while traditional mathematics was taught in the Center City school.

The abstract of Dr. Zdep's article notes that the various tests and results that followed were basically similar to the report given to the public.

> Except for the attitude inventory (in the Primary School) all tests were standard for the particular grade involved.

There are other statements in Zdep's report worth noting — for instance, that the selection was made randomly from a total of 170 students whose parents had indicated an interest. The 38 were chosen — 37 actually participated — through a lottery procedure under the guidance of a representative of the New Jersey Department of Education.

The counterpart group who would remain at the inner city school was selected from the remaining children whose parents had given permission for them to participate. In anticipation of a high student turnover rate in the city school, a larger number of counterparts were selected. This selection of counterparts was done by Educational Testing Service personnel without any personal knowledge of the students. From each grade level, names were chosen if they corresponded to both the sex and age of a transported child. This selection resulted in at least one counterpart being selected for every transported child. Matching of counterparts, rather than random selection, was used to balance the small groups on potentially confounding variables. When the matching had been completed, the vice principal of the city school commented that, to her knowledge, the children in both groups were representative of neighborhood socio-economic background, and that neither group contained children who were considered to have behavior or emotional problems.

The large number of volunteers and the relatively low number of students that Verona would take must have caused disappointment to some parents. Dr. Zdep pointed out that these were parents who wanted to further their children's education. But those who were not picked by the lottery and did not attend the schools in Verona surely were also watched to some degree at home — as is evidenced by the interviews with some of the Hawthorne parents and teachers today. Since the matching group that remained also was chosen from the same group of willing parents, the large differences in the various skills encountered after only one year is even more surprising.

Over the last year the Verona Board of Education has been in the midst of a continual downhill slide. . . . Grown adults sit at these meetings booing, shouting out and generally being more childish than children.

The displeasure over the busing issue led to the election of a reactionary candidate, . . . The budget was defeated, . . . in the long run it is only the students and the caliber of their education that suffers. . . . — Verona High School *Fairviewer*

Chapter 21

Related Issues

IT DID NOT SEEM A coincidence that the Vietnam question engaged most of the same players in Verona. Most of those who had supported the Sharing Plan either were against the war in Vietnam, or at a minimum supported an open and frank discussion. And many of the leaders who opposed the Sharing Plan also opposed student demonstrations, or believed that any discussion of the Vietnam problem would be biased and should not be permitted.

A new problem, which erupted like a volcano at the next Board meeting, was the issue of Vietnam War moratorium activities held at Verona High School. Emil Tomecek charged in the *Newark*

Evening News that a public school had no right to sponsor a "protest" on a political issue. If Tomecek had attended the program, or had asked what really occurred at Verona High School, however, he would have found that the program was less a protest than a dialogue on the war. The newspaper responded that

> ... the Moratorium ... was an educational program, with both aspects of the question of U.S.-Vietnam policy presented. The tabulated results of a questionnaire circulated to the students and teachers document the overwhelming success of the fundamental learning experience that occurred. ... We are anxiously awaiting the day when Verona residents will look beyond their petty prejudices and politics and start thinking about the education of their children.

The *Verona-Cedar Grove Times* did not help with its headline of October 16, 1969: "Students Join War Protests." Yet a careful reading of the article contradicted the headline. The second paragraph read: "A formal program was presented in Verona starting with an assembly panel discussion, with speakers taking pro and con sides on the war." The article went on to say that in neighboring Cedar Grove no formal discussion had been offered, but that in both schools 200 to 250 students had been marked absent, probably not all for the same reasons. All over America that day, students had been called to participate in protests or hold discussions.

Don Ellicott, chairman of the social studies department at Verona High School, was reported as saying the moratorium program had been triggered by students, and Ellicott said,

> ... in keeping with school policy the decision was reached to obtain speakers who would present both sides to the war question. Unfortunately, rumors had circulated that the program would be one-sided and of a controversial nature. But this was not true. Every effort was made to have a well-balanced presentation and in this, I believe, we were successful.

One week later, the local paper was overflowing with comments and letters to the editor. A questionnaire, which had been distributed in home room classes at the Verona High School, showed that 66 percent of those who attended said they learned "much more" than during a normal day of classes. Eighteen percent had not attended because they were enrolled in Distributive Education classes or were ill, and 11 percent did not attend because they did not wish to participate, or because their parents forbade them to attend. A similar questionnaire filled out by the faculty revealed that 95 percent approved of this gathering as a profitable educational experience, and 70 percent were in agreement that the program dealt with both sides of the question "very well."

"High on the Hilltop," Ed Fox's weekly column in the *Verona-Cedar Grove Times* gave credit to the Verona High School officials who had granted permission for the program, and credited the students with presenting both pro and con views "in peaceful fashion."

There were numerous letters to the editor, by parents, students, and teachers — for the most part congratulatory. One man wrote that as a result of the day, he had decided the complete withdrawal of our forces from Vietnam must commence immediately. Another reader commended the principal of the high school, and reported that her two children had found the day a most worthwhile experience. Walter M. Wermuth, a mathematics teacher, wrote that the Board of Education should be proud of the students who gave credit to and showed respect for speakers of various viewpoints. S. William France, president of the Verona Senior Class of 1970 (and son of a Republican councilman), wrote about the learning experience and stressed that there were no acts of violence, vandalism, or disrespect. He wrote:

> On a day when, for the most part the nation's youth struck out blindly at the Nixon administration, our high school took no official stand, but presented a program designed to give all the facts and allow each student to see the problems before rushing into a protest.

Thelma Zukosky had decided to keep her daughter at home, but she attended the assembly herself and was impressed with the presentation. Yet she still objected, mainly that it was held on that particular day, and she worried that the broad participation all over America may have sent the wrong message to Hanoi. A letter by Edwin Willard, the high school principal, took issue with Tomecek's position, and questioned whether he

recognized the fundamental responsibility of the Board to develop policy
and not to administrate.

> I hope I will never have to ask permission of the Board of Edu-
> cation to permit me to innovate any Assembly program. This
> aspect of the school system is left to the discretion of the
> Administration. I trust that this prerogative will continue to
> remain in effect.

Board president John McDonald had announced at the start of the October meeting that in the future all of the meetings would be opened with a
prayer, followed by the Pledge of Allegiance. In attendance were two jour-
nalists and 500 citizens, including 250 students of the social studies classes of Verona High School.

Tomecek introduced a resolution that began with the words,
"Appropriate exercises for the development of a higher spirit of patriotism
shall be held in all public schools. . . ." The motion was designed, according to Tomecek, to "give assurance . . . that our schools are being
conducted in accordance with specific state school laws, [and] these
statutes require appropriate patriotic exercises before certain patriotic
holidays."

Superintendent Mattis felt that the resolution merely echoed already
existing laws, and he only questioned it because he wanted to be sure that
the resolution did not infer that they had not been observing patriotic
holidays, or that there was a lack of patriotism on the part of school personnel.

Tomecek had apparently not been swayed at all by the letters and statements commending the Moratorium Day program at the high school. He
complained:

> On Wednesday, October 15, Verona High School held a Viet
> Nam War Moratorium. This means that the students of our high
> school took part in a national protest against our U.S. Govern-
> ment's position in Viet Nam, all explanation to the contrary
> notwithstanding. . . . Wednesday's activities at the high school
> were not authorized by the Verona Board of Education. It is the

board's responsibility to determine whether such an all-day program will or will not be held. . . .

John McDonald wanted it clearly understood that while he would vote
for the "patriotic" resolution, Verona had always complied with any law
required under the state statutes.

Next, Emil Tomecek introduced a resolution that each Board meeting
should be opened with a prayer, followed by the Pledge of Allegiance to
the flag. In response, Ed Wizda commented, "I hope the public does not
judge our degree of faith, nor our degree of patriotism by the fact that we
hold a public prayer or the pledge of allegiance to the flag." He added that
there were numerous other ways to express patriotism or religion without
a public display — and, it was pointed out, the Board meetings had for
some time already opened with a prayer.

Another resolution, moved "proudly" by McDonald, commended "the
students, staff and administration of Verona High School for their initia-
tive in planning and carefully presenting the [*moratorium*] program . . . to
consider the issue of war and peace in Vietnam, with which all the people
of the United States are actively concerned." This resolution initiated a
lengthy discussion, and Hilda Jaffe, who had spent the whole day at the
Verona High School to evaluate the proceedings, seconded the motion.

In a long speech, Emil Tomecek reiterated the role of the Board and the
employees. In his opinion, the most important statute stated that "no
course of study shall be adopted or altered except by the recorded roll call
majority vote of the full membership of the board of education of the district." This offered the citizens control through the ballot box over what
was taught in the schools. He warned, "Don't fall for the smokescreen
'academic freedom'."

Tomecek wondered who had the authority to "pay a teacher when the
teacher does not teach?" and he also noted that it cost approximately
$6,000 per day to operate the Verona High School. He said, "[*Principal*]
Willard must learn that the board decides where the taxpayers' money will
be spent."

Marshall Butler and John McDonald then exchanged verbal blows.
Butler wanted to know on what basis McDonald had commended the staff,
and whether he had actually been present. McDonald replied that he had
based his findings on the reports he had received, and when Butler asked
why the other Board members had not received such reports, McDonald

explained that he had made it a point to contact some of the teachers. When McDonald explained that he needed to investigate what had transpired, Butler said that he found it unfortunate that McDonald had had to go to extremes to find out what was going on. In response, McDonald did not think it extreme to call a teacher for information.

Butler, in general agreeing to the relevance and importance of the program offered at the high school, felt he was not in a position to accept the resolution McDonald had presented, because McDonald did not have any firsthand knowledge.

Subsequently, Edward Wizda tried to explain that there was a fundamental difference between "schooling" and "education." Tomecek, Wizda said, seemed to be more concerned with the mechanics of schooling — attendance, school bells, class hours, and procedures. While the Board should be concerned with these, Wizda said, education should permit an open discussion on issues, not only the issues of war or peace in Vietnam, but also on issues such as drugs, air and water pollution, problems in the cities, or transportation. Wizda named a number of such topics and hoped that the faculty had the freedom to discuss both sides.

Emil Tomecek then sought an explanation of the term "academic freedom." Was it used as in believing in motherhood? Or in sex education? General terms, Tomecek said, should not be used without those terms being defined.

John McDonald asked Ed Wizda what his definition would be, and Wizda replied, ". . . in blunt simple terms . . . 'academic freedom' is not to have an administrator or board of education breathing down your neck at every moment." Tomecek felt that Wizda's explanation meant that the teacher could hold classes when he chose to hold classes, and if not, then no classes would be held.

Superintendent Mattis assured the Board that both he and Principal Edwin Willard had insisted that during the program both sides of the questions would be discussed. Mattis said, "It was the freedom of the teachers, using other resources, to approach a problem of national interest, and to approach the problem from all points of view. . . ."

McDonald's resolution passed — Tomecek voted against it and Butler abstained.

A "code of ethics" resolution was then introduced by Hilda Jaffe. She explained that this was the second time she had prepared this resolution; at first, it had been discussed at a Board meeting, and since no comments had been forthcoming at that time, Jaffe had decided to use it as a personal statement. Now that the State Federation of School Boards, of which the Verona Board was a member, had adopted its 15-point code, Jaffe was introducing this resolution to remind the Board members that they were serving a larger interest than just their own.

To Butler's question as to what purpose this would serve, Jaffe replied that she would be rather disappointed if it did not change the conduct of this Board.

> If nothing else — it should make us stop and consider how we should behave, and what our responsibilities are toward each other and toward our school system in the community, and it will give the members of the community a yardstick by which to measure the conduct of the individual board members. . . .

She did not convince Butler. He did not want a code of ethics to tell him how to behave in a specific way. Jaffe, in answer, told him that she had no intention of reminding any member about the code of ethics during any particular meeting but, rather, it was her opinion that the members would have to control themselves and would need to use their own interpretations. The public, she said, needed to realize that the Board members were not "free-wheeling agents . . . that there are some common ethical precepts to which we must conform. . . ."

Emil Tomecek had a lot to say on a number of the 15 points that composed this code of ethics. After his lengthy speech, in which he addressed specific concerns about this code, Hilda Jaffe agreed that he had made some good points. But, she said, "each board member will interpret this code of ethics in his own individual fashion. . . ." Further, it was Jaffe's opinion that the people might be the boss, but Board members have a higher boss as well, and "that boss is the State of New Jersey and the State Board of Education and the State Legislature which passes the laws by which we operate and are governed."

Marshall Butler spoke next. "I have matured enough," he said, "to determine what my own Code of Ethics would be in the best interests of the community under the guise of the State, the oath that I took to serve the community, the youngsters and education. . . ."

The vote was finally called, and with Butler and Tomecek dissenting, the code of ethics resolution passed, three votes to two.

Read into the record were 17 letters praising the Board and Principal Willard for the program on Moratorium Day; there were three letters in opposition.

The meeting was then opened for public comment, and there ensued a contentious debate that touched on, among other things, the high school program on Vietnam, academic freedom, communism, and the credentials of the high school principal. The meeting adjourned at 12:30 a.m.

"Conflict Marks Board Meeting" was the headline of the October 30 *Verona-Cedar Grove Times*. The overflow audience, the paper reported, listened to Emil Tomecek attack the school administration, staff, and the high school principal for arranging the program in connection with the nationwide Moratorium Day.

A letter to the editor of the *Times*, signed by Edwin A. Willard, took issue with Tomecek's statement, which had been printed in the *Newark Evening News*. Willard wrote:

> . . . Verona High School has had and always will have appro-priate programs for special days. . . . It is a sad commentary on our school life that any member of the School Board should try to inflict his own personal points of view on the administration of the school.

On October 31, 1969, the staff of the *Fairviewer*, the Verona High School paper, printed the following editorial:

> Over the last year the Verona Board of Education has been in the midst of a continual downhill slide. They have not been able to get the original school budget passed, and so due to a lack of funds have been providing Verona students with second rate educational facilities. The outspoken and many times unjustified criticism of the Board by Mr. E. Tomecek has resulted in splitting the borough of Verona into two openly hostile camps. The reason for this situation is a complicated one. Perhaps it began a year and a half ago when the Board offered a plan to share educational opportunities with forty Newark children. The first Board meeting following the pro-posal hangs like a bad dream in your memories, a dream which is now reoccurring. Grown adults sit at these meetings

booing, shouting out and generally being more childish than children.

The displeasure over the busing issue led to the election of a reactionary candidate, Mr. Marshall Butler, who joined with Mr. Tomecek against the sharing of educational opportunities. The budget was defeated, a move advocated by Mr. Tomecek, as an expression of anger of the Board's handling of the busing issue. The students of Verona High School resent being used as the tool for punishing the Board of Education, for in the long run it is only the students and the caliber of their education that suffers when the budget is defeated.

At the next Board meeting in November 1969, George Buermann, the Board's attorney, announced that the appeal brought by Amy Bostwick and her group regarding the Sharing Plan had been dismissed by the Superior Court.

The appeal, heard by Judges Goldmann, Lewis, and Matthews, had been considered by the Superior Court on November 10 and decided on November 17. Anthony F. Ditri and Sam Weiss had appeared as counsel for the appellants, and George Buermann and Grant M. Gille for the respondent. The Judges' decision read:

> The resolution and ordinance have already run their course. The appeal is moot and is hereby dismissed.

After Buermann's report, John McDonald, having accepted the challenge made at the previous month's meeting to take a position on "academic freedom," defined it as the freedom of a teacher to speak, to write, and to carry on research, and the freedom to deal with controversial matters and to state opinions, as well as to speak freely outside of the classrooms on matters that claim the teacher's attention. Students should have similar rights, he said, as well the right to petition the faculty on matters in which the students have a direct concern.

The term then elicited further discussion. According to Hilda Jaffe, it described the educational atmosphere of a community, and like fresh air, it cannot easily be created, she said, but can very easily be polluted. She went on:

> If you stop up our mental breathing equipment, deprive us of ideas and experiences, we become spiritless living vegetables, capable of being manipulated easily by people with special interests.

Edward Wizda added:

> If education is nothing more than the delivery of information by teachers to students, the issue of "academic freedom" would never arise in Verona. The students and the faculty are to probe and share all issues, to hypothesize and to discuss things openly.

Butler and Tomecek declined to define "academic freedom" for lack of preparation; both agreed that it would require a careful choice of words.

Tony Iuso, a guidance counselor at Verona High School, addressed the Board and asked which of the members could have told the *Star-Ledger* that Verona's guidance counselors are the "highest paid clerks in Essex County." Iuso, directing his remarks to Tomecek, explained that an investigation had been made, and according to the reporter, Tomecek had made the remark.

> It would seem, then, that either the reporter is lying, or you were lying. Since there is no conceivable reason for the reporter to lie, one would have to assume that it was, in fact, you who was not truthful. . . . In view of your eloquent denials . . . and the fact that you refused to accept the Code of Ethics, as proposed by your colleagues, I seriously question your fitness to sit as a member of the Board of Education. . . .

Emil Tomecek again denied making the statement. Quoting the reporter who had used the offending statement, Tony Iuso said that the only reason Tomecek had not been named was because the reporter "didn't want to discredit the article." Tomecek thanked Iuso for the "compliment," then added:

I know school systems where this kind of a thing at a public meeting on the part of a school teacher would have serious consequences. That's all I'd like to say, and the reason why I say that is this . . . I really believe that one of the problems that we have is when employees of the School Board get involved directly in the politics of the School Board . . . because then it becomes very difficult for those individuals to keep that kind of politics out of the classroom, and I would suggest that you consider this kind of thing very, very seriously before you get involved in the internal politics of this particular split School Board.

John McDonald then declared that when a "derogatory remark" has been made, it should be admitted to, "not hide behind some grandiose statements of staying out of politics on the School Board." He added that in his personal dealings with the guidance department, he had found that they were doing an excellent job.

Bernard Sterling felt the need to comment. The previous Sunday evening, he said, several hundred Veronans and teenagers had met under the auspices of the Concerned Citizens of Verona to discuss the problems of the teenagers and to talk about the "generation gap." The youngsters were mostly talking about the hypocrisy of the adult world, he said, including the admonition to *"don't do what we do, or don't act as we act."* Sterling was appalled that Tomecek, a member of the Board,

has taken a public forum and, if I interpreted the words correctly, threatened a member of the faculty of our high school, and I think if nothing else, he should withdraw his statement and apologize. . . .

He also suggested a resolution acknowledging the fine work of the guidance department.

Ed Wizda agreed and offered the resolution expressing fullest confidence in the guidance department. The motion was seconded by Hilda Jaffe. Marshall Butler unhappily explained that he was being asked to vote on something on which no information had been provided other than what he had heard that evening. He and Tomecek then abstained on the vote while the other three members voted for the resolution.

Richard Meehan also had been appalled by what he heard, but for exactly the opposite reason — that a professional educator had decided to make this known at a public meeting. He requested the name of the reporter. He also asked why there had been a delay of a discussion of the "Health and Safety" report, which he felt should be called, "Health, Safety and Sex Education." Superintendent Mattis and McDonald explained that this had been a temporary postponement only due to insufficient time, because of other problems. Still, Meehan continued,

> One of the issues involved here is a sex education program in Verona, which also has become an emotional issue throughout the State — throughout the country — and I think the people are interested in finding this out. . . .

Tomecek interrupted the proceeding, feeling that his vote on the previous resolution might have been misinterpreted, and wondering if he might feel differently later, when he had received a full report.

John Burguillos, also a teacher, interpreted the "veiled threat by Tomecek as an eloquent discourse on his feelings on academic freedom," and therefore did not think it necessary for Tomecek to write his opinion on that subject. The generation gap that had been described earlier, he went on to say, was not only between teenagers and adults, but also between teachers and Board members who were living in the "Dark Ages," and he insisted that members of the teaching profession would not buckle down under that kind of a threat.

Emil Tomecek apologized for the "implied threat." He indicated that he did not intend his statement to be such, and that he has had "the highest regard for [*Tony Iuso's*] work in the guidance department." Iuso replied that he had felt it to be a threat.

"All right," Tomecek said, "I'd like to withdraw the threat then, if you felt that it was."

The meeting ended after Walter Wermuth appealed to both factions to discipline themselves:

> So again I make this appeal, in an emotional way, probably, but I hope in a little bit of an intellectual way . . . the world is changing at a fast rate and the school system was behind. Let's face the facts, let's discuss . . . and all I can say again is that I

hope that both factions will get together and resolve the issues rather than throw eggs at one another.

The headline of the October 22 *Newark Evening News* read: "School Trustee Raps Moratorium Program." It reported in detail the clash between Emil Tomecek and Edwin Willard.

The *Newark Evening News* of December 31, 1969, declared: "VERONA OFFICIAL ASKS BUSING PLAN REPEAL." A similar story on the same date ran in *The Star-Ledger*. The previous evening, the Verona Board of Education had announced a dual decision by New Jersey Commissioner of Education Carl Marburger concerning two appeals filed by Emil Tomecek, Verona Board member. Tomecek had claimed that the agreement between the Newark and Verona School Boards became invalid when a third party, Educational Testing Service, took part. Tomecek asserted that the Commissioner had not taken into account a state law forbidding Boards from entering into contracts prior to the presentation of those contracts at scheduled board meetings. Commissioner Marburger, however, had ruled that authorization was implicit in the original contract approved on June 25, 1969, between the two Boards and should stand. Tomecek said he would appeal to the state Board of Education.

In another ruling, Marburger decided that a newspaper advertisement placed by the Board during February explaining the school budget was proper, but should have been decided at a public meeting and not during a caucus.

"Verona High Teens Tutor Newark Pupils" — a continuation of the special relationship between Verona and the Hawthorne Avenue School — was the gist of a story in the *Evening News* during November. "The children love this one-to-one confrontation," Woodrow L. Davis, principal of Hawthorne Avenue School, was quoted as saying. "We think we have a great school, but despite the best efforts of dedicated teachers, the learning process sometimes seems impersonal in too much of a crowd. Personal contact is needed."

The story went on to say that volunteer drivers would bring the Verona teens to Hawthorne School around 3:30 and that they would devote about 45 to 60 minutes to intensive study. Each member of the group of about

90 volunteers, it was reported, spent about one afternoon with the assigned Hawthorne child, who had also volunteered.

The report quoted a 14-year-old Verona freshman who considered tutoring a great opportunity, as she had hoped to become a teacher. She tutored a sixth-grader in math, her favorite subject. Chuck Daume, a senior, taught English to a group of about 20 youngsters of Puerto Rican background. "Many of them speak nothing but Spanish at home and with their friends," he said. "The language barrier ruins their confidence and makes them tense in regular classes. . . . In the after-class session they feel freer and discover learning isn't so difficult after all."

A 15-year-old sophomore youth taught reading because music — his original choice — was not yet completely organized. His 17-year-old sister, who tutored piano, complained that the study periods went too fast, and that there was just not sufficient time.

Although the Verona Board of Education may have had to discontinue its relationship with the Hawthorne Avenue School, some of the citizens of Verona were willing to keep up the contacts they had made. On December 4, 1969, the *Verona-Cedar Grove Times* announced that all Verona High School volunteer tutors were requested to attend a special in-service teachers' workshop conducted by Hawthorne Avenue School teachers and administrators. The program, sponsored by Verona's Educational Task Force, attracted more than 70 Verona students, who were tutoring Hawthorne youngsters four days a week in reading, math, and science and were conducting special classes in Spanish, French, Algebra, piano, and cheerleading. Principal Davis was quoted as saying, "We at Hawthorne are tremendously pleased by the effort of the Verona High School students and we aim to make our tutoring program as effective as possible. . . ."

Davis believed that the programs in Spanish, French, and Algebra, which were not taught at the Hawthorne School, were important in helping students make the transition to high school. Hawthorne Avenue Vice Principal Elizabeth Quinlan told the Verona teenagers that even though the regular tutoring program had been called off to allow time for this special workshop, some of the little children had come to school anyway. "You can tell how they feel when their faces light up as you [*students*] arrive," she stated.

Two years later, this special relationship between Verona and Hawthorne continued. On August 12, 1971, the *Verona-Cedar Grove Times* ran a photo on its front page picturing three black Newark youngsters on ponies, helped by three white volunteers from Verona. That August, the third successful year of the Verona summer program ended, which involved 50 children from Newark's Hawthorne Avenue School. More than 100 adult volunteers and their children celebrated with a festive day that included live band music, an exhibition of precision marching by the Royaleers — the junior drill group of the award-winning Soul Stompers from St. Peter Claver Church in Montclair — pony rides, and refreshments including fried chicken and cakes, prepared and contributed by Verona residents. More than 250 people, from children to honored guests, participated in the final program, which was held in Verona County Park and Our Lady of the Lake Church.

On December 30, 1969, the *Verona-Cedar Grove Times* wrapped up the year's news. Even though Mayor Walter McKinley had pleaded for harmony, the article read, "in the beginning of the year, not much attention had been paid, and many feared the polarization [*that*] had become an integral part of the borough's social structure." Dissension marked many lengthy School Board sessions, the story continued, as well as divisiveness within the Board membership and among the public.

Life was continuing in Verona, but it would take many years to heal the wounds.

*. . . Almost a year later Verona remained divided. . . . The **Verona-Cedar Grove Times** summed up 1970 as "Mostly Normal," but stated that there were changes in the fabric of community life.*

Chapter 22

The Year 1970

THE *NEWARK* Evening News of April 30, 1970, marveled that even though the busing plan had been terminated, almost a year later Verona remained divided. The newest members of the School Board, who had received their support from the conservative Citizens for a Fair Decision, were pressured to toe the line. A long-time education observer in the community talked about the cleavage of the Conservative versus the Progressive. "The small homeowner is aligned against the intellectual," the article asserted.

The former supports the Vietnam war, or at least supports the president, is against sex education in the schools, is less tolerant of dissent and less empathetic toward the aspirations of blacks. And despite the heavy tax burden already placed on them, they would favor additional pay raises for police and firemen. This group generally remains politically apathetic except when a gut issue confronts them. Busing children from Newark and teaching sex education in school are gut issues. . . .

The *Verona-Cedar Grove Times* summed up 1970 as "Mostly Normal," but stated that there were changes in the fabric of community life.

The rebellion of young people was evident on a wide front, most noticeably in dress and hair fashions. Students did not give up their protest of the war, [*and*] took pride in gathering 2,000 signatures of residents calling for a cessation of the hostilities. . . .

These were inflationary times — the cost of living index rose, the real estate market slowed, and rents increased. The tangled array of emotions and prejudices that emerged as a result of the Sharing Educational Opportunities plan faded gradually into a more subdued form as the months unfolded.

State Commissioner of Education Carl Marburger dismissed the appeal filed by Emil Tomecek. Neither Tomecek nor John McDonald wanted to seek re-election. The Verona Board of Education announced its budget, an increase of $397,852, and an impasse was reported in the contract negotiations with the Verona Teachers Association. Assemblyman John Dennis assured residents opposed to school consolidation that the controversial Mancuso Report must be implemented by legislation before it could be enacted into law. And the Citizens for a Fair Decision discussed school redistricting at their meeting.

The Verona Educational Task Force continued its volunteer work with the Hawthorne Avenue School. Additional volunteer drivers were needed to transport Verona High School students who were tutoring the Hawthorne children. No less than 20 Verona volunteers were on the waiting list, and could not participate unless more drivers were found.

The two candidates of the Fair Decision group won the School Board election, and Marshall A. Butler was elected president of the Board. The Board voted approval of the teacher's new salary guide.

Edwin A. Willard, high school principal, resigned effective the following February, 1971. Hilda Jaffe and Ed Wizda indicated that they believed that "harassment" was the reason for his decision. Wizda also charged that public and Board interference with Mr. Willard's administrative duties had a bearing on his action. These statements, however, were termed "assumptions" by newly elected Board member Richard Meehan.

Emil Tomecek, former Board member, declared that Principal Willard had been made the "scapegoat" for Board members who failed to set proper policy. Meehan and Jaffe clashed on the merits of the Bateman Bill, which had been designed to provide more state funds for education. Petitions were circulated urging Principal Willard to reconsider, but he announced in a letter to the residents that he could not alter his decision.

The Verona summer recreation program for the Newark youngsters was supported by four churches and the Junior Women's Club, in addition to the Verona Task Force. Meanwhile, over 150 windows had been broken at the Verona schools, and the Verona Council for Inter-Religious Affairs called on Mayor McKinley to establish an "advisory group on inter-personal relationships." This was related to an independent study on prejudices, which revealed unfavorable attitudes toward those with strong Liberal or Conservative views. Some prejudices were also held against blacks, Italians, and Jews. Councilman Jim Orr asked for the creation of a borough-sponsored commission to promote inter-group harmony.

The Board of Education set desirable qualifications and characteristics for candidates hoping to fill the post of the high school principal. Board president Marshall Butler reviewed the steps taken following the announcement that Willard was resigning.

And thus the year ended, with the Sharing Plan still reverberating and the fallout continuing.

Slowly the wounds healed and normalcy returned — at least on the surface. Some 250 people attended a meeting aimed at improving athletic facilities, and two residents spent time participating in budget meetings!

Both sides in the Sharing Plan conflict in Verona no doubt could have found solace in the Mancuso Report. Those in favor of the Plan could claim that based on the recommendations, Verona was one step ahead; those who opposed the Sharing Plan could see the very ogre they had feared — loss of local control.

Chapter 23

Aftermath

ON APRIL 2, 1969, Chairman Ruth H. Mancuso had signed a letter on the stationery of the New Jersey School Board Association addressed to Dr. Carl L. Marburger, Commissioner of Education of the State of New Jersey. The letter, along with a 23-page attachment, comprised the report of the Committee to Study the Next Steps of Regionalization and Consolidation of School Districts — commonly referred to as the Mancuso Report. The committee had been appointed two years earlier, in January 1967. Acting Commissioner of Education Dr. Joseph Clayton had charged the committee with its goal. The letter urged that the summary of the report be printed for general distribution, and that hearings should be held. It had also recommended legislative action.

The Mancuso Report's foreword explained that in New Jersey, contrary to a national trend toward consolidation, the number of school districts were growing — and with that expansion, services were being duplicated. The question to be studied was whether a reduction of school districts would provide a better educational program for all young people of the state. Three study subcommittees had been formed. The first looked at the "Qualitative and Quantitative Factors required to Provide Quality Educational Opportunity"; the second dealt with "Current and Feasible Patterns of School District Organization"; and the third delved into "Legislation and Finance in School District Organization."

All of the members of the committee were in one way or another connected to the educational process, mostly Superintendents of Schools or members of Boards of Education. The chair, Ruth Mancuso — a member of the Glassboro Board of Education — had been the president of the National School Boards Association. There were at least three representatives of regional school districts, as well as Superintendents of counties. However, none of the members were from New Jersey's larger cities — Morristown, Union, and East Orange were likely the largest among the 20 localities represented. Even the county Superintendents — of Salem, Bergen, and Warren — did not truly represent any area with a large minority population.

The issues addressed near the beginning of the report were the apparent disparities, differences, and inequalities throughout the state's educational system.

> The equalized valuation behind each pupil is more than ten thousand times as great in New Jersey's *wealthiest* district as it is in the poorest.

The differences lay also in enrollment and geographic size: the Greater Egg Harbor Regional High School District covered 339 square miles, Victory Gardens in Morris County encompassed a mere 0.13 square miles and operated only a kindergarten, and Newark had the largest system in enrollment. Some systems offered fewer than 50 courses, while others offered 120 or more. School libraries were ill-equipped: 432 elementary schools had centralized library collections without a librarian; 512 schools had only classroom collections; and of 1,816 elementary schools, only 64 met the American Library Association standards of at least 6,000 volumes.

> There are schools without specialized guidance personnel, psychologists, provisions for feeding students, special education, vocational training, art and music.

When the future was contemplated, the study said, the situation seemed to be approaching crisis proportions. The problems of the cities were unique and the schools were unable to offer children "an education relevant to their needs."

> The damage done by raising children in a substandard environment that frustrates rather than satisfies their basic needs is compounded by the inability to equip them in their educational environment to improve their situation.

The committee's conclusion was that there was a definite correlation between enrollment, wealth, quality education, and efficiency. Therefore, equal quality educational opportunities were not available to all young people in New Jersey, in large part due to socio-economic factors. School districts, the report concluded, should be reduced by reorganization, and the state's share in costs must be increased.

The recommendations of the committee were that all school districts should be organized on a K-12 basis with a minimum of 3,500 pupils projected by 1973, unless the district was so extensive that it would require transportation greater than 45 minutes one way. It was also felt that these districts should remain mostly within a county, with exceptions which were noted.

> Each newly created district shall respect, as nearly as practicable, a natural geographic, social and economic community providing equalization of opportunity for all students, to avoid the creation or perpetuation of racial imbalance.

The county was to be the basic unit for planning school district reorganization, with all school districts to be part of the study. Several pages of the report spelled out details as to how these county master plans should be developed, how the members of the reorganization committee would be selected, who should chair these commissions, and how often the committees were to meet. The expenses were to be paid by the State Department of Education. Each master plan was to be completed by January 1971.

Step by step, the committee envisioned how these county master plans would be submitted to the State Board of Education, how a new State Commission on School District Reorganization would be appointed by the governor to review the plans, and, finally, how these approved reorganized school districts would go into operation. There were other recommendations, especially those dealing with State Equalization Aid, "incorporating a guaranteed financial base equal to at least the state average equalized property value per pupil."

Both sides in the Sharing Plan conflict in Verona no doubt could have found solace in the Mancuso Report. Those in favor of the Plan could claim that based on the recommendations, Verona was one step ahead; those who opposed the Sharing Plan could see the very ogre they had feared — loss of local control.

Probably the surprise was that this committee, representing neither minorities nor large cities, arrived at such conclusions. Not surprisingly, New Jersey did not enact these recommendations, and to date it is still among the very few states that have more than 600 individual School Boards.

A fascinating story, never revealed before, appeared in the December 31, 1969, *Newark Evening News*. Franklyn Titus, Newark's Superintendent of Schools, and Marshall Lambert, assistant principal of the Carter County High School in Ekalaka, Montana, population 900, had been discussing a plan to bring 10 or 12 black Newark high school students to Montana, and to send an equal number of Montana juniors to Newark. This discussion had been held during a dinner at Princeton University at the same time Newark was negotiating the pilot student exchange program with Verona.

The Montana proposal gained widespread publicity on the ranch lands of Montana, but was never disclosed to the people of Newark. The plan, together with a coupon, was printed in Montana's *Ekalaka Eagle*, the local newspaper. It was found that the majority of the population was against the plan.

> It was not so much that we are prejudiced out here (though we do have our prejudices); it is that we did not want the national publicity. [*The plan would*] catapult Carter County and the high school into the news all over the country.

The real purpose of the plan, according to Assistant Principal Lambert, was

> not to relieve overcrowding in Newark, but to give a worthwhile broadening experience to severely deprived kids. We are faced with lots of wide open spaces with few students. Newark has no wide open space and thousands of students.

Many of the Ekalaka citizens did pledge to take Newark students into their homes as boarders, but as it was noted, the Newark children would have found it very different:

> For instance, it must be down to near 50 below right now and our school buses haven't been running for several days.

On May 19, 1971, *The New York Times* reported that a special three-judge panel in federal court had refused to

> nullify existing public school district lines in New Jersey to force racial integration. Although the court declared that the state's school system had "degenerated to extreme racial imbalances in some districts," it refused to order that new lines be drawn.

Racial segregation in New Jersey is caused by housing patterns similar to those in North Carolina. The United States Supreme Court left such segregation in North Carolina unresolved by upholding the busing of children.

The Times noted that a federal civil suit had been brought as a class action, in the name of two black Jersey City children, on the behalf of all black students in New Jersey. Defendants named were State Attorney General George M. Kugler Jr., Dr. Carl L. Marburger, the State Commissioner of Education, and the State Board of Education.

Previously, in 1964 and 1965, the court had turned down three such suits, but Harold J. Ruvoldt, Jr., the attorney in the New Jersey case, indicated that this case might eventually test the constitutionality of *de facto* school segregation. Under New Jersey law, virtually all of the state's school districts conformed to municipal lines. In their suit, the plaintiffs had contended that to end *de facto* segregation, black school districts should be required to merge with predominantly white school districts in the suburbs.

In 1981, the Education Law Center in Newark brought a suit on behalf of students in four communities. It was not until nine years later, after the New Jersey Supreme Court found the reliance on property taxes to be the heart of the inequity in financing the school system, that the headlines in *The New York Times* of June 6, 1990, reported:

NEW JERSEY RULING TO LIFT SCHOOL AID FOR
POOR DISTRICTS; LEGISLATURE TOLD TO ACT
Case Comes as Other States Are Upsetting or Revising
Education Fund Laws

A "thorough and efficient" education was mandated by the New Jersey Supreme Court, which insisted that the poorest cities must ensure spending as much on their children's education as wealthy suburbs. This would include not only money for basics, but also for music and sports or any other program that completed the school experience. Specifically, the court complained that students in the poorest districts "have already waited too long for a remedy, one that will give them the same level of opportunity, the same chance, as their colleagues who are lucky enough to be born in a richer suburban district."

Chief Justice Robert N. Wilentz said that the debate "shows beyond doubt that money alone has not worked, but it does not show that money makes no difference." The court had found that urban schools could not compete in virtually any area with those in richer districts and that they taught students in buildings that were "crumbling."

This made headlines. *U.S. News & World Report* of June 25, 1990, wrote, "Courts nationwide are challenging funding inequities," emphasizing that the New Jersey Supreme Court became the third top state bench in a year to strike down the system of financing public education, which shortchanged disadvantaged students. This story and a summary in *The New York Times* made several points:

- poor districts must receive sufficient state aid to enable them to spend about as much per pupil as wealthy districts;
- wealthy districts can continue to increase their spending if they choose, but then the state must increase aid to poorer districts;
- the state's "minimum aid" program that gives some money to wealthy districts regardless of need is unconstitutional;
- how to close the spending gap between poor districts and rich ones is up to the Legislature, except that poor districts cannot be forced to raise property taxes.

To quote from the court's opinion:

Nevertheless, we reject the State's claim that in these poorer urban districts a "thorough and efficient education" has been or will be achieved. The extent of failure is so deep, its causes so embedded in the present system, as to persuade us that there is no likelihood of achieving a decent education tomorrow, in the reasonable future, or ever. The State's argument is strong on paper: districts can raise all the money they want, districts must raise all the money they need to provide a thorough and efficient education. But for ten years and more there has been no thorough and efficient education in these districts.

The court specifically stated that its mandate did not permit it to consign poorer children permanently to an inferior education. Specific instances were cited, such as Princeton's 1 computer per 8 children versus East Orange's 1 computer per 43 children, or Camden's 1 computer for 58 children. Princeton taught science in 7 laboratories in its high school, each with built-in equipment, while many poorer urban districts had laboratories built 60 or 70 years before with sinks that did not work and without equipment such as microscopes. Montclair's students began instruction in French or Spanish at the preschool level, while Jersey City started its foreign language program in the ninth grade. In Montclair, every elementary school had at least one art classroom and one art teacher, while in Jersey City, art was available to only about one-third of the city's students. Many affluent districts offered instruction in gymnastics, swimming, basketball, baseball, soccer, lacrosse, field hockey, tennis, and golf. In East Orange, the track team practiced in a classroom-building corridor.

In 1989-1990, Princeton raised $8,346 per student with a modest tax rate of 67 cents per $100 of assessed property value, while Camden taxed its residents more than double that amount, $1.62 per $100, but raised only $4,186 per student.

An editorial in *The New York Times* of June 7 declared,

> The New Jersey Supreme Court's remarkable decision on poor school districts deserves national notice for reasons of justice and elemental decency. . . .

The paper lauded the court for moving past other state courts with its insistence that New Jersey provide sufficient aid to poor districts "to allow them to provide a 'thorough and efficient' education as guaranteed by the State Constitution."

Whether money alone could fix the woes of the urban schools was the question raised by *The New York Times* of June 8. Quoting again Chief Justice Wilentz's comments that money alone did not work but that there was no proof that money made no difference, Dr. Ernest Boyer, president of the Carnegie Foundation for the Advancement of Teaching, said that it would be unfortunate if the issue of money became the end of the debate. "It should get us to what's an adequate education." Without going into specifics, the court suggested:

> If the educational fare of the seriously disadvantaged student is
> the same as the "regular education" given to the advantaged

student, those serious disadvantages will not be addressed. In poorer urban districts something more must be added to the regular education in order to achieve the command for the Constitution.

And if money alone was not a cure, money would help.

Dr. Susan H. Fuhrman, director of the Center for Policy Research in Education at Rutgers University, stated that nobody knew what money would buy, and that there were gaps in knowledge on linking money to classroom practices and programs that could promote learning. She suggested bonuses that would encourage schools to start using programs that improved performance.

Dr. Frank Newman, president of the Education Commission of the States in Denver, added

> Unless you change the fundamental way schools are operating, you're not going to get there. And remember where "there" is. We want schools that are focused on getting kids to think and reason and write effectively, use their minds well and handle math reasoning with ease. . . ."

The Times article concluded

> In its mandate to equalize spending, the New Jersey court argued that if money was unimportant, why did the affluent suburbs continually increase their school budgets year after year?

The headlines of 1995 might seem familiar to those who remember 1968. Saturday, April 14, the headline in the Newark *Star-Ledger* read, "Judge urges quick takeover of Newark school district." On page 12, the same edition recounts the past under the heading, "Twenty-seven years of frustration and futility." Year by year, the newspaper article follows the tortuous path that started in 1968, when the Governor's Select Commission on Civil Disorder — the panel assigned to study the causes of the 1967 riots — warned of future problems unless the schools were improved. Governor Hughes had called for a state takeover of the Newark schools but the Legislature never acted.

On May 20, 1995, *The Star-Ledger* reported "Klagholz orders takeover to 'liberate' Newark Schools." Quoting a 24-page decision written by the Commissioner of Education, Leo Klagholz, the paper stated, "The children in Newark have been served by a failing school district for too long." An editorial in the same newspaper tried to answer the question of why the takeover had been delayed.

> There is a one-word answer . . . Politics. A school system does more than simply educate children. It also supplies a substantial number of jobs to adults. It can also be a source of graft. Because there was a generation of delay in implementing Governor Hughes' wishes, it is reasonable to conclude that there was a generation of school children that were deprived of the "thorough and efficient" education the state constitution proclaims is legally theirs. This mistake can never be rectified. . . .

The history of the takeover is repeated again in *The Star-Ledger* of July 13, when the headline read, "State takes control of Newark schools as court appeal fails." Subsequent editions tell of the work force hired to try to get the schools ready for the September opening. In print and with photos, the paper describes in great detail the dilapidated school buildings and how the first order of business was to clean the dirty and stinking bathrooms, paint over the graffiti-covered walls, and fix all the other housekeeping problems prevalent in most of the facilities.

Hartford, Connecticut, was also in the news in 1995. *Time*, on April 24, headlined an article "Segregation Anxiety." When Verona was debating the Sharing Plan, Hartford was cited as a forerunner, an area where suburban communities took the lead to take in ghetto children. Many years later, *Time* noted that the problem Hartford faced was "by now a familiar one" — an inner-city school system "burdened by structural decay and besieged by the pathologies of urban poverty." Over 90 percent of Hartford's students were African American or Hispanic, and the high school dropout rate was more than three times the state average. The Connecticut

Supreme Court that very week had ruled that because the state did not create the segregation, it did not have to take measures to dismantle it.

The state had tried, pouring money into the system, promoting racial balance by supporting magnet schools, school choice, charter schools — and yet it failed. "The quickest fix — though it is one most parents hate — would be to bus pupils across district lines . . . ," the closing paragraph said, not reminding readers that some 27 years earlier this "quick fix" had indeed been tried by a group of volunteer suburban communities.

The Sunday edition of *The New York Times* of May 14, 1995, reported the Hartford story as well, headlining its article "For Schools, Sad Echoes of Hartford." This time, the reporter probed some of the suburbs, which were looking at their own schools and at the increasing numbers of poor families moving into their communities. In Hartford itself, the consultant to the School Board suggested laying off teachers and instead using the money for computer laboratories, books, and classroom supplies. One professional was quoted as saying, "We organize schools on the assumption that students will come for the most part in good shape, that they will have slept the night before, that they have a place to do homework, that they have parents at home. . . ." Another stated, "These kids are in dire need of more attention, not less attention. . . ."

The problem was universal. The best of the Hartford schools, in the most affluent neighborhood, where only 53 percent of the pupils qualified for free or reduced-price lunches, compared favorably in their reading goals with the poorest of the suburban schools of Manchester, where similarly some 50 percent of the pupils qualified for free lunches and which also had the highest concentration of minority children — 40.4 percent.

And again, *The New York Times* article did not devote a single word to what had happened in that area 27 years before.

In the early 1990s, Verona once again had strife due to a program suggested by the Board of Education. Facing a falling enrollment and increased costs, the Board, proposing a five-year plan, had suggested the closing of two schools. The money saved would be used to improve the plants, books, and computers, and to add kindergarten time. Once again, groups formed. One called itself the Coalition for a Quality Education, the other was named the Committee to Preserve Verona. Neither group was able to unseat the two incumbents who had endorsed the five-year plan. School elections in 1995 subsequently saw the incumbents win and soon after it was announced that the Brookdale School would be closed and leased. This, however, never happened.

It is ironic that in 1995 the residents of Verona were fighting each other over whether to close one, two, or no schools, while in 1969, 37 black children had been denied access to the schools of Verona, ostensibly due to lack of space.

"Back to Segregation" was the lead article in *Time* magazine on April 29, 1996. The topic was described in the brief subhead, "A four decade effort is being abandoned, as exhausted courts and frustrated blacks dust off the concept of 'separate but equal'." *Time* noted that:

> . . . since the onset of widespread desegregation in 1971, black 17-year-olds have closed roughly a third of the reading-score gap that separated them from whites.

Citing the Columbia University study by Debora Sullivan and Robert L. Crain, the magazine noted that among 32 states,

> the gap between black and white fourth-grade reading scores is narrowest in West Virginia and Iowa, where blacks are least isolated from whites, and largest in Michigan and New York, where blacks are the most racially isolated.

The article added that Crain, and others, had found that academic-achievement tests are only "one measure" of a school:

> . . . another important one being what researchers call "life chances." The "great barrier to black social and economic mobility is isolation from the opportunities and networks of the middle class," Crain says. School desegregation puts minority students in touch with people who can open doors to colleges and careers.

The article cited the 1966 Hartford, Connecticut, experiment with a randomly selected group of children from kindergarten through fifth grade,

nearly all black. These children had attended school in essentially "all-white suburbs," and some 16 years later over 1,000 were "tracked down" by researchers. Dr. Crain found that:

> males in the test group were significantly more likely to have completed two or more years of college and less likely to have dropped out of high school or got in trouble with the police, and females were less likely to have had a child before age 18. . . .

After discussing my project with Professor Crain, he sent the complete 85-page report, dated June 1992, signed by the four participants of the study at the Institute for Urban and Minority Education, Teachers College, Columbia University. The report details how the Hartford program started, how it still works today, the way the children to be studied were found, interviewed, and classified, and what conclusions had been drawn. The Abstract at the beginning of the report, the source of much of the *Time* material, stated:

> The desegregation program — Project Concern in Hartford, Connecticut — began in 1966 by randomly selecting one group of students to be offered the opportunity to attend suburban schools and a second group as controls. Both groups, along with other Project Concern participants, were traced, and they and their parents surveyed in 1982, after they had finished secondary school.
>
> We concluded that attending suburban schools reduced high school dropout rates, increased adult contacts with whites socially, and increased the number of blacks choosing to live in interracial housing. Male participants had less difficulties with police and perceived less discrimination in colleges and in employment. Female participants were less likely to have a child before age 18.
>
> Desegregated male students are considerably more likely to succeed in college — it is unwise to attempt an exact estimate, but it seems very likely that for males, the chance of obtaining two or more years of college are at least one-and one-half times greater if he received a desegregated education.

Similar to the experiment in Verona, often only a small number of black students were present in the all-white suburban Hartford schools, and often the teaching staff was entirely white. That happened even though Hartford had selected entire classrooms to be sent to the suburbs, along with the teachers of these classes, who had been loaned to the suburban schools for the support of the children. Most of the observations noted in the study seemed to have nothing to do with the actual quality of the school; it is segregation that limits intergroup contact, permits stereotyping and prejudice, freezes minority attitudes about the majority, and reinforces non-equal distribution of resources. For instance, none of the graduates of a Project Concern high school say that they experienced discrimination in college, while 22 percent of control group members who attended college say they did.

Transportation, just as in Verona, was a problem in Hartford, even though "it is particularly surprising that Project Concern students who finished their education in suburban schools had a higher level of participation in extracurricular activities than did non-Project Concern students in central city schools."

Obviously there was a difference between the Hartford participants, who were high school students, and Verona Sharing Plan children, who were in the lower elementary grades. There would have been more after-school interaction between the Newark and Verona children if they had had the means to return to their homes without depending on the bus.

Similar to Verona, Hartford students spent a long time on buses, between 25 minutes and 53 minutes (depending which school they attended) each way. Even more difficult, the students, who had been bused in the beginning, later had to use public transportation. On the other hand, this change permitted the students to participate in after-school activities, since they always could catch a later bus.

A companion report to the Crain study, from the Center for Social Organization of Schools, authored by R. Crain and J. Strauss and called "School Desegregation and Black Occupational Attainment: Results from a Long-Term Experiment," describes the effect of desegregation on occupational success.

In a series of articles starting in July 1997, *The Star-Ledger* wrote about

"Newark, the Next Chapter." Ted Sherman of *The Star-Ledger* staff began with:

> It happened 30 years ago this week, but people talk about it like it was just yesterday.
>
> The Riots. Five days of self-destruction, indiscriminate shooting by State Police and National Guard troops, looting, violence and bright fires in the night that still seem to smolder three decades later.

Noteworthy in the article is the fact that in the past 30 years, one out of three residents left Newark; the total population declined from 402,000 to less than 259,000. Jobs in the private sector declined 23 percent, while jobs statewide increased 36 percent. The number of retail stores dropped more than half since 1967, a loss of more than 1,300 shops. In 1967, Newark had six major department stores; now there are none. According to current census figures, 22.8 percent of all Newark families live below the poverty line. The 1997 *per capita* income in the city, which is the largest in Essex County, was $9,424 versus $17,574 for Essex County and $18,714 for the state.

In 1996, Newark's school system scores ranked among the lowest test scores in the state, even though $2,000 more per pupil was spent above the state's average. School enrollment dropped from 78,712 to 44,981. And the dropout rate went up, from 7.1 percent to 8.4 percent. Nearly one-quarter of all fourth-grade students failed reading, 23 percent failed writing, and 34 percent failed math.

On December 19, 1997, *The Star-Ledger* carried a follow-up story with the banner heading "Study asserts schools need more libraries, gyms." Due to the dwindling number of students, the article noted, classroom space was no longer a problem; however, the space available for its libraries, cafeterias, auditoriums, and gymnasiums was inadequate. The two-year study pointed out that in the last 12 years, Newark had lost about 19 percent of its school population, while at the same time, private and parochial schools gained 25 percent. Only 914 students, about two-thirds of previous years, now attend Weequahic High School, while enrollment at magnet high schools remained steady.

Nearly half of the public schools were a minimum of 50 years old; age and overuse demanded extensive repairs. This coincided with a report by the New Jersey Department of Education, which concluded that it would take $335 million to bring Newark schools up to code and create more classroom space.

On January 8, 1998, *Education Week* magazine reported that New Jersey had some of the best and the worst schools in the United States. New Jersey, the second wealthiest state in the country, has some of the nation's poorest cities — Camden, Newark, Paterson. Using fourth graders for comparison at a basic level or higher, New Jersey was fourth in the nation in non-urban districts and next to last in urban districts.

At least since 1989, the New Jersey Department of Education has published an annual report card for every public school in New Jersey. Below are listed only parts of the complete report, the percentages of the eighth grade performance in reading, math, and writing.

Reading

	Level 1	Level 2	Level 3
Hawthorne Avenue School	10.0	55.0	35.0
Verona Middle School	69.6	28.6	1.8

Math

	Level 1	Level 2	Level 3
Hawthorne Avenue School	5.0	33.3	61.7
Verona Middle School	52.7	43.8	3.6

Writing

	Level 1	Level 2	Level 3
Hawthorne Avenue School	32.2	32.2	35.6
Verona Middle School	77.5	18.9	3.6

Students who scored in Level 1 showed "clear competence in critical thinking skills," those on Level 2 showed "at least minimal competence" and may or may not need additional help. Level 3 are "below the state level of proficiency" and are in need of additional help.

The Department of Education cautions that students are not placed in

classes solely according to the Early Warning Tests; other assessment information is considered. The Early Warning Test given to all eighth graders in New Jersey is not a pass/fail test. It is designed to identify whether a student requires remedial attention in reading, writing, or math — subjects that will be tested again in 11th grade on the High School Proficiency Test.

The DFG column (district factor group) was created by the state to divide districts into socio-economic categories. The state arrived at these one or two-letter designations by weighing demographic factors: levels of education, income, unemployment, and population density. They are used to compare similar districts and range from A (the lowest socio-economic districts) to J (the highest).

			PERCENT CLEARLY COMPETENT	
	DFG	**ENROLLED**	**1997**	**1998**
Newark-Hawthorne E.S.	A	63	5.0	0.0
Verona-Whitehorne M.S.	I	112	44.6	44.1

Professor Robert L. Crain and Rita E. Mahard authored Chapter 3, "Minority Achievement: Policy Implications of Research," in *Effective School Desegregation*. In this chapter, the effects of school desegregation on minority achievements are discussed. "The studies are usually small, unpublished . . . dealing with single cities." Very few of the papers had been published in journals or books, but after a lengthy search, the authors located 93 studies that measured the impact of desegregation on minority achievements. One of the studies was the one done for Verona, New Jersey, and could have been written especially to those who had decried the test results in Verona.

It was unfortunate that the Sharing Plan children were not tested a year after they returned to their segregated school. Yet, as Crain and Mahard noted:

> We found that the duration of desegregation made no difference. Students, who had experienced 4 years of desegregation did not show a stronger effect of desegregation that those desegregated only 1 or 2 years. This is a very surprising

conclusion. We also discovered that the age which desegregation began made a very important difference. We found 11 samples of students who were desegregated at kindergarten, and found the effects of desegregation to be positive in every case. At the other extreme, when students were desegregated for the first time in secondary school, less than half of the samples showed positive effects of desegregation.

Further studies suggest that desegregation creates a sudden burst of achievement growth lasting through the early grades of elementary school, and that at a later date this growth is maintained but not increased. No difference was found between mandatory or voluntary plans.

In those places where voluntary plans were started — and Newark/Verona is mentioned — the number of students willing to attend suburban schools far exceeded the number of spaces offered.

Two findings came from the literature. The first is that the various large-scale studies of schools have found black achievement directly related to the percentage of white students in the school — the whiter the school, the higher the minority achievement. The second, from the National Opinion Research Center, was that there was an optimal point in the percentage of white students, that when the percentage of whites exceeded 80 percent, achievement began falling.

We can see from this analysis that desegregation is indeed beneficial, although it must begin in the earliest grades. We have also seen what research has led us to suspect for some time — that desegregation in a predominantly white society requires predominantly white schools, and desegregation in a society where whites have run to the suburbs to establish a "white noose" around declining minority central cities requires metropolitan desegregation. We have also learned some things that were not expected. The discovery that a school can have too many white students and thus harm black achievement confirms what up to now had been a largely speculative argument for a "critical mass" of black students in desegregated schools. ... The success of voluntary one-way transfer programs to suburbs is particularly relevant.

Verona, which was torn apart by the voluntary invitation to bring in up to 40 children, can find solace in this report. Those who were in favor should be pleased to learn that even a one-year program, especially a voluntary one, could cause a "burst of achievement." Without knowing this, it seems that everything Verona did was done in the right way to achieve the most benefits. Those who were opposed should take note that in no way did the Sharing Plan harm either Verona, the children of Verona, the educational system, or the black visitors. As a matter of fact, Verona has been recently cited for its outstanding school system.

And nowhere in all of the press clippings, reports, or books used to research this manuscript is there a record of volunteers working as hard as those in Verona.

Epilogue

*I*T COSTS thousands of dollars to educate one child. But this book is not about dollars; it is about education. Oddly, it is not even about the education of children, but rather the education of Verona, New Jersey, a small suburban town.

NIMBY — Not In My Backyard — is a favorite suburban expression. Build wherever and whatever you wish, but *not in my backyard*. Do whatever you want, but *not in my backyard*. Invite whomever you want, but *not in my backyard*.

Some 30 years ago, many cities faced riots, school desegregation, and busing. But not in Verona; *not in our backyard*.

Although there were residents in our town who suspected that Verona was part of a larger universe, others cared about the outside only as long as it did not infringe on their home turf. And as a result, the educational process started for everyone. The good people of Verona did not ask for it; indeed, some were shocked when confronted with the possibility that 40 little black children would be our guests. But the children came, and most of the townspeople treated them with civility.

But then, after only one year, the children were told not to return. Eventually, Verona recovered from the bitterness.

All children, white and black, gained from the brief encounter. Some remember the experience to this day, more than 30 years later.

The *not in my backyard* syndrome cropped up again years later, when a large Verona edifice, located at the edge of one of our tranquil residential areas, was offered to an institute teaching disabled children. Local citizens retained legal services to fight the project. . . . *Not in my backyard.* This time, race was never mentioned, only traffic or tumult. The residents lost their fight.

The learning process moved on. Toward the end of 1999, the Verona Board of Education suggested that we name our sports fields after well-known local persons. The first name suggested was that of Bucky Hatchett — the record-breaking sports icon who had been denied several jobs in Verona because of his race. But nobody remembers why he no longer lives in Verona.

The education of Verona, New Jersey, will continue.

Sources

Board of Education, Newark, New Jersey. *Minutes*. 1968.

Board of Education, Verona, New Jersey. *Minutes*. 1968, 1969.

Bowen, William G. and Derek Curtis Bok. *The Shape of the River: Long-Term Consequences of Considering Race in College and University Admissions* (Princeton, NJ: Princeton University Press, 1998).

Bryant, W. C. *Picturesque America or The Land We Live In*, Vol. II (New York: D. Appleton and Company, 1874).

Coleman, James. *Equality of Educational Opportunity* (Washington, D.C.: Government Printing Office, 1966).

Burnett, Kenneth W. *Verona Master Plan of 1946* (Verona, NJ: Burrough of Verona).

Crain, Robert L., *et al. Finding Niches: Desegregated Students Sixteen Years Later* (New York: Institute for Urban and Minority Education, Teachers College, Columbia University, 1992).

Crain, Robert L., and Rita E. Mahard. "Minority Achievement: Policy Implications of Research," in Willis Hawley, *Effective School Desegregation: Minority Achievement* (Beverly Hills, CA: Sage Publications, 1981).

Crain, Robert L. *The Politics of School Desegregation: Comparative Studies of Community Structure and Policy-Making* (Chicago, IL: National Opinion Research Center, 1968).

Cunningham, John T. *Newark* (Newark: New Jersey Historical Society, 1994).

Cunningham, John T., and Charles F. Cummings. *Remembering Essex: A Pictorial History of Essex County* (Virginia Beach, VA: The Donning Company, 1995).

Cunningham, John T. *This is New Jersey* (New Brunswick, NJ: Rutgers University Press, 1994).

Educational Testing Service, Princeton, New Jersey. *The Newark-Verona Plan for Sharing Educational Opportunity.* 1969.

Emmens, Carol A. *An Album of the Sixties* (Danbury, CT: Franklin Watts, Inc., 1981).

Evans, Rowland, Jr., and Robert D. Novak. *Lyndon Johnson: The Exercise of Power* (New York: New American Library, 1966).

Governors Select Commission on Civil Disorder, *Report for Action* (New Jersey, February 1968).

Harvard Civil Rights Group. *City-Suburban Desegregation,* by Gary Orfield *et al.*, press release.

Hawley, Willis. *Effective School Desegregation: Equity, Quality, and Feasibility* (Beverly Hills, CA: Sage Publications, 1981).

Kaas, Grace. *History of Verona, New Jersey 1702-1907.* (1940).

Landsberger, Kurt. *Between the First and Second Mountains: Verona, New Jersey* (1996).

League of Women Voters, Verona, New Jersey. "Know Your Town," in *Verona-Cedar Grove Times*, 1953.

New Jersey School Boards Association, Trenton, New Jersey. *Regionalization and Consolidation of School Districts.* April 1969.

Pack, Kenneth David. *The New Jersey Department of Education; The Marburger Years; A Case Study of Bureaucratic Innovation, Planning and the Politics of Education at the State Level* (Ph.D. diss., Rutgers University, New Brunswick, NJ, 1974).

Queale and Lynch, Inc. *Housing Element and Fair Share Plan.* (Verona, NJ: Planning Board, 1991).

Queale and Lynch, Inc. *Verona Master Plan Background Studies* (Verona, NJ: Planning Board, November 1991, rev. April 1992).

Shachtman, Tom. *Decade of Shocks: From Dallas to Watergate, 1963-1974* (New York: Poseidon Press, 1983).

Stummer, Helen M. *No Easy Walk: Newark 1980-1993, Visual Studies* (Philadelphia, PA: Temple University Press, 1994).

Sullivan, Robert. *The Meadowlands: Wilderness Adventures at the Edge of a City* (New York: Scribner, 1998).

Wells, Amy Stuart, and Robert L. Crain. *Stepping Over the Color Line: African-American Students in White Suburban Schools* (New Haven, CT: Yale University Press, 1997).

Williams, Bob. *The Other Side of the White Mountain*: *Another Verona, The Early History of Verona, New Jersey from 1700-1907.* Unpublished mimeograph. Verona (NJ) Public Library.

Witcover, Jules. *The Year the Dream Died. Revisiting 1968 America* (New York: Warner Books, 1998).

Wofford, Harris. *Of Kennedys and Kings: Making Sense of the Sixties* (Pittsburgh, PA: University of Pittsburgh Press, 1992).

Yergin, Daniel. *The Prize: The Epic Quest for Oil, Money, and Power* (New York: Touchstone Books, Simon & Shuster, 1993).

Zdep, Stanley M. "Educating Disadvantaged Urban Children in Suburban Schools: An Evaluation," *Journal of Applied Social Psychology*, vol. 1, no. 2 (Apr.-June 1971): 173-186.

Newspapers and Publications:

The Advocate
Asbury Park (NJ) *Press*
Catholic Transcript
The Christian Science Monitor
Courier News (Plainfield, NJ)
Education News
Education Week
Fairviewer (Verona High School, NJ)
The Free Lance-Star (Fredericksburg, VA)
Independent Press
Journal of Applied Social Psychology
New York magazine
New York Post
The New York Times
Newark Evening News
Newsday
Passaic (NJ) *Herald News*

Plainfield (NJ) *Courier News*
Saturday Review
Scholastic Teacher
School Board Notes, Verona, New Jersey
School Management
The Star-Ledger (Newark, NJ)
Time
Urban New Jersey
U.S. News and World Report
Verona-Cedar Grove (New Jersey) *Times*
West Essex Record
West Essex Tribune

Index

by
Lori L. Daniel